It is hard to overstate the timeliness and in
peacemaking and reconciliation. While su
an abstract and general level this collectior
moving account of on-the-ground efforts and
historical resources. Once you begin reading
it down, and you will come away with renewed inspiration to be part of God's
program of reconciliation.

William Dyrness, PhD
Senior Professor of Theology and Culture,
Fuller Theological Seminary, Pasadena, California, USA
Author of *Insider Jesus*

Can peace and justice embrace in our violent and unjust world? This rich
compilation probes the depths both of the biblical narrative as well as the
stories of contemporary peacemakers in a hope-inspiring and practically rooted
response to that urgent question. I have no doubt that readers will share my
gratitude to the editors and authors for opening up new vistas and laying new
stepping stones for our shared journey as followers of the Prince of Peace.

Ruth Padilla DeBorst, PhD
Provost, Center for Interdisciplinary Theological Education
Coordinator, International Fellowship for Mission as Transformation (INFEMIT)

We live in a world of conflict and in need of peace, yet a great number of
the followers of Jesus are ill-equipped, ineffective, and in some cases even
uninvolved in the task of peacemaking, despite the Beatitudes reminding us
that peacemakers will be called the children of God. Too often, Christian
believers do not appreciate the importance of this divine task or do not feel
competent to carry it out. This compendium presents an invaluable tool that
will enable the Body of Christ to overcome our deficiencies in the realm of
peacemaking and fulfill the mission of our Lord, the Prince of Peace.

Bishop Efraim Tendero
Secretary General/CEO, World Evangelical Alliance

How Long, O Lord?: The Challenge and Promise of Reconciliation and Peace is a collection of engaging essays presented at a theological forum sponsored by the Asian Theological Seminary in Manila in 2016. This book takes the Western evangelical into another world – a world almost ignored in popular evangelical literature. The primary focus of the book is the Philippines, where the churches are strong in numbers, but great disparity continues in wealth, poverty, injustice, the abuse of women, and civil war. Nevertheless, the wider world is never ignored. Thus, for example, the injustices and pain of the Israeli-Palestine conflict and the Rwanda genocide have chapters. The constant question put to the reader is, What does the Bible say about peace and reconciliation in a world where division, injustice, and conflict prevail? What struck me most forcibly was that the essay writers turned to the Bible, often the Old Testament, to find perspectives and answers. This is a wonderful book, but the pain it reflects makes it a challenging read.

Rev Kevin Giles, DTh
Pastor, Theologian, Writer
Melbourne, Australia

It is a must for us to be equipped in biblical knowledge by all means possible, especially on subjects like peace, a foreign concept in many parts of the world. How we can extend peace to a war-stricken world? This book presents to various Christian leaders and theologians, God's revelations on the reconciliation and healing brought about by Christ in different contexts. I highly encourage every pastor and church leader to have a copy of this book.

Bishop Noel Pantoja
National Director,
Philippine Council of Evangelical Churches

How Long, O Lord?: The Challenge and Promise of Reconciliation and Peace is a timely book! Those of us who self-define and self-identify as "being in Christ in the world" should be troubled that in spite of (and sometimes because of) the growth and spread of Christianity globally, the world of the twenty-first century is characterized by violent strife and conflicts, gross inequalities, devastating natural disasters, and moral decay. The promise of the gospel narrative – that followers of Jesus, wherever they are, shall have impact on society as salt and light – seems to be a far cry from the experience today.

This book speaks directly to the distortions of the gospel narrative, which have shaped a form of Christianity that is interwoven in the story of discrimination and oppression, violent strife and conflicts, gross social-economic inequalities and moral decay. It also elucidates what the true gospel is – good news of justice, peace, and reconciliation, with testimonies of how it works in different contexts and communities.

I commend *How Long, O Lord?* to all who define their life in the world by the dictates of the gospel story, but especially to those that are troubled, restless, and dissatisfied with the way things are in the church and in our world today.

Bishop David Zac Niringiye, PhD
Senior Fellow,
Institute for Religion, Faith, and Culture in Public Life (INTERFACE)
Visiting Fellow,
Fuller Theological Seminary, Pasadena, California, USA

ATS Theological Forum Series

How Long, O Lord?

Langham

GLOBAL LIBRARY

How Long, O Lord?

*The Challenge and Promise of
Reconciliation and Peace*

General Editors

Athena E. Gorospe
Charles R. Ringma

© 2018 Asian Theological Seminary

Published 2018 by Langham Global Library
An imprint of Langham Publishing
www.langhampublishing.org

Langham Publishing and its imprints are a ministry of Langham Partnership

Langham Partnership
PO Box 296, Carlisle, Cumbria, CA3 9WZ, UK
www.langham.org

ISBNs:
978-1-78368-493-9 Print
978-1-78368-494-6 ePub
978-1-78368-495-3 Mobi
978-1-78368-496-0 PDF

Athena E. Gorospe and Charles Ringma hereby assert their moral right to be identified as the Author of the General Editor's part in the Work in accordance with sections 77 and 78 of the Copyright, Designs and Patents Act 1988.

The Contributors hereby assert their moral right to be identified as the Author of their Contribution in the Work, in accordance with the Copyright, Designs and Patents Act 1988.

All rights reserved. No part of this publication may be reproduced, stored in a retrieval system or transmitted, in any form or by any means, electronic, mechanical, photocopying, recording or otherwise, without the prior written permission of the publisher or the Copyright Licensing Agency.

All Scripture quotations, unless otherwise indicated, are taken from the Holy Bible, New International Version®, NIV®. Copyright ©1973, 1978, 1984, 2011 by Biblica, Inc.™ Used by permission of Zondervan.

Scripture quotations marked NRSV are from the New Revised Standard Version Bible, copyright © 1989 National Council of the Churches of Christ in the United States of America. Used by permission. All rights reserved.

British Library Cataloguing-in-Publication Data
A catalogue record for this book is available from the British Library

ISBN: 978-1-78368-493-9

Cover & Book Design: projectluz.com

Langham Partnership actively supports theological dialogue and an author's right to publish but does not necessarily endorse the views and opinions set forth here or in works referenced within this publication, nor can we guarantee technical and grammatical correctness. Langham Partnership does not accept any responsibility or liability to persons or property as a consequence of the reading, use or interpretation of its published content.

CONTENTS

Section III. Healing and Forgiveness

Section IV. Liturgical and Cultural Resources

Section V. Partnership and Cooperation

List of Abbreviations

AFP	Armed Forces of the Philippines
AHB	*Australian Hymn Book*
ARTS	*The Arts in Religious and Theological Studies*
BAS	*The Book of Alternative Services of the Anglican Church of Canada*
BFBS	British and Foreign Bible Society
BofW	*Book of Worship*
CCC	*Catechism of the Catholic Church*
CDP	*Celtic Daily Prayer*
COP	Culture of Peace
DSWD	Department of Social Welfare and Development
FOTL	The Forms of the Old Testament Literature
GCF	Greenhills Christian Fellowship
GCF-OC	Greenhills Christian Fellowship-Operation Compassion
GNT	Good News Translation
IDPs	Internally Displaced Persons
IMC	Immaculate Conception
ISIS	Islamic State of Iraq and Syria
JBL	*Journal of Biblical Literature*
JBQ	*Jewish Bible Quarterly*
JES	*Journal of Ecumenical Studies*
JSNT	*Journal for the Study of the New Testament*
JSOT	*Journal for the Study of the Old Testament*
MBB	Magandang Balita Biblia / Meaning-Based Bibles
MILF	Moro Islamic Liberation Front
MNLF	Moro National Liberation Front
NGO	Non-Government Organization
NIV	New International Version
NKJV	New King James Version
NRSV	New Revised Standard Version
OMF	Overseas Missionary Fellowship

OMF-IRD	Oblates Missionary Foundation-Inter-Religious Dialogue
PBS	Philippine Bible Society
RQ	*Restoration Quarterly*
TDOT	*Theological Dictionary of the Old Testament*
TinS	*Together in Song*
UBS	United Bible Societies
UNHCR	United Nations High Commissioner for Refugees
WBC	Word Biblical Commentary

List of Figures and Tables

List of Photos

Foreword

This book comes at a most auspicious time as we face the challenges of a world that continues to be marred by war and other forms of conflict, including cyber warfare, so that peace seems ever further away. In the Philippines and in many parts of the world, geopolitical tensions abound with neighboring countries. News of interreligious as well as intrareligious strife are also commonplace in cable news and social media. In the local context, our television networks focus a lot on violence, conflict, and crime, embroiled as they are in another form of war – the war on ratings!

Peace seems to be increasingly distant because of increasing suspicion among the major global players and a shift towards an isolating nationalism on the part of many countries. In the Asian context, there are worrying signs of the weakening of societal institutions so that people look for quick fixes for major social problems. It is apparent that our world has become more polarized and conflicted rather than marked by cooperation and peacemaking.

What does the Christian faith say about peace and reconciliation in our world, where conflict and strife are so real and peace is so elusive? How do we become Christ's agents of peace and reconciliation?

This book seeks to listen to Scripture's good news of reconciliation while understanding the ways that the church has sought to be a healing presence throughout history and also critically assessing the ways it has failed to do so. Most of the essays were presented during a theological forum sponsored by Asian Theological Seminary (ATS) in February 2016. The forum provided a wonderful opportunity for the church in the Philippines, along with evangelicals from other parts of the world, to grapple with this relevant topic.

As we face the challenges of conflicts in our world and even within the body of Christ, we are guided and energized by Jesus's words: "Peace I leave with you; my peace I give you. I do not give to you as the world gives. Do not let your hearts be troubled and do not be afraid" (John 14:27). We pray that the peace of Christ will continue to be God's healing presence in our churches and the world, for Christ himself has already "broken down the dividing wall of hostility" (Eph 2:14), and we continue to bear that promise and victory as part of his body.

While ATS has published several volumes of theological forum books in past years, this is the first time that this collection of conference papers will be published by Langham Literature. We hope that this will enable a cross-fertilization of ideas about common challenges facing our world, especially by Majority World nations in Asia, Latin America, and Africa.

We want to express our thanks to the general editor, Athena E. Gorospe, and her co-editor, Charles Ringma, together with Karen Hollenbeck-Wuest, who meticulously worked through the manuscripts to make them more accessible to a worldwide audience. Ruth Orteza contributed much in coordinating the publication process and in checking consistency of style and format. Lastly, we are grateful for the authors who willingly worked through their forum presentations so that they could be presented in a publishable format.

Soli Deo Gloria!

Timoteo D. Gener, PhD
President, Asian Theological Seminary,
Quezon City, Philippines

Foreword

As Christians, we are called to a life of discipleship and this involves carrying the cross as we follow Jesus. Moreover, we are called to proclaim in both word and deed the good news of God's coming kingdom that entered human history through the life, death, and resurrection of the Lord Jesus Christ. These imply that we are also called to be peacemakers, for the cross and the good news of the kingdom both point to God's divine initiative through Jesus to bring perfect reconciliation and peace – the *shalom* of God – to broken humanity and fallen creation. Thus God's message is called "the good news of peace" (Acts 10:36), which as God's gift encompasses all of life. For this reason, the heavenly hosts offered praises to God upon the announcement of the Savior's birth, saying, "Glory to God in the highest heaven, and on earth peace to those on whom his favor rests" (Luke 2:14).

However, God's concern for peace "on earth" has time and again been overlooked in favor of peace "in the highest heaven." That is to say, the spiritual has been deemed more valuable than the bodily, the individual more than the social, the inward more than the outward, and the future more than the present. This has weakened the church's engagement with and concern for peace and justice issues that confront the wider society. Sadly, this posture has further fractured our world and the gospel message itself. Can such a gospel be deemed good news among those living in contexts wherein discrimination, oppression, conflict, and violence are deeply embedded? Was not Jesus's announcement in Luke 4 at the beginning of his ministry (vv. 16–19) good news to the poor precisely because he did not relegate God's shalom to an entirely future and otherworldly realm?

Manifesting the biblical notion of peace and reconciliation in the here and now should be a central concern for all who follow Jesus, particularly in view of the multi-layered discord that is rampant in our society. Scripture reminds us that "[p]eacemakers who sow in peace reap a harvest of righteousness" (Jas 3:18) and "the work of righteousness will be peace" (Isa 32:17, NKJV). Peace and righteousness (*tsedakah*) or justice (*mishpat*) are thus intrinsically and causally intertwined. While shalom is ultimately God's gift, as it has its foundation in the Christ event, its outworking on earth is through ethical works of peace, righteousness, and justice (Deut 16:20; Mic 6:8), which not only aim towards transformed personal relations but also social structures that engender injustice and oppression. The gospel is not, to use Nicholas

Wolterstorff's description, "de-justicized,"[1] for when righteousness and justice are absent or perverted, a nation is thrust towards deterioration and eventual destruction (cf. Amos 5).

Scripture frequently portrays the victims of unrighteousness and injustice as vulnerable people, such as widows, the poor, orphans, and prisoners. At the Philippine Council of Evangelical Churches (PCEC), we encounter the vulnerable ones in the faces of the poor Muslims of Mindanao, marginalized members of the LGBTQ community, families of victims of extra-judicial killings (EJKs), oppressed members of indigenous peoples, and victims of political repression, among others. Such diverse social issues with differing root causes and social expressions certainly require varied approaches, but it has been crucial for PCEC to recognize that Philippine Christianity has participated in and perpetuated many acts of injustice towards our nation's marginalized sectors, whether intentionally or unintentionally, actively or passively. Thus PCEC leaders, as recipients of divine forgiveness, have publicly sought forgiveness from Muslim and LGBTQ participants in a sincere effort to heal and restore relationships with their communities, which have long been defined by prejudice and exclusion. While forgiveness necessitates further and sustained actions, it carries a sense of promise for both offender and offended that genuine reconciliation, peace, and justice are already on the horizon.

This volume of incisive and engaging essays that draw from various disciplines is an important and welcome contribution to the much-needed literature that aims to cultivate peace, justice, and reconciliation in our society today. Written by scholars and practitioners who are both reflective and practical, this book will surely be of great value to those who seek fresh perspectives in following the path taken by Jesus, the Prince of Peace.

Aldrin M. Peñamora, PhD
Executive Director, PCEC Justice, Peace and Reconciliation Commission
Executive Director, Center of Research for Christian-Muslim Relations

---

1. Nicholas Wolterstorff, *Justice: Rights and Wrongs* (Princeton, NJ: Princeton University Press, 2008).

Introduction

"How Long, O Lord?"

The Challenge and Promise of Reconciliation and Peace

Most people long for peace, well-being, and human flourishing, but what we long for so often alludes us. There are many reasons for this discrepancy. We ourselves are not always the bearers of peace, as we tend to be insecure, assertive, and conflict-oriented. What is so sadly true at the personal level is also the case at the communal, national, and international levels.

There have been fourteen major wars and numerous smaller conflicts since World War II, which claimed to be the war to end all wars. However, at this point in history, we live with fear that other major conflicts will soon erupt due to significant power shifts in our world. In addition, our societies are not only marked by all-out war, but also by marginalization, discrimination, and oppression. And at the personal level, relationship breakdowns mar the human landscape.

Thus our lives, communities, and societies are not flourishing as they can or should. In response, we need to find inner spiritual resources and practical strategies so that we can become the handmaidens of peace, even as we learn how to walk the difficult road of reconciliation that leads to well-being and shalom.

In taking up this challenge, this collection of essays from the 2016 Asian Theological Seminary Theological Forum seeks to inspire and encourage us to be bearers of peace in a world of conflict. This vision is drawn from the biblical narratives and theological reflections (section I), contemporary practical engagement in the work of peacemaking, reconciliation, and justice

1

(sections II and III), and the history and praxis of the church in seeking to follow the Prince of Peace into the world (sections IV and V).

In developing the first section, "Biblical Perspectives," Christopher Wright gives us a panoramic view of Scripture's articulation of peacebuilding and reconciliation, exploring both the theme of ethnic reconciliation in the book of Ephesians and cosmic reconciliation in Colossians. He makes the point that this task should not be peripheral to the ministry of the faith community but part of the mission of the church. In carrying out this task the church is not only called to communicate the message of God but also to reflect the character of God as peacemaking communities. In this challenging task, the church needs to recover the vision and practice that there cannot be peace without mercy, truth, and justice.

Takamitsu Muraoka further develops these biblical and theological perspectives by exploring the relationship between memory and reconciliation, which he grounds in his reflections on the Japanese invasion of the Philippines and his own witness as a bearer of repentance, healing, and reconciliation. He reminds us that in a world of personal and collective evil, forgetting is never an option. Both perpetrators and victims need to face their respective histories so that peace may truly flourish.

This theme is also illustrated in Alvin Molito's discussion of the Jacob and Esau narratives. In tracing the work of transformation in these narratives, he explores the themes of ritualization and liminality developed by A. Van Gennep, along with Athena Gorospe's work on narrative and identity. He makes the challenging point that we can read our own narratives of disharmony and conflict in light of the biblical narratives; moreover, we can discern wisdom that will guide us towards freedom and wellness.

The second section, "The Ways of Peace," explores practical strategies for peacebuilding and the work of reconciliation based on hard-won experience. While the first section establishes a biblical and theological vision for peacebuilding, this section traces the sociology of working for peace. Salim Munayer's work with *Musalaha*, an organization that provides reconciliation encounters between Israeli and Palestinian youth, tackles the challenge of gaining traction in peacemaking strategies and identifies a range of common obstacles that can be overcome by following various steps in the stages that foster and facilitate reconciliation. This engaging account outlines a praxis that is based on the wisdom of experience and shaped by social theory.

Fermin Manalo Jr. continues this theme in the Philippine setting, focusing on the long history of armed conflict in Mindanao and targeting three people groups impacted by armed conflict and disruption. He explores the conflict within the domain of peace and conflict studies and provides theories for peacebuilding, focusing on effective strategies from below. He identifies the importance of creating safe spaces to provide the setting for the onerous task of rebuilding. In this wide-ranging discussion, Manalo gives credence to the role of faith-based initiatives. Thus, he challenges evangelicals to take up this difficult work.

Jeremy Simons also locates this theme in Mindanao but reaches further back in history, focusing on the role of the *datu* (tribal chieftain) in indigenous communities (*Lumad*) in that region. He notes that the role of the *datu* has much to do with problem-solving and maintaining peace and order, particularly among feuding families. In this process, the issue is not so much the vindication of a particular family but the maintenance of community harmony. Simons suggests that for *Lumad* communities that have been Christianized, the story of Moses raises possibilities for the process of peacemaking and maintaining communal harmony. Here again the work of Athena Gorospe is formative. The overarching theme in Simons's treatment is that in familial conflict, the focus is on restorative practices that contribute to communal peace and harmony.

The third section, "Healing and Forgiveness," engages several studies that reflect the experience and insights of practitioners who are developing healing strategies in the most extreme circumstances. John Steward takes us to the horrendous genocide in Rwanda in 1994, when over eight hundred thousand Tutsis and Hutus slaughtered each other, recounting his years of involvement in post-genocide reconciliation workshops. Steward maps out important steps in the forgiveness process, highlighting what is counterproductive as well as steps that lead to healing and reconciliation.

Annabel Manalo brings us to the decades-long armed conflict in Mindanao that has traumatized and displaced hundreds of thousands. She maps out the history, setting, and her own involvement, drawing on psychosocial and spiritual strategies for working with traumatized and displaced survivors of armed conflict. Grounded in Manalo's credible wisdom, this study provides an important map for facilitating reconciliation and healing.

Finally, Tricia Mazo explores the oft hidden pain of abuse within families, including sexual abuse and incest. Profiling a number of representative case studies, Mazo not only provides insight into the damage caused by such abuse, but also how to work with those who have been traumatized by these tragic circumstances.

All three authors reveal the terrible ways humans treat each other while at the same time giving us hope that certain strategies can help bring about restoration.

In the fourth section, "Liturgical and Cultural Resources," Charles Ringma demonstrates how peace themes are embedded in Christian hymns and liturgical practices and how these resonate with peace themes that are intrinsic to Franciscan spirituality and missional practices. This chapter argues that the life of St Francis continues to be a relevant example for the church in its peacebuilding mission in the world.

Ronaldo Magpayo continues the liturgical theme by demonstrating how the reading of the *Pasyon* during Holy Week in the Philippines leads not only to the memory of God's sacrifice in Christ, but also to the practices of sacrificial love for the other. Insights in this chapter, which are gained from participant observations and interviews, show how liturgy spills over into ethical behavior, including peacemaking and reconciliation.

Finally, John Rances provides an extended philosophical discussion of the use of violence in all forms of artistic expression. While viewing violence as desensitizing and leading to various forms of disengagement, the creative depiction of reality can also shape imaginations and values. Thus the aestheticization of violence can lead a viewer towards repulsion so that he or she is moved never to do such a thing or to do something about what he or she has seen, thereby contributing to peacebuilding processes.

In the final section of this volume, "Partnership and Cooperation," Glicerio Manzano Jr. demonstrates how peacebuilding is part of the church's mission. Manzano reports on how a major evangelical church in Metro Manila provided medical and other services to an urban poor Muslim community in Zamboanga City, Mindanao. While this was challenging enough, the church continued its involvement with this community even after bombings occurred and when the city was under siege by the Moro National Liberation Front. Throughout the conflict, Muslims turned to Christians for help and shelter.

The final chapter, written by Christine Martinez and Leizl Ocampo, provides the reader with an extended history of Bible translation in the Philippines, highlighting issues experienced by the Philippine Bible Society in its work in interconfessional Bible translation and the challenge in dealing with controversial passages in Scripture. The chapter highlights how combined Bible-related activities have helped to build bridges in the broader Christian community.

As editors of this far-ranging volume, we trust that this book will help readers make inroads for peace in our deeply divided world.

While many people of other faiths as well as people without faith also work for peace, this volume reflects Christian perspectives. These are offered with humility, since Christians have not always followed the Prince of Peace, but regrettably, have sometimes borne the sword into the world. Therefore, in repentance, we offer the fruit of this forum in the hope that the church may be a community that serves the rule of God by bringing peace and justice into our world. Our prayer is that shalom will flourish in all places of devastation, harm, neglect, and violence.

We want to thank Langham Partnership International and Scholar Leaders International for supporting the travel expenses of the international speakers in the 2016 ATS Theological Forum. We would also like to thank Karen Hollenbeck-Wuest for her masterful and nuanced copyediting. Finally, we are gratefulto Langham Literature for their partnership and to their staff for making the production process an agreeable experience.

Athena E. Gorospe and Charles R. Ringma
Editors

Section I

Biblical Perspectives

1

"Righteousness and Peace Kiss One Another" (Ps 85:10)

Biblical Perspectives on Peace and Reconciliation

Christopher J. H. Wright

The vision of reconciliation and peace could be said to be the overarching theme of the whole Bible, from the alienation and brokenness of creation and humanity in Genesis 3–11, through to the restoration of creation and the healing of the nations in Revelation 21–22. The central act of the whole drama of Scripture is the atoning work of the cross and resurrection of Jesus Christ, through whom, as Paul says, God reconciled "to himself all things, whether things on earth or things in heaven, by making peace through his blood, shed on the cross" (Col 1:20). In another epistle, Paul reiterates, "God was reconciling the world to himself in Christ . . . And he has committed to us the message of reconciliation" (2 Cor 5:19).

The biblical narrative contains remarkable stories of reconciliation, which serve as models for those engaged in this ministry today (e.g. Jacob and Esau, Joseph and his brothers). But here we shall focus first on the distilled insight of Israel at worship in Psalm 85, in which the psalmist declares on God's behalf some core conditions for the peace for which we all long. According to the psalm, there can be no peace without God, no peace without justice, and no peace for humans without the earth as well.

From that comprehensive Old Testament vision, we will move to scan the vistas of Paul's equally creational vision of *cosmic* reconciliation in Colossians 1:15–20, of which *ethnic* reconciliation is a sign and foretaste, as expressed in Ephesians 2:11–22 – both dimensions being accomplished through the cross of Christ. Finally, we shall respond to Paul's call for missional reconciliation in Romans 14–15.

For only when the church grasps the gospel of peace and reconciliation that God has created in Christ, and then lives in unity as a fellowship of reconciled sinners, can we carry an authentic and credible message and engage the task of reconciliation in the world – a mission that we must embrace.

The Criteria of Peace – An Old Testament Perspective (Psalm 85)

The heart of Psalm 85 is God's promise of peace in verse 8, but it only comes to those who are carefully defined by the words they pray and sing. God's promise of peace is, first, for people who know God's mercy.

People Who Know God's Mercy (vv. 1–7)

The psalmist, speaking on behalf of the whole people, looks back, remembering the many times in the past when his people experienced the forgiveness and mercy of God (note that the verbs in the psalm are all past tense). There were so many times when Israel, under judgment or in great danger, cried out to God, and God restored them because of God's grace ("favor"), forgiveness, and atonement of their sins.

> ¹ You, LORD, showed favor to your land;
>   you restored the fortunes of Jacob.
> ² You forgave the iniquity of your people
>   and covered all their sins.
> ³ You set aside all your wrath
>   and turned from your fierce anger. (vv. 1–3)

Remembering that history of God's mercy, the psalmist asks God to extend it again (vv. 4–7). He is clearly aware that the people have, yet again, gone astray and need forgiveness, life, renewal, and salvation.

> ⁴ Restore us again, God our Savior,
>   and put away your displeasure toward us.
> ⁵ Will you be angry with us forever?
>   Will you prolong your anger through all generations?

⁶ Will you not revive us again,
    that your people may rejoice in you?
⁷ Show us your unfailing love, LORD,
    and grant us your salvation. (vv. 4–7)

Israel, who has been taught by psalmists such as this son of Korah, knew there could be no peace without God's mercy and reliable love. The peace of God is for those who remember God's mercy and repent of their failures. Remembrance provokes repentance, and repentance is a necessary first condition for seeking or building peace.

Old Testament Israel had plenty to remember in terms of God's mercy, but Christians have even more. For those great statements about God in verses 1–3 – *favor, restoration, forgiveness, and covering of sin* – are ultimately true because of the cross and resurrection of Jesus. That is the foundation of the peace that Christ accomplished and which God grants.

"Peace on earth . . ." the angels sang, announcing the birth of Jesus. But we can't have the peace of Christmas without the self-giving sacrifice of Calvary – either for ourselves or for others. This means that we cannot pursue the mission of reconciliation, peacemaking, and peacebuilding if it is *divorced from the mission of evangelism.* For the peace of God – both vertically and horizontally – is dependent on the mercy and love of God, which is expressed by bringing people in repentance and faith to the foot of the cross and the victory of the resurrection. The *fact* of peace and the *gift* of peace are integral to the gospel itself as good news. As Christians, therefore, we can only *seek* peace because of the gospel, and we must share the gospel as the only truly effective roadmap to peace.

This is consistent with an integral understanding of mission, in which all that we do (in word and deed) as those who have been sent into the world is centered around and ordered by the gospel. And by "gospel," I do not mean a formula that gets us to heaven, but rather the good news of how the God of Israel has kept his promise of blessing and healing to the nations and all creation through the life, death, resurrection, ascension, and promised return of his Son, Jesus Christ, the Savior, Lord, and King. Just as there can be no peace without the saving action of God in the context of human and cosmic brokenness, there can be no effective peacemaking by Christians if it does not flow from that good news and bear witness to it.

People Who Seek God's Justice (vv. 8 – 9)

Returning to Psalm 85, the psalmist, who is praying on behalf of the people, seems to be standing in the temple, in the presence of God, waiting to hear God's answer to the plea he expressed in verses 6–7. What will be the "word"?

> 8 I will listen to what God the LORD says;
>> he promises peace to his people, his faithful servants – (v. 8a–b)

To his great relief and all who are waiting, that "word" from God is "PEACE" – *shalom*. But the promise of peace comes with strong words about how people who want peace need to live:

> 8 but let them not turn to folly.
> 9 Surely his salvation is near those who fear him,
>> that his glory may dwell in our land. (vv. 8c–9)

This warning leads us to the central section of the psalm, where the psalmist makes it clear that the condition of peace is for those who both know and bear witness to God's mercy and also seek God's justice.

Not Reverting to the Old Ways (v. 8c)

The phrase "let them not return to their folly" (v. 8c) means not going back to living in the way that brought about the present mess in the first place. It is amazing how quickly we forget and go back to the same old ways – individuals, countries (war, pollution), banks, military options, and so on.

A friend involved in reconciliation initiatives in Israel-Palestine told me how he and some colleagues took a group of youth from both sides away for a camp, where they interacted with one another and learned biblical principles of relating in mutual respect and love. But when they got back home, and news of fresh violence broke out on the news media, many of the young people started blogging and emailing in the same old vicious and hate-filled language as before. Genuine heart-changed reconciliation is a hard road with many setbacks. It takes people of courage to persevere on this road.

Having Peace on God's Terms (v. 9)

The next line "surely, his salvation is near to those who fear him" (v. 9) shows that only those who take God seriously – and don't think that we can live in selfish autonomy, in the spirit of "I'll do it my way" – can have the peace God promises. If we want the peace of God, which is included in his salvation, we will have it on God's terms, not our own.

The Group Hug of Peace (v. 10)

Verse 10 is one of the most beautiful pictures in the Bible:

> [10] Love and faithfulness meet together;
> righteousness and peace kiss each other. (v. 10)

The psalmist identifies four things that are essential in the pursuit of reconciliation and peace: *love, faithfulness (or truth), righteousness, and peace.* Then he personifies them – that is, he imagines them as people with names, having a group hug! He imagines them walking towards one another: "Here comes Love! Oh look, there's Truth coming, too! And who's this? Righteousness! And last but not least, here comes Peace! And they are embracing one another!"

What do these words mean? "Love" (*hesed*) means faithful, reliable love and is often translated as mercy or kindness. "Faithfulness" *('emet)* would be better translated as truth, integrity, honesty. It describes people who are true in word and trustworthy in character. "Righteousness" (*tsedeq*) describes what is right and fair, straight, matching the standard, as it should be. It is often translated simply as justice – what makes things right, puts relationships right. "Peace" (*shalom*) includes total well-being, freedom from fear, violence, or hunger, flourishing of body and mind, and living in a wholesome and restored relationship with God, with others, and with creation.

Now think about how the psalmist puts them all so close together, embracing, kissing one another. His point is – *if you want one, you must want them all. You can't have peace without embracing the other three as well.*

There can be no true peace – certainly no peace with or from God – without mercy, truth, and justice. Peace comes only when mercy, truth, and justice are at work. Otherwise peace remains a sentimental slogan, a fragile patching-up, or a utopian dream.

Once again, we know that these great realities came together at the Cross of Christ, where the love, faithfulness, and justice of God all met in perfect harmony and accomplished peace. First, God's justice was at work, dealing with our sin and rebellion. Second, God's love was at work, bearing all our sin on himself in the person of his Son. Third, God's truth and faithfulness were vindicated when he raised Jesus from the dead. So verse 10 was fully embodied at the cross. When we read that verse with Calvary in mind, it makes perfect sense.

But verse 10 is not just something for God. It is also intended by the psalmist as the pattern for us – for all who are asking God to come to us with words of restoration, forgiveness, and peace. Peace and peacemaking are for those who are committed to the other three partners in this great group hug. We cannot long for *peace* in our world without willingness to exercise *mercy* – even towards the perpetrators of evil (as Jesus did at the cross).[1] We cannot seek peace without the painful task of facing up to the *truth* (as the Truth and Reconciliation Commission in South Africa understood – and which is now emulated elsewhere, e.g. in Canada). We cannot call for peace without also calling for *justice*. Indeed, we should not pray for peace without also praying for justice.

Jesus said, "Blessed are the peacemakers" (Matt 5:9), but only after he said, "Blessed are those who hunger and thirst for righteousness" (Matt 5:6). Jesus's words reflect this psalm and many other Old Testament texts, which inextricably link peace and justice.[2] The petitions of the Lord's Prayer, "May *your kingdom* come, may *your will* be done on earth as in heaven" (Luke 11:2), speak of the reign of God and the will of God, which hold together this vision of justice and peace together. So if our lives are going to match our prayers, we cannot separate justice from peace.

The prophet Isaiah reflects on this link between experiencing peace on earth and the practical, hard work of seeking justice and caring for the needy. Isaiah 57 echoes the movement of thought in Psalm 85, first recognizing God's past judgment and mercy, and then promising healing, restoration, and, above all, peace.

> [17] "I was enraged by their sinful greed;
>> I punished them, and hid my face in anger,
>> yet they kept on in their willful ways.
> [18] I have seen their ways, but I will heal them;
>> I will guide them and restore comfort to Israel's mourners,
> [19] creating praise on their lips.
>> Peace, peace, to those far and near,"
>> says the LORD. "And I will heal them."
> [20] But the wicked are like the tossing sea,
>> which cannot rest,

---

1. This is a point that is strongly emphasized by Miroslav Volf in his classic study of reconciliation, *Exclusion and Embrace: A Theological Exploration of Identity, Otherness, and Reconciliation* (Nashville: Abingdon, 1996).

2. Cf. Isa 32:16–18; Isa 59:8.

> whose waves cast up mire and mud.
> [21] "There is no peace," says my God, "for the wicked." (Isa 57:17–21)

Notice that there is "no peace for the wicked," which further mirrors Psalm 85. We can't go on following the same old ways of cruelty, violence, corruption, and exploitation and expect peace!

But Isaiah offers his people a remedy for putting things right, so they can expect God's blessing.

> [6] "Is not this the kind of fasting I have chosen:
> to loose the chains of injustice
> and untie the cords of the yoke,
> to set the oppressed free
> and break every yoke?
> [7] Is it not to share your food with the hungry
> and to provide the poor wanderer with shelter –
> when you see the naked, to clothe them,
> and not to turn away from your own flesh and blood?
> [8] Then your light will break forth like the dawn,
> and your healing will quickly appear;
> then your righteousness will go before you,
> and the glory of the LORD will be your rear guard.
> [9] Then you will call, and the LORD will answer;
> you will cry for help, and he will say: Here am I." (Isa 58:6–9)

God's promise of *peace* is to people who are committed to God's standards of *justice, truth,* and *compassion* in the world. There are no shortcuts for this hard work, and those who commit to it usually pay a high cost. But the cross of Christ reminds us that there is no other way.

People Who Honor God's Earth (vv. 11–12)

Yet the psalmist isn't finished, for the scope of his vision is not confined to people. Already he has spoken twice about the context – "your land" (v. 1), "our land" (v. 9). In verses 11–12, he returns to the land for the third time. For God's promise of peace is not only for those who know God's mercy and those who seek God's justice, but also for those who honor God's earth.

Those who "honor" God's earth don't merely see the earth as a place where we live, material stuff, or disposable property, but rather as God's creation, the object of God's love, and the beneficiary of God's provision. Those who honor God's earth take seriously the opening verse of the Bible – "God created the heavens and the earth" (Gen 1:1) – and understand the wonderful harmony that God wants between heaven and earth. Those who honor God's earth remember that the opening words of the "Great Commission" – "All authority in heaven and on earth has been given to me" (Matt 28:18) – are Christ's claim over all creation as Lord of heaven and earth.

In verse 11, the psalmist pictures this harmony in another attractive metaphor. He takes two of those personified words from verse 10 – *faithfulness* (or truth) and *justice* – and pictures them as rain coming down from heaven, meeting the crops growing up from earth. He binds together human and divine qualities (truth and justice) with creation itself (rain and crops), which are also gifts of God.

> [11] Faithfulness springs forth from the earth,
>   and righteousness looks down from heaven.
> [12] The LORD will indeed give what is good,
>   and our land will yield its harvest.
> [13] Righteousness goes before him
>   and prepares the way for his steps. (vv. 11–13)

When people on earth live by God's standards, there will be genuine fruitfulness in creation. This fruitfulness is part of the *shalom* that God grants.

Verse 12 expresses a beautiful balance and a simple biblical understanding of God and creation: God gives what is good (Gen 1), and the land gives back its productivity. This giving of nature is in response to the giving of God, and so we give thanks to *God* for what *the earth* gives us.

Yet we have made this beautiful picture almost unrecognizable. We want peace on earth, but there can be no peace for humanity as long as we rape the earth upon which we depend. Though God gives what is good, our earth is poisoned, stripped bare, fracked, exhausted, spoiled, stolen; our seas are over-fished, polluted, and warming; climactic extremes are hurting the poor of the world. The effects of climate change on whole populations are already fueling regional conflicts over scarce and dwindling resources. If war generates massive migrations, so will water – or the lack of it. People can survive war; we can't survive without water. Nor, indeed, can we survive if there is too much water, such as when whole islands and low-lying coastal areas are slowly submerged by rising ocean levels. What can reconciliation and peace possibly mean for people who suffer these massive environmental calamities?

Surely these are the massive contemporary "follies" from which verse 8 calls us to turn away. This psalm – only one fraction of the Old Testament – makes key points that we must take seriously as we pursue peace and reconciliation for the earth and all it contains. First, *there is no peace without God* – specifically without the forgiving grace and mercy of God. Therefore, we cannot separate our search for peace from the mandate of evangelism. Horizontal and vertical reconciliation must remain integrated in our understanding of the gospel and our practice of mission. Second, *there is no peace without justice.* Therefore, we cannot seek peace without advocacy and action for justice, however partial and provisional our efforts may seem. Third, *there is no peace without the earth.* Therefore, we cannot respond to human needs without seeing them in relation to their environmental and social contexts.

Psalm 85 affirms some key ingredients of what has come to be known as "integral mission" – living in God's earth, in God's way, for God's purposes, which is the *shalom* that will bring integration and wholeness to both humanity and creation, when truth, mercy, righteousness, and peace not only embrace one another, but also embody the reign of God.

The Scope of God's Peace – A New Testament Perspective

The creational note on which Psalm 85 ends provides a suitable transition into a New Testament perspective. For as Paul writes in one of his classic reconciliation texts, "God was reconciling the world to himself in Christ" (2 Cor 5:19). The "world" here includes the creation, which is very much in Paul's mind as he writes that when anyone is in Christ, the new creation is already there (5:17).

Cosmic Reconciliation (Colossians 1:15–20)

Colossians 1:15–20, perhaps the most exalted piece of writing in all Paul's letters, concerns the cosmic-creational significance of Christ's life and death. Paul wrote this letter to a church that seems to have been infected by some incipient Gnostic ideas, some of which included the idea of cosmic healing and unification. People in the ancient world were as much aware as we are today of the brokenness of our world and the realities of conflict and violence. Yet they more readily included the unseen world of spiritual or divine forces within that conflict-ridden worldview than our demythologized, post-enlightenment modernity worldview would acknowledge in this age.

People in first-century Palestine longed for peace. At one level, Octavian, Caesar Augustus, the first Roman emperor, claimed to have given it to them through the *Pax Romana*. By his victory over Antony at the Battle of Actium, 33 BC, Augustus claimed to achieve peace for the whole world and all nations. Contemporary Roman inscriptions proclaimed that this good news (*evangelium*) was accomplished by Caesar Augustus, "our great god and savior." This political peace was achieved by military force and through the suppression of rebels. By crucifying its opponents, Rome also made peace by the blood of the cross. Paul preached a very different peacemaking, a very different good news, but it also had a cross at its heart – the cross on which Jesus died.

At another level, cults and philosophies promised peace in the cosmic realm by placating the powers and divinities that stood behind human conflicts.

Paul did not preach this transcendent, non-historical, supra-mundane transaction in the heavenly realms, but rather the victory of the one who was himself the creator and sustainer of all created reality – both physical and spiritual. This victory was accomplished through the brutally physical reality of the cross on which Jesus of Nazareth shed his blood.

> [15]The Son is the image of the invisible God, the firstborn over all creation. [16]For in him all things were created: things in heaven and on earth, visible and invisible, whether thrones or powers or rulers or authorities; all things have been created through him and for him. [17]He is before all things, and in him all things hold together. [18]And he is the head of the body, the church; he is the beginning and the firstborn from among the dead, so that in everything he might have the supremacy. [19]For God was pleased to have all his fullness dwell in him, [20]and through him to reconcile to himself all things, whether things on earth or things in heaven, by making peace through his blood, shed on the cross. (Col 1:15–20)

Reconciliation, according to Paul, is neither an enforced political and military submission, nor a mystical or heavenly alignment of spiritual powers, but rather the plan and purpose of God for his whole creation, which was actually and historically accomplished through the bodily death and resurrection of God's Son, Jesus Christ.

Ralph Martin notes that this Christological and cross-centered exposition by Paul envisages a cosmic reconciliation that provides space and hope for reconciliation at the human level. He writes:

> The essence of Gnosticism was a dualism that set the high God and the material world in antithetical relationship. Our passage by asserting that "all the fullness" chose to reside in Christ is opposing any such dichotomy between the creator and the creation. "Reconciliation" takes on the meaning of harmony and peace with the cosmic order . . . [people in Graeco-Roman society lived with]

a sense of life's meaninglessness and lack of purpose since their fate rested in a cosmic strife over which they had no control and had little power to resolve . . . To such people the Christological tribute to the lordly Christ who embodied in himself the total pleroma of the creator would come as good news of hope and freedom . . . The universe was no longer to be regarded as an alien, threatening sphere; its "principalities and powers" were dethroned because of the supreme lordship of Christ . . . A new beginning in world history had been made (v. 18) with his elevation to supreme power as "firstborn from the dead;" and by that act of enthronement all the refractory elements of the universe had been united under his headship and authority.[3]

However, Martin continues, Paul does not remain purely at the cosmic level. By adding the crucial words, "making peace by the blood of his cross," Paul ensures that the personal dimension of reconciliation is clearly brought into the foreground. Martin observes that Paul's language of reconciliation:

. . . now embraces both the overcoming of the cosmic hostility through the lordship of Christ (explained in Col 2:15) and the restoration of sinful men and women to God's favor and family (1:22) . . . Paul can glide smoothly [from the reconciliation of creation in verse 20] to the discussion of verses 21–22 where both pronoun ("And you") and verb ("he has now reconciled by his death") stand in an unusual and emphatic position . . . Now the reconciliation touches human lives and produces the effect of a changed human character and conduct.[4]

But it was also at the cross that "the cosmic forces that were thought to control and tyrannize over human lives" were confronted and defeated – thus liberating human lives for reconciled freedom in Christ.[5]

That engagement between the *stoicheia* and Christ, Paul says, took place at the cross where the issue of God versus the powers was joined (Col 2:14–15). Their accusation and condemnation of humankind was levelled at Christ who in his representative person met the demand and took it upon himself. He both submitted

---

3. Ralph P. Martin, *Reconciliation: A Study of Paul's Theology* (London: Marshall, Morgan & Scott, 1981), 119–120.

4. Martin, *Reconciliation*, 122.

5. Martin, 122.

to and triumphed over the spirits; but it was no show of force or display of omnipotence that won the day. He died on the cross and shed his blood. Only then did his reign begin and only thus does it continue. Reconciliation whether of super-beings or of mortals was not easily secured as an other-worldly drama or automatic process.

The "subjugation" of demonic agents, following on their resounding defeat and open ignominy on Jesus's cross, is the scenario used to establish more firmly these infant believers in their knowledge of personal reconciliation to God by the same historical event of Jesus's death on the cross and to give them renewed assurance that as they have been forgiven by that death, so they may be set free from any kind of bondage that would rob them of their liberty as God's children. The dear son of God has undertaken a cosmic reconciliation that can never be reversed; it is their privilege as children of the same Father to rejoice in their reconciliation, actualised in forgiveness of sins.[6]

What this means is that all our human efforts for reconciliation and peace, provisional and imperfect though they will remain in this fallen world, are nevertheless carried on in a context in which the forces that instigate conflict and violence have themselves been defeated and shamed by the decisive victory of the cross. We are still on a battlefield, but the enemy has already been defeated. Ultimate, cosmic, creational reconciliation is already accomplished, though not yet fully consummated. We live, work, and struggle between the victory of the cross and the coming of the new creation, which will usher in the messianic reign of justice and peace. So our struggles for reconciliation and peacemaking are slung between those two poles, sustained, motivated, and guaranteed by both.

Ethnic Reconciliation (Ephesians 2:11–22)

It is generally assumed that Paul wrote this letter as a kind of "circular" to the churches in the same region as Colossae, most probably at the same time, or immediately after, he wrote the letter to Colossae.[7] There are striking similarities

---

6. Martin, 123–126.

7. A very thorough discussion of all the critical issues involved in the authorship and dating of Ephesians and Colossians, which concludes in favor of Pauline authorship of both, is provided by P. T. O'Brien, *The Letter to the Ephesians* (Grand Rapids: Eerdmans; Leicester: Apollos, 1999), 4–47.

in structure and theme, such that the wording of one often helps to illuminate the meaning of the other. The closest summary of what we have just read in Colossians 1:15–20 comes in Ephesians 1:9–10:

> [9][God] made known to us the mystery of his will according to his good pleasure, which he purposed in Christ, [10] to be put into effect when the times reach their fulfillment – to bring unity to all things in heaven and on earth under Christ.

Here again we see this divine plan and purpose expressed in cosmic-creational terms. The mission of God is to bring healing, reconciliation, unity, and wholeness to the whole creation – "all things in heaven and on earth" – and to accomplish that through Christ.

In the second half of Ephesians 1, Paul dwells on the cosmic significance of that plan:

> [19]That power is the same as the mighty strength [20]he exerted when he raised Christ from the dead and seated him at his right hand in the heavenly realms, [21]far above all rule and authority, power and dominion, and every name that is invoked, not only in the present age but also in the one to come. (vv. 19–21)

By his victorious resurrection, Christ now exercises supreme rule over all powers and authorities in the universe – whatever they may be. This is identical to the points made in Colossians 1.

But in chapters 2 and 3, Paul moves on from cosmic unification to ethnic reconciliation – from the heavenly to the earthly outworking of God's reconciling plan. Ephesians proclaims that the alienation between Jews and Gentiles has been overcome through the cross of Christ – just as Colossians proclaims that creation itself has been reconciled to God through the cross.

> [11]Therefore, remember that formerly you who are Gentiles by birth and called "uncircumcised" by those who call themselves "the circumcision" (which is done in the body by human hands) – [12]remember that at that time you were separate from Christ, excluded from citizenship in Israel and foreigners to the covenants of the promise, without hope and without God in the world. [13]But now in Christ Jesus you who once were far away have been brought near by the blood of Christ.
>
> [14]For he himself is our peace, who has made the two groups one and has destroyed the barrier, the dividing wall of hostility, [15]by setting aside in his flesh the law with its commands and regulations. His

purpose was to create in himself one new humanity out of the two, thus making peace, [16]and in one body to reconcile both of them to God through the cross, by which he put to death their hostility. [17]He came and preached peace to you who were far away and peace to those who were near. [18]For through him we both have access to the Father by one Spirit. (vv. 11–18)

Strikingly, Paul uses the word *peace* three times in this passage in relation to Christ. "He himself *is* our peace . . . thus making peace . . . He came and preached peace . . ." (vv. 14, 15, 17). Thus, the reconciliation of Jew and Gentile to each other creates "one new humanity" and enables them, in that one body, to be reconciled to God through the cross. This reconciliation is simultaneously and inseparably both horizontal and vertical.

Paul portrays the reconciled unity that has been created through the cross and is manifested in the church as the essential human dimension of cosmic unification (see Eph 1:9–10). God's purpose for the whole creation is to be modeled and anticipated in the church. Later Paul says that God displays his amazing wisdom to the spiritual powers – and signals to them their decisive defeat – precisely "through the church":

His intent was that now, *through the church*, the manifold wisdom of God should be made known to the rulers and authorities in the heavenly realms. (Eph 3:10, emphasis mine)

Now the object of Paul's teaching in Ephesians 2 and 3 is specifically the enmity between Jews and Gentiles – enmity which the cross destroyed. But in view of the scriptural role of Israel as God's means of bringing God's blessing to all nations, Paul may well see the reconciliation between Jews and Gentiles as paradigmatic of the wider power of the cross to bring reconciliation between ethnic groups in general. In other words, the cross is not only God's answer to the problem of Genesis 3 (all human beings are sinners who need God's mercy and forgiveness), but also God's answer to the problem of Genesis 11 (humans live in divided, confused, and conflicting nations and are in dire need of reconciliation). The gospel is good news not only for the forgiveness of sins, but also for the ultimate healing of the nations (Rev 22:2).

The global church, therefore, has the immense privilege and responsibility of demonstrating in advance that multiethnic reconciliation is God's purpose for all humanity, for those who will be redeemed by the blood of Christ from every tribe and language, nation and people.

Accordingly, in the wonderful flow of thought demonstrated in Ephesians, Paul moves from *cosmic integration* in chapter 1, to *ethnic reconciliation* into one new humanity in chapters 2 and 3, to *ecclesial unity* in chapter 4. At the head of his instructions in chapter 4 is the command to *maintain* the unity that God has already created:

> [1]As a prisoner for the Lord, then, I urge you to live a life worthy of the calling you have received. [2]Be completely humble and gentle; be patient, bearing with one another in love. [3]Make every effort to keep the unity of the Spirit through the bond of peace. (vv. 1–3)

This instruction in Ephesians reflects a more amplified teaching about unity and peace than the previous epistle to the Colossians:

> [12]Therefore, as God's chosen people, holy and dearly loved, clothe yourselves with compassion, kindness, humility, gentleness and patience. [13]Bear with each other and forgive one another if any of you has a grievance against someone. Forgive as the Lord forgave you. [14]And over all these virtues put on love, which binds them all together in perfect unity. [15]Let the peace of Christ rule in your hearts, since as members of one body you were called to peace. (Col 3:12–15)

Paul's teaching is very simple, utterly demanding, and regretfully ignored almost everywhere. Those whom God has reconciled to himself through the cross of Christ must live in reconciled love and unity with one another – even (and especially) across barriers of ethnicity, gender, and social class.

Though Paul was not present during the last hours that Jesus spent with his disciples before his crucifixion, Paul's teaching reflects both the command and prayer of Jesus that is recorded in John's Gospel, along with the same missional reasons – that the world will come to know who Jesus is, who sent him, and to whom his followers therefore belong:

> [34]"A new command I give you: Love one another. As I have loved you, so you must love one another. [35]By this everyone will know that you are my disciples, if you love one another." (John 13:34–35)

> [20]"My prayer is not for them alone. I pray also for those who will believe in me through their message, [21]that all of them may be one, Father, just as you are in me and I am in you. May they also be in us so that the world may believe that you have sent me. [22]I have given them the glory that you gave me, that they may be one as we are one – [23]I in them and you in me – so that they may be brought to complete unity. Then the world will know that you sent me and have loved them even as you have loved me. (John 17:20–23)

The Cape Town Commitment binds the command and the prayer together in this way:

> *Love calls for Unity.* Jesus's command that his disciples should love one another is linked to his prayer that they should be one. Both the command and the prayer are missional – "that the world may know you are my disciples," and that "the world may know that you [the Father] sent me."[8] A most powerfully convincing mark of the truth of the gospel is when Christian believers are united in love across the barriers of the world's inveterate divisions – barriers of race, colour, gender, social class, economic privilege or political alignment. However, few things so destroy our testimony as when Christians mirror and amplify the very same divisions among themselves. We urgently seek a new global partnership within the body of Christ across all continents, rooted in profound mutual love, mutual submission, and dramatic economic sharing without paternalism or unhealthy dependency. And we seek this not only as a demonstration of our unity in the gospel, but also for the sake of the name of Christ and the mission of God in all the world.[9]

Paul teaches us that Christian unity is the creation of God, based on our reconciliation with God and with one another. This double reconciliation has been accomplished through the cross. When we live in unity and work in partnership with one another, we demonstrate the supernatural, counter-cultural power of the cross. But when we demonstrate disunity through our failure to partner together, we demean our mission and message, and we deny the power of the cross.

Missional Reconciliation (Romans 14:1–15:13)

Recognizing the missional dimension of the imperative of reconciliation and peace brings us to Paul's letter to the Romans, the one specific case where Paul pleads, with the fullest range of personal and scriptural appeal, that a particular community of believers should live in peace with one another. What is most interesting here is not only the range of arguments that Paul brings to bear, but also the missionary motivation that surrounds his appeal.

---

8. John 13:34–35; 17:21.

9. The Lausanne Movement, "The Cape Town Commitment: A Confession of Faith and a Call to Action I.9.a," 2011, https://www.lausanne.org/content/ctc/ctcommitment.

We need to approach Romans 14:1–15:13 through the lens of all Paul has said so far in this great letter and then look further to what follows his appeal in the rest of Romans 15. We can lay it out as follows: Look what the gospel has created! Look what the gospel demands! Look where the gospel leads!

Look What the Gospel Has Created

Paul's whole argument in Romans (as in Galatians and Ephesians) is that the God of Israel has kept his promise to Abraham by fulfilling the mission of Israel in the person of the Messiah, Jesus of Nazareth, through whose death and resurrection God's blessing has now come to all nations – just as God promised. Thus, people from any and every nation can now become part of the people of God through faith in Jesus. Accordingly, Paul's central missionary goal is to bring about the obedience of faith among all nations (Rom 1:5; 16:26).

By going out to the nations, the gospel has created a multiethnic community of Jews and Gentiles in Christ. For Paul, the very essence of the gospel is that the old barriers have been broken down, and so he can declare to Gentile believers that, along with believing Jews, they are "all one in Christ Jesus" (Gal 3:28).

Paul then spends Romans 9–11 demonstrating that this inclusion of the Gentiles, far from being contrary to the Scriptures or in any way a failure of God to keep his promise to Israel, is the very fulfillment of the Scriptures and the paradoxical way in which God faithfully honors his promise to Abraham and achieves the purpose of Israel's election – the blessing of all nations.

In other words, the ingathering of people from all nations into unity with Israel fulfills the Scriptures. Reconciliation is not merely a byproduct or happy outcome of the gospel, but rather the proof of the gospel's truth and effective power.

Look What the Gospel Demands

With this vision of a reconciled humanity established through chapters 1–11, Paul turns to the specific issue in the church at Rome that is troubling him – the apparent disunity between Jewish believers and Gentile-background believers. The opening verses of Romans 14 indicate that there are serious disputes between the believers concerning some of the most precious and conscientious aspects of Jewish identity – food and Sabbath. These issues are apparently generating contempt on one side and condemnation on the other (v. 3). They are not minor differences of opinion, but serious theological and ethical disputes that could cause (and have caused) long-term fractures to arise within the church.

Paul responds to these divisions with a single command, "accept one another," which comes at both the beginning and the end of the section (14:1; 15:7). This command has the flavor of a welcoming and farewell embrace (like Ps 85:10), which he intersperses with a range of arguments.

And why should believers with so much difference between them accept one another and "make every effort to do what leads to peace" (Rom 14:19)? Paul weaves in and out of his passionate appeal for mutual acceptance, but three things stand out as major considerations.

First, because *we are subject and accountable to the same Lord* as master, savior, and judge (vv. 1–10), we have no right to judge or reject one another.

> ⁷For none of us lives for ourselves alone, and none of us dies for ourselves alone. ⁸If we live, we live for the Lord; and if we die, we die for the Lord. So, whether we live or die, we belong to the Lord . . . ¹⁰You, then, why do you judge your brother or sister? Or why do you treat them with contempt? For we will all stand before God's judgment seat. ¹¹It is written:
> "'As surely as I live,' says the Lord,
> 'every knee will bow before me;
>   every tongue will acknowledge God.'"
> ¹²So then, each of us will give an account of ourselves to God. (vv. 7–12)

Second, *we are constrained by love* (vv. 13–23), and therefore to act without love is to sin against Christ himself.

> ¹⁵If your brother or sister is distressed because of what you eat, you are no longer acting in love. Do not by your eating destroy someone for whom Christ died. (v. 15)

Third, *we are to be shaped by the example of Christ* (15:1–8), who followed the way of self-denial, suffering, and death so that we, as Jews and Gentiles, might praise God for the privilege of belonging together to God's people. (Notice how the cross is once again in the background of the call to reconciliation.)

> ²Each of us should please our neighbors for their good, to build them up. ³For even Christ did not please himself but, as it is written: "The insults of those who insult you have fallen on me."

> ⁷Accept one another, then, just as Christ accepted you, in order to bring praise to God. ⁸For I tell you that Christ has become a servant of the Jews on behalf of God's truth, so that the promises

made to the patriarchs might be confirmed ⁹and, moreover, that the Gentiles might glorify God for his mercy. (vv. 2–3, 7–9)

Look Where the Gospel Leads

Paul builds towards the climax of his argument in this section by piling up scriptural quotations from the Old Testament that all relate to God's promise to the Gentiles that they will rejoice and praise God for including them in his people along with Israel (15:9–12). This, of course, is precisely the mission to which Paul has given his life.

More particularly, he has immediate plans for this mission. As soon as he finishes his exhortation, he moves on to outline his plans for the next phase of his mission to these quarrelsome believers in Rome – including the part he wants them to play in it. Paul intends to carry on his evangelistic mission further westward to Spain, and so he wants to use the church in Rome as his base and sending church. But this mission demands the church to manifest reconciliation and peace with God and one another.

Paul makes this plea for unity in the church in Rome because he has experienced disunity in his "home church" in the past, which disrupted and hindered his mission – a situation we read about in Galatians 2.

Paul began his missionary career preaching the good news among the Gentiles of Asia Minor and then Greece from his church base in Antioch, where he taught that Gentiles and Jews could both be saved and belong together to God's people through faith in the Messiah Jesus. Paul's gospel was accepted by the apostles of the "mother church" in Jerusalem:

> They recognized that I had been entrusted with the task of preaching the gospel to the uncircumcised, just as Peter had been to the circumcised. ⁸For God, who was at work in Peter as an apostle to the circumcised, was also at work in me as an apostle to the Gentiles. ⁹James, Cephas and John, those esteemed as pillars, gave me and Barnabas the right hand of fellowship when they recognized the grace given to me. They agreed that we should go to the Gentiles, and they to the circumcised. (Gal 2:7–9)

Antioch was a well-mixed and well-taught church, as we read in Acts (11:19–30; 13:1–3). But then problems arose, as Paul explains in the verses that immediately follow the encouraging passage above:

> ¹¹When Cephas came to Antioch, I opposed him to his face, because he stood condemned. ¹²For before certain men came from James, he used to eat with the Gentiles. But when they arrived,

he began to draw back and separate himself from the Gentiles because he was afraid of those who belonged to the circumcision group. [13]The other Jews joined him in his hypocrisy, so that by their hypocrisy even Barnabas was led astray.

[14]When I saw that they were not acting in line with the truth of the gospel, I said to Cephas in front of them all, "You are a Jew, yet you live like a Gentile and not like a Jew. How is it, then, that you force Gentiles to follow Jewish customs?" (Gal 2:11–14)

"Even Barnabas was led astray!" The issue came between Paul and his closest companion in their combined teaching and missionary ministries. For Paul, this issue was contrary to "the truth of the gospel." If Jewish and Gentile believers could not live together – and eat together – in reconciled unity and equality, then the gospel was hollow and ineffective.

As Paul explains in Romans 15, his mission in the eastern Mediterranean basin has accomplished God's purposes, and now he intends to head further west to Spain, and he wants to make Rome his base for that mission.

[23]But now that there is no more place for me to work in these regions, and since I have been longing for many years to visit you, [24]I plan to do so when I go to Spain. I hope to see you while passing through and to have you assist me on my journey there, after I have enjoyed your company for a while. [25]Now, however, I am on my way to Jerusalem in the service of the Lord's people there . . . [28]So after I have completed this task and have made sure that they have received this contribution, I will go to Spain and visit you on the way. [29]I know that when I come to you, I will come in the full measure of the blessing of Christ. (Rom 15:23–29)

But there are problems in the church at Rome! The Gentile believers (probably the majority) are treating the Jewish believers with contempt for their adherence to Jewish practices, while the Jewish believers are condemning the Gentile ones for the apparent laxity of their "freedom." But this division is a denial of the truth of the gospel and a betrayal of Christ's sacrificial death. Furthermore, it will seriously hinder Paul's mission. Paul needs a united church in Rome as his sending church to Spain, for how can he preach the good news of the reconciling power of the gospel if the church he comes from is fractured and divided?

In other words, *the integrity of Paul's gospel and the integrity of Paul's mission are both at stake* in this issue of reconciliation within the church – and they still are today. Paul wants the Gentile believers in Rome to understand

God's love and purpose for the Jews (the thrust of Rom 9–11), and he wants both Jews and Gentile believers to love and accept one another as God in Christ has accepted them both (Rom 14–15). Otherwise his gospel and mission will lack credibility.

This recognition that reconciliation, unity, and peace between Christians demonstrate the gospel and are essential components of effective mission lies behind the exhortation of the Cape Town Commitment:

> A divided Church has no message for a divided world. Our failure to live in reconciled unity is a major obstacle to authenticity and effectiveness in mission.
>
> (A) We lament the dividedness and divisiveness of our churches and organizations. We deeply and urgently long for Christians to cultivate a spirit of grace and to be obedient to Paul's command to "make every effort to maintain the unity of the Spirit in the bond of peace."
>
> (B) While we recognize that our deepest unity is spiritual, we long for greater recognition of the missional power of visible, practical, earthly unity. So we urge Christian sisters and brothers worldwide, for the sake of our common witness and mission, to resist the temptation to split the body of Christ, and to seek the paths of reconciliation and restored unity wherever possible.[10]

Conclusion

Following are concluding statements about efforts to achieve reconciliation and peace among Christians and to engage in conflict-resolution and peacemaking in the wider world. First, we cannot hope to succeed without God's mercy, without a commitment to truth and justice, and without attending to the environment in which people live as well as their social, political, and economic circumstances. Second, our efforts must always follow the way of the cross. Third, our efforts must recognize both cosmic and spiritual dimensions, for we wrestle not against flesh and blood only, but against a powerful but defeated enemy (see Eph 6:12). Finally, the work of reconciliation must be a core part of an integrated understanding and practice of mission, which will authenticate the message we bring.

---

10. The Lausanne Movement, "The Cape Town Commitment: A Confession of Faith and a Call to Action II.F.1," 2011, https://www.lausanne.org/content/ctc/ctcommitment.

Ralph Martin's reflections on the classic reconciliation text in 2 Corinthians 5 conclude as follows:

> The call of Paul's gospel was to live "in peace" (1 Cor 7:15; 14:33; 2 Cor 13:11; Rom 12:18; Col 3:15; 1 Thess 5:13). The scope of such a term is wide . . .
>
> Reconciliation is more than a theological code-word for God's work of restoring men and women to himself. It marks the way of life to which those people are summoned by the fact that they are reconciled and share in God's continuing ministry of reconcilement in the world. The life of the Pauline congregations was for the apostle one of the most telling methods of evangelism since that corporate life was meant to reflect both the character of God and the outworking of the message as it applied to the human context. As Christians loved one another, forgave and were compassionate to one another, showed forth in their mutual attitudes that they shared a new spirit which was not self-centered, hard-hearted or spiteful but one that made for unity and harmony, so they were giving expression to the authenticity of the message of reconciliation . . .
>
> Bound up with this far-reaching prospect of a transnational, multi-racial Christian community as a novel entity on the world stage is the promise that this society mirrors as in a microcosm the hope of the world and the universe, at present divided and at odds with its creator.[11]

Such is the scope of God's mission – and the context and assurance of ours.

---

11. Martin, *Reconciliation*, 229–230.

2

"What's Your Name?"

Biblical Perspectives on Memory and Reconciliation

Takamitsu Muraoka

Reconciliation lies at the core of the Christian biblical message. Here I would like to look at reconciliation with reference to a few key passages in the Scriptures: Genesis 32:1–32, Mark 5:1–13, and Jeremiah 31:27–34.[1] I would like to show their implications for the work of reconciliation, particularly in regards to Japan's responsibility towards the peoples and countries it colonized during World War II.

Preconditions for Reconciliation (Gen 32:1–32)

This well-known chapter is a story of a reconciliation in progress. What can we learn from this Scripture about reconciliation?

First, humility on the part of perpetrators and wrongdoers is an absolutely necessary precondition for reconciliation. We see here the humility of Jacob. More than once, he calls his brother, "my lord, my master," instead of "you,"

---

1. *Editor's Note*: This was originally a public lecture given by Prof. Takamitsu Muraoka at Asian Theological Seminary on February 13, 2017. Upon retirement, he and his wife, Keiko, decided to devote a minimum of five weeks of every year to teaching and sharing his expertise in Hebrew, Aramaic and the Septuagint to the countries that were colonized and invaded by Japan in World War 2, as reparation for the atrocities of the Japanese army in the war.

and he calls himself, "your servant," instead of, "I," "my," or "me." This is a remarkable stance on the part of Jacob. When he was still in his mother's womb, she was told by God, "the elder boy will serve his junior" (Gen 25:23), and Esau, the senior, was told by his father, "You shall serve your younger brother" (Gen 27:40). Jacob's humility is displayed not only towards his brother, but also towards God, when he confesses, "I am unworthy of all the kindness and faithfulness you have shown your servant. I had only one staff when I crossed this Jordan, but now I have become two companies" (32:10).[2]

This humility is a spiritual price that Jacob had to pay before he could settle back in the land to which he yearned to return for so long, the land where he could build up his family with peace of mind, free from the fear of retaliation by his aggrieved elder brother.

Second, reconciliation sometimes entails a material price. In the case of Jacob, the price tag is pretty stiff: an assortment of livestock totaling 550 heads (32:14–15). By the end of 2005, Germany had paid out a staggering amount of €63,224 billion as compensation for Nazi crimes. I expect the country is still paying surviving victims. The payment is financed from taxes paid by all German citizens, who must have reckoned that peace and harmony with their neighboring nations and moral integrity in relation to the Jewish nation are worth the ongoing financial cost.

Our sense of guilt and remorse can be effectively communicated to the aggrieved party not only through our words, or what we say by way of apology, but also in material ways, through our deeds.

Third, a sense of guilt and remorse on the part of the perpetrator is another necessary precondition for reconciliation. When it is getting light and Jacob's opponent begs to be released, Jacob insists that he will not let his opponent go unless he blesses him (32:26). Then the anonymous opponent asks, "What's your name?" (32:27). This seems to be a very simple and obvious question, since the opponent surely knows with whom he has been wresting all night. He knows that Jacob asked God to rescue him from Esau and that he is fearful of his elder brother (32:11). The opponent also knows that Jacob is very desirous of reconciliation and peace with Esau (32:20). By putting this seemingly obvious question to Jacob, the opponent is trying to make Jacob see why he had to spend twenty long years away from home, away from his doting mother, and why he finds himself still cornered, fearful of his only brother. The opponent is reminding Jacob, "Jacob, O yes, that is the answer you should have given

---

2. Most Bible translations are from the author.

when your father asked you, 'What's your name, my son?' But you lied and said: 'I am Esau, your firstborn'" (Gen 27:19).

On hearing Jacob's honest answer, without excuses, the opponent blesses him straightaway and then renames him "Israel" (32:28). His response may be paraphrased, "Through your humility, honesty, and moral integrity, you have come out a winner, you have won peace with the God of justice, and you are on the way to achieving reconciliation with your brother."

Remembering the Name (Mark 5:1–13)

The name a person bears is not "just a name." When Esau discovers that he has been tricked and fraudulently robbed of his blessing, he utters a heartbreaking cry: "Jacob – that name is a perfect reflection of what he is" (Gen 27:36). A name embodies the bearer's past and present – who the person was and what he or she did as well as who the person now is and what he or she does.

When God creates animals, cattle, and birds, he brings each to Adam in order to ascertain Adam's name for it (Gen 2:19). We see that God is interested even in animals' names.

Jesus compares himself to a good shepherd, who calls each sheep by its own name when he leads the flock out of its sheepfold to pasture every morning. He doesn't say, "Hey, sheep, follow me, all of you!"

In the 1980s, when I taught at the University of Melbourne, Australia, I got to know the principal of a local Jewish day school. He once shared with me that he knew the names of all his six hundred or so pupils, not only the problem kids or academically outstanding pupils. When he would run into a pupil on the school playground, he would say, "Hi, Simon, I heard your father had been hospitalized. How is he doing?"

Why does Jesus need to know the name of the demoniac of Gerasene before proceeding to treat him? The man comes up to the Lord, shouting, "Jesus, Son of the Most High God," so he already knows the physician's name (Mark 5:7). But when Jesus asks, "What's your name?" the miserable man's reply is, "legion," a Latin word denoting a military unit of some six thousand soldiers (5:9). This is a most unusual diagnosis, for the poor man is possessed of six thousand mini-demons. The patient's reply shows his total confusion: "My [singular] name is *legion*, for we [plural] are many" (5:9). The only effective remedy is to restore his true identity – his real name (5:15).

Peter, addressing the Sanhedrin after the Pentecost, declares, "The salvation does not come through anybody other than Jesus Christ the Nazarene; there is no other name given under the heaven with which we need to be saved" (Acts

4:12). Thus the name of Jesus itself has a saving power. The name embodies a Savior. Jesus, which is a Hebrew name, also means "savior."

A Memorial without Names

On the occasion of my annual return to my hometown in Japan two years ago, seventy years after the defeat of my country in the Pacific War, I visited a spot which I had long wanted to visit, a humble stone memorial in a forest beside a railway.

Five days after Japan's defeat, a trainload of soldiers was heading home. At that spot in the forest, there begins a steep upward climb. As a child, I sometimes went there with friends, racing with a train. On that particular day after the war, the train – which was loaded beyond capacity with soldiers, many sitting on the roof – suddenly came to a halt in the middle of a tunnel that was some six hundred meters long. The soldiers, who were choking on the smoke belching from the locomotive, got off the train and began to walk back out of the tunnel. When the train started rolling back, fifty-six soldiers were killed beneath the train's wheels. What a tragedy for them and for their waiting families and friends!

When I looked at the inscription on the memorial, which was built on the seventeenth anniversary of the accident, I was deeply shocked. Though the stone identifies the date and the number of the victims, not a single name is inscribed – even though the memorial is large enough to accommodate all fifty-six names. The inscription also states that since the building of the memorial, the bereaved families have been coming there to commemorate their dear ones. Regretfully, the individual dead soldiers have become mere statistics.

A Face-off with God

Although Jacob cannot elicit the name of his opponent, he names the memorable place *Peniel*, a Hebrew expression that means "the face of God" (Gen 32:30). Though it is not apparent in translation, the Hebrew word *panim*, meaning "face," appears to be the keyword in this story. A literal translation of Genesis 32:20–21 would read, "You should say, 'Look, sir, your servant, Jacob, is also behind us.' For he had thought: with this gift going before my *face* I would like to cleanse his dreadful *face* of anger and hate, and then later I might be able to look him straight in the *face*, and perhaps he may say, 'Look me up in the *face*,' and the gift proceeded before his *face*, and that night he lodged in the camp." Later, in Genesis 33, we see Jacob in his brother's arms, saying,

"As I look you in the *face*, it looks like God's *face*" (v. 11). At Peniel, Jacob has a *face*-off with God. For Christians, our Peniel is Calvary, where every time we realize we have committed a sin, we have a *face*-off with God, as we listen to Jesus asking us, "What's your name?"

When Jacob's opponent is gone, the sun shines for him (not "above him," as in the NIV, 32:31). He is now out of a long, pitch-dark tunnel of fear, anxiety, uncertainty, and guilty conscience, and so he marches on in the broad daylight – though he is limping. In the rest of the book of Genesis, we never read of Jacob being cured of this handicap. For the rest of his life, whenever he needs to hurry, he is reminded of the incident at Peniel and all that it implied.

Some time ago, we had a Korean missionary staying with us. During breakfast one morning, he told us an interesting story about a naughty boy. One day his father said to him, "Listen, if you misbehave next time, I shall hammer an iron peg in the wooden wall of our living room." Pegs kept increasing. After some time, there were twenty of them! The boy was despondent. Then he had a bright idea: "Dad, if I do a really good thing for you, will you pull one of the pegs out?" The pegs kept disappearing, and after a while there were none left. The boy was overjoyed. However, when he took a close look at the wall, he saw twenty holes still remaining. Yet he did not ask his father to fill them in.

Coming back to Genesis 32, Jacob's limp remains stuck not only in Jacob's memory, but also in the national memory. Even hundreds of years later, when the book of Genesis was written down, his descendants still did not eat the tendon attached to the socket of the hip of any animal (v. 32). They needed to be reminded that even though they were named after this forefather as "children of Israel," and even though they had been chosen by their God for a special blessing and a unique mission for humankind, this blessing was not *because of* their forefather, but rather *in spite of* him. This also applies to us as Christians – we are the New Israel.

A name is borne not only by an individual person, but also by a group of individuals, a family, a church, a theological seminary, a company, or a nation. There is no group which does not have dark pages in their history. It is necessary for us to remember and learn from our history, both personal and collective, the bright side as well as the dark side. I would even say that this knowledge is necessary not only for perpetrators, but also for victims, however painful it may be. We are all fallible humans. The victims of yesterday could degenerate into victimizers tomorrow.

The Bridge on the River Kwai

Since 2003, when I retired from Leiden University, every year I have been visiting an Asian country for voluntary teaching, tithing my time, returning to God a minimum of five weeks per year. This is an act of penance against the background of incalculable damages, losses, and sufferings – physical, material, and mental – inflicted by my Japanese compatriots during the first half of the last century.

During the three years of occupation of the Philippines, the Japanese army inflicted horrible damages and sufferings on hundreds of thousands of Filipinos. Some other Asian peoples suffered as badly or even far worse, such as Koreans and Chinese. Unlike Germany, one of our allies at the time, my country has done little since the end of the war to deal with this past. In the 1970s, when we lived in Manchester, Great Britain, every year on the second Sunday of November, Remembrance Sunday, the British Broadcasting Corporation (BBC) would telecast a well-known film, "Bridge on the River Kwai." It is a film about the infamous 415 kilometer Thai-Burma railway built by the Japanese Army during World War II with the illegal use of Prisoners of War (POW) of the allied forces. Because of harsh working conditions, poor nutrition, insufficient medical supplies, and physical violence, an estimated thirteen thousand out of about sixty-one thousand POWs perished.

We also know that to construct the death railway, a huge number of laborers were brought, often by force or deception, from some neighboring Southeast Asian countries under Japanese occupation. Of the estimated two hundred thousand laborers, some ninety thousand are said to have perished. Unlike the case of the Allied Forces, there are no precise statistics for these deaths, which does not, by any means, diminish the scale of the tragedy nor the extent of the injustice.

I once read of an Indonesian forced laborer who survived the ordeal. However, at the end of the war, he was penniless and could not pay for a journey home. Thus he decided to stay put and marry a local Thai woman. Some years later, he was met in his village by an ex-Japanese soldier named Nagase, who had served as an interpreter at one of the railway construction sites. Nagase took pity on him and offered him some money for a return air ticket. One evening, at a meeting in his village in Indonesia, he talked about his experiences in Thailand. At the end of his talk an old woman came up to him and asked, "Do you remember me?" Hard as he tried, he could not remember who she was. Then she muttered, "I was your fiancée, and I still am!" Thereupon the old man broke down and burst into tears.

Near the bridge on the River Kwai stands a stone memorial built by ex-POWs who survived the ordeal. Engraved on the memorial are the names of all their colleagues who didn't make it, and there is an inscription at the bottom: "We forgive you, but we shall never forget." One Japanese Christian minister, referring to this inscription, said, "How wonderful that we believe in a god who forgives and forgets." Two years ago, when I taught in Taiwan, I preached at a church in Taipei. The title of my sermon was, "Is our God forgetful?" My answer to this rhetorical question was a resounding, "no." Our God is not in the business of revising, doctoring, or polishing up our spiritual curriculum vitae (c.v.). If we truly confess a sin and are forgiven, God will draw a line across the relevant page of our c.v., but will not tear the page off or blot it over with correction liquid.

Forgive and Forget? (Jeremiah 31:27–34)

Some of you might contradict me by referring to Jeremiah 31:34, where we read, "I will forgive their iniquity, and their sin will I remember no more." This verse concludes the announcement of the arrival of a new age with a new covenant, as seen in the following:

> [27]"Behold, the days come," says Yahweh, "that I will sow the house of Israel and the house of Judah with the seed of man, and with the seed of animal. [28]It shall happen that, like as I have watched over them to pluck up and to break down and to overthrow and to destroy and to afflict, so will I watch over them to build and to plant," says Yahweh. [29]"In those days they shall say no more, 'The fathers have eaten sour grapes, and the children's teeth are set on edge.' [30]But everyone shall die for his own iniquity: every man who eats the sour grapes, his teeth shall be set on edge. [31]Behold, the days come," says Yahweh, "that I will make a new covenant with the house of Israel, and with the house of Judah: [32]not according to the covenant that I made with their fathers in the day that I took them by the hand to bring them out of the land of Egypt; which my covenant they broke, although I was a husband to them," says Yahweh. [33]"But this is the covenant that I will make with the house of Israel after those days," says Yahweh: "I will put my law in their inward parts, and in their heart will I write it; and I will be their God, and they shall be my people: [34]and they shall teach no more every man his neighbor, and every man his brother, saying, 'Know Yahweh'; for they shall all know me, from their least to their

greatest," says Yahweh: "for I will forgive their iniquity, and their sin will I remember no more." (Jer 31:27–34, World English Bible)

It appears that this announcement is being made against the background of a fundamental error made by Jeremiah's contemporaries of the famous statement in the Decalogue, the backbone of the old covenant: "I, Yahweh your God, am a jealous God, visiting the iniquity of the fathers on the children, on the third and on the fourth generation of those who hate me" (Exod 20:5). Some people apparently misinterpreted this as meaning that people could be punished for the sins of their forefathers, which they themselves did not commit. Our God of justice is absolutely fair and would not do such a thing. What is meant by the text is that if we commit sins like those committed by our forefathers, God will punish us just as he punished our forefathers. If we commit a sin and confess it and are forgiven by God, we have to transmit that personal history to our children, grandchildren, and so on.

Is Jeremiah saying that there is no connection, no historical continuity between the past and the present, between the past generation and the present? Hardly. The "new" covenant he is speaking about is not new in content, but rather the *renewal* of the old covenant. The old covenant was engraved on two stone tablets, but the new covenant will be put in our hearts.

The principle of individual responsibility mentioned in Jeremiah 31:30, "But everyone shall die for his own iniquity," harks back to Deuteronomy 24:16: "The fathers shall not be put to death for the children, nor shall the children be put to death for the fathers. Every man shall be put to death for his own sin." It is not as if God was unforgiving in the past and only recently emerged as a forgiving God. God has always been a forgiving, merciful god. Even Jeremiah readily admits that his God is still the God of Abraham, Isaac, and Jacob. The God of Israel was, is, and will continue to be a god who works in history: "God, who is and who was and who is to come" (Rev 1:4); "I am Alpha and I am Omega" (Rev 21:6). We, whether as individuals or groups, are historical beings, and we will neither be punished for our forefathers' sins nor rewarded for their merits.

When we remember the grievous sins for which we have been forgiven, we can be truly grateful to God for his love and mercy. I do not think the message encoded in the inscription on the memorial near the River Kwai is at all unbiblical or un-Christian. To imagine that our God forgives our sins and then forgets about them is cheap grace. When the Lord says, "I will forgive their iniquity, and their sin will I remember no more" (Jer 31:34), this does not mean that he cannot recall the sins his people committed or what sins he forgave. God does not suffer from amnesia, whether temporary or chronic.

You can be sure that God remembers all the details of our spiritual c.v. The Hebrew verb translated as "remember" here means "to act on one's memory." The cross on which our Lord died had two bars of wood diametrically crossing each other: the one symbolized God's justice, and the other symbolized God's love and mercy. This is the only cross that can save us from eternal perdition.

It may be emotionally easier to forgive the wrongs and injustices that have been inflicted on us by other generations and to leave the painful past behind us once and for all. However, the scribes had a point when they protested to Jesus, "Who can forgive sins except God alone?" (Mark 2:7). For the truth stands: "If we confess our sins, God is faithful and just to forgive our sins and cleanse us of any unrighteousness" (1 John 1:9). The Greek verb translated here as "confess" means, "to say the same thing." Both parties need to face each other and reach basic agreement about what happened between them. If the perpetrator begs for forgiveness, the victim might be moved to forgive the perpetrator in the presence of God, and only then can true reconciliation take place.

If one of the parties, or neither party, does not recognize the biblical God, then a principle which transcends the horizontal, interpersonal relationship may be invoked. The military court held in Munich after the Second World War introduced a new principle called "crime against humanity." Any sin or crime is, after all, a violation of the humanity and human dignity with which every human being is endowed as a descendant from Adam and Eve who is created in God's image and likeness.

Taking Responsibility for the Sins of the Past Generation

By admitting or confessing wrongdoing, an individual or a group of individuals takes responsibility for that wrong.

One Saturday, during my second visit to the Philippines, my wife and I visited the municipality of Lumban, one of the oldest towns in the province of Laguna, about a hundred kilometers from Metro Manila. We stood in front of a huge marble stone, the Yamashita Shrine. On the right side, there was a monolingual inscription in Japanese – "In memory of the Japanese war-dead in the Philippine islands" – while on the left corner, there was a Japanese-English plaque – "Built in 1979 by the Japanese Government with assistance of the Philippine Government."

We ran into a group of local school children and asked their teacher what she had told the pupils about the monument. "I tell them it symbolizes the friendship between our country and Japan," she told us. However, she was unaware that, at the hands of many of those fallen soldiers (a little over half a million), about twice as many Filipinos were killed.

Our Lord told his disciples: "Nobody can display greater love for his friends than laying down his life for them" (John 15:13). When I mentioned this fact to one of the guards nearby, he pulled out a newspaper clip of a visit made to the site by the Japanese Emperor Akihito and Empress Michiko. When asked if the imperial couple expressed any remorse for the Filipino victims of the war, he answered in the negative. Japanese media reported that the couple met with Japanese citizens, whose fathers or brothers were among the half a million Japanese soldiers who had died in the war, expressing sympathy about how difficult it must have been for them over the years. One could sense the depth and sincerity of the emperor's sentiments from his words and facial expressions. In contrast, however, there was no word of apology to the Filipino victims on behalf of his father, Hirohito, who had been the emperor during World War II.

But Filipino victims were not the only ones who suffered the effects of the war. Every Japanese soldier was taught to die for the emperor and many did. If the war was wrong, the emperor is responsible not only for the victims and the damages caused by the war, but also for the Japanese soldiers and their families. One of these was Onoda, an ex-sublieutenant of the Imperial Japanese Army, whose story hit the news headlines in 1973 after he returned to Japan. He hid in the jungles of the Philippines for twenty-nine years, not knowing that Japan had already been defeated. However, there was no apology from the emperor or his son. The emperor merely expressed his sympathies but did not say anything about the war being wrong.

Nine years ago, I gave a lecture at the University of Nanjing in Jiangsu province, China. I was introduced to the audience as "Muraoka," though I was fully aware that on August 15, 1945, when I was only seven years old, my late father, Muraoka Yoshie, was in the city as a lieutenant colonel of the Imperial Japanese Army. In December 1937, when the massacre of Nanjing took place, I was still in my mother's womb. Yet I agree with Richard von Weizsäcker, former president of Germany, who delivered a famous speech to the German Parliament on May 8, 1985, the fortieth anniversary of the defeat of Germany:

> One who closes his eyes to the past becomes also blind to the present. Most of our German citizens today were either children or not yet born during the war. They cannot confess sins which they did not commit personally. However, guilty or innocent, young

or old, we are all responsible for what we make of this historical legacy and how we relate to it.[3]

Conclusion

The relationship between the Philippines and Japan was gravely damaged following Japan's invasion in 1942 and the Japanese army's treatment of the Philippines during their occupation. Even though it has been more than seventy years since the cessation of hostilities, in the eyes of God the relationship is far from repaired.

Conflicts, armed or otherwise, sadly appear to be a permanent feature of human existence, though that was not how God created the first human couple (Gen 2:18–25). It is incumbent on us to strive to resolve these conflicts in order to make our lives worth living. For this reconciliation to be achieved, both perpetrators and victims need to face their history. The former need to admit their guilt honestly and sincerely ask for forgiveness. Only then can the way be open for reconciliation to take place. Though this will not be easy, there is no other way to arrive at genuine reconciliation. This is true not only at the individual level, but also at the collective level, between groups and nations.

This path has been manifested through the cross. Jesus Christ, hanging on the cross, visually unifies the principle of justice with the principle of empathy and love.

---

3. Translated by the author from the German text, "Von Weizsäckers berühmte Rede vom 8. Mai 1985," *Welt*, January 1, 2015, https://www.welt.de/politik/deutschland/article136982300/Von-Weizsaeckers-beruehmte-Rede-vom-8-Mai-1985.html.

3

God in the Face of the Other

A Biblical Model for Resolving Conflicts (Genesis 32–33)

Alvin M. Molito

This essay is a study of the fascinating biblical story of reconciliation between Jacob and Esau.[1] The story is familiar, especially for Christians who grew up in Sunday School. Most tend to see this narrative as a classic example of sibling rivalry brought about by parents' attitudes towards their children. The father, Isaac, favors Esau, while his wife, Rebekah, favors Jacob. On the other hand, some see this as a homecoming story of the estranged son/brother after a period of exile. Others tend to read this narrative in light of God's overall redemptive plan in the way that the sovereign God chooses to bless Jacob and make him the heir of the Abrahamic covenant in spite of his limitations and weaknesses. From Jacob comes Israel, and through the line of Israel comes the Messiah, through whom God redeems his people. In short, this narrative is either read in terms of the bigger narrative of God's redemptive plan or in light of familial conflicts.

---

1. I developed this paper from my two previous works, "Transformation in the Context of Divine-Human Confrontation: A Narrative Reading of Genesis 32–33," in *Phronesis* 17–20 (2010–2013): 111–130 and "From Jacob to 'Israel,' Transformation Through Divine Confrontation: Narrative, Ritual, and Etiological Analysis of Genesis 32:23–33" (master's thesis, Asian Theological Seminary, March 2015). In this paper I will specifically look at the angle of reconciliation.

In this essay, through a close reading of the narrative, I shall attempt to offer a perspective that can help appropriate this story in relation to the theme of peace and reconciliation. To this end, I shall employ *narrative criticism*,[2] particularly the analysis of the plot structure.[3] Then I will draw connections between the narrative structure and the framework of a rite of passage. Finally, I will identify some ethical principles by which we can appropriate this narrative to our present context by examining the "face of God" motif in relation to conflict resolution.[4]

Conflict, Confrontation, and Reconciliation in the Jacob Narrative

From beginning to end, Jacob's life is marked by conflict and struggle. While in his mother's womb, Jacob and his twin brother, Esau, *struggle* (Gen 25:22). On his deathbed, when he is blessing his children, he mentions Simeon's and Levi's act of violence against the men of Shechem (Gen 49:5–7; cf. 34:13–31); he describes how Dan and Gad will be attacking the *heels* of horses and raiders, respectively, a metaphor for deception and treachery (49:17, 19; cf. 25:26; 27:36), and how Joseph is attacked by archers yet prevails because of his strength and because of the Lord's blessing (49:22–26); finally, he describes Benjamin, his youngest son, as a "ravenous wolf" who devours its prey and divides the plunder (49:27). All these descriptions imply that the lives of Jacob and his children will be marked by deception, violence, and survival.

In Genesis, the *Jacob cycle* covers a large portion (Gen 25:29–35:29).[5] George Coats describes this cycle as a novella with different twists and turns of events towards the dramatic resolution of tensions in the life of the hero.[6] Coats notes that the primary intention of the Jacob novella is to describe the growth of Jacob's family under the theme of *strife* or *conflict*. In other words,

---

2. See Robert Alter, *The Art of Biblical Narrative*, rev. ed. (New York: Basic Books, 2010); Yairah Amit, *Reading Biblical Narratives* (Minneapolis, MN: Fortress Press, 2001); Shimon Bar-Efrat, *Narrative Art in the Bible* (Sheffield: Sheffield Academic Press, 1989, 1997); Jerome T. Walsh, *Style and Structure in Biblical Hebrew Narrative* (Collegeville, MN: The Liturgical Press, 2001).

3. Alter, *The Art of Biblical Narrative*, 20.

4. See Emmanuel Levinas, *Otherwise Than Being*, trans. Alfonso Lingis (Dordrecht: Kluwer Academic Publishers, 1991). Also, Philippe Nemo's interview with Emmanuel Levinas, "Ethics and Infinity," *Cross Currents* 34, no. 2 (1984): 191–203.

5. Genesis 32–33 fits within the frame of the story about the family of Isaac (Gen 25:19–35:29) known as the "Jacob cycle." See Thomas Mann, *The Book of the Torah: The Narrative Integrity of the Pentateuch* (Atlanta, GA: John Knox Press, 1988), 51.

6. George W. Coats, *Genesis with an Introduction to Narrative Literature*, FOTL 1 (Grand Rapids: Eerdmans, 1983), 265.

the narrator depicts a family that continues to survive despite the conflicts that threaten to break it apart.[7]

Robert Cohn identifies three large sections in this novella. In between the conflicts and confrontation between Jacob and Esau (Gen 27–28; 32–33), Jacob has conflict and confrontation with Laban (29–31). According to Cohn, "these long narratives enable the author to probe deeply into the character of Jacob and his relationships with his brother and father-in-law, as well as with his mother, his father, and his wives."[8] Following Cohn, the plot of the narrative can be structured as follows: (1) the Jacob–Esau Conflict (Gen 27–28); (2) the Jacob–Laban Conflict (Gen 29–31); (3) the Jacob–Esau Conflict (Gen 32–33).

However, within these large sections, there are also narratives that concern Jacob's relationship with Yahweh. When Jacob leaves the house of his father (Isaac) to flee the wrath of Esau, he encounters Yahweh through a dream in Bethel (28:10–22). Later, when he departs from his father-in-law (Laban), Jacob has another encounter with God, first through God's angels in Mahanaim (32:1), then through an unknown attacker at Jabbok (32:22–32). According to Cohn, these divine encounters act as hinges that connect the Jacob–Esau stories with the Jacob–Laban story as they relate to the journey of Jacob away and back to the Promised Land. In other words, in these narratives, God appears at the borders, blessing Jacob's exit and entrance.[9]

Taking into consideration these elements, including the motif of conflict and confrontation in the Jacob cycle, the plot of the novella looks like this:

Jacob–Esau Conflict: Jacob leaves Canaan (25:22–23; 27–28)

Jacob–Divine Confrontation in Bethel (28:10–22)

Jacob–Laban Conflict: Jacob in Haran (29–31)

Jacob–Divine Confrontation in Mahanaim and Peniel (32:1–32)

Jacob–Esau Conflict Resolved: Jacob arrives at Canaan (33:1–17; 35:28–29)[10]

---

7. Coats, *Genesis with an Introduction*, 222.

8. Robert L. Cohn, "Narrative Structure and Canonical Perspective in Genesis," *JSOT* 25 (1983): 8.

9. Cohn, "Narrative Structure," 9.

10. This is my own structure of the Jacob cycle, but the same kind of structure with minor differences is found in Jerome T. Walsh, *Style and Structure in Biblical Hebrew Narrative* (Collegeville, MN: Liturgical Press, 2001), 31.

This is a chiastic pattern, or a reverse symmetry, that emphasizes the contrasts and reversals in the life of Jacob.[11] The first part of Jacob's journey is comprised of his moving away from Canaan into Haran (25:22–23; 27–28). Prior to his arrival at Haran, Jacob has an encounter with God in Bethel (28:10–22). The second part of his journey consists of his journey from Haran and back to Canaan (31:1–33:20; 35:28–29). In this return journey, Jacob has another encounter with God, this time in Mahanaim and then in Peniel (32:1–2, 23–33). When Jacob leaves Canaan, it is to avoid Esau's death threats (27:42–28:2). When he returns, he discovers that Esau is as changed as Jacob himself by his encounters with Yahweh (33:1–16). Thus, the Jacob–Esau conflict is resolved, and Jacob settles in Canaan (33:17–20).

In this structure, the reconciliation between Jacob and Esau (Gen 32–33) highlights the conclusion of the cycle. This final section can be divided into five scenes, which follow a concentric structure, in which Jacob's struggle with an unidentified attacker (32:22–32) is sandwiched between Jacob's preparations to meet Esau and their meeting (32:3–21; 33:1–16), and also between his journey towards and his arrival at Canaan (32:1–2; 33:17–20).

Scene 1: Jacob travels to Canaan (32:1–2)

Scene 2: Jacob prepares to meet Esau (32:3–21)

Scene 3: Jacob wrestles with an unidentified adversary (32:22–32)

Scene 4: Jacob meets Esau (33:1–16)

Scene 5: Jacob arrives at Canaan (33:17–20)

The narrative structure reveals the reconciliation process between Jacob and Esau. It is quite interesting how the redactor of this entire novella arranged these events in order to show to readers the unfolding drama about Jacob's transformation and his reconciliation with Esau as well as the essential elements of this process.

The story of Jacob's journey away from his family and his return resembles the plight of many people today. A lot of people are forced to leave their families behind, some due to conflicts in their own families or communities, while others are forced to leave because of the difficult social or political situation in their home countries (i.e. poverty, political instability, and armed conflicts). Through the story of Jacob, I hope that people today can find inspiration and

---

11. Walsh, *Style and Structure*, 31. Walter Brueggemann also sees chiastic structure, but he places the fertility of Jacob's family and livestock (Gen 29:31–30:24) at the center. See Brueggemann, *Genesis* (Atlanta, GA: John Knox Press, 1982), 213.

wisdom in dealing with our sense of displacement and unrest so that we might be able to find our way towards transformation and peaceful reconciliation.

Rite of Passage and Jacob's Transformation

Through the previous analysis of the plot structure, I identified the major events in Jacob's life, which is characterized by a series of journeys away from his family in Canaan to a place of temporary shelter (in Haran) until he finally returns to Canaan. This journey, however, is not a simple story of going away and returning to one's homeland; rather, "it represents a journey with multiple dimensions: geographical, psychological and religious; individual and communal; human and divine."[12] Throughout his journey, Jacob has several encounters with God and men, and these encounters shape him into becoming *Israel,* through whom God fulfills his promise to Abraham and his descendants (Gen 28:13–15; 35:11–12).

The story of Jacob's life shows the process of individual transformation. From being branded as a deceiver and a usurper of blessing since birth, Jacob becomes the *blessed* one who prevails over God in a wrestling match. Another mark of transformation is Jacob's noticeable humility before Esau (Gen 33:3).[13] There are three key stages in Jacob's life that reveal this transformation process: first, his departure from his family in Canaan; second, his life in Haran, which serves as a threshold in his journey;[14] and third, his return and reconciliation with his family. Interestingly, Genesis 32–33 follows a pattern of separation, transition, and re-incorporation, which results in the reconciliation of Jacob and Esau, a process that can be compared to a *rite of passage.*[15]

A *rite of passage* is a ritual or ceremony conducted to mark an individual's or people's "succession of states," either from one place to another, or from one social state to the next.[16] A rite of passage involves three stages: separation (*pre-liminal*), transition (*liminal*), and re-incorporation (*post-liminal*).[17] This process enables an individual or community to overcome the challenges and difficulties associated with change once the transformation is complete. In

---

12. Mann, *Book of the Torah,* 65.

13. Gordon Wenham, *Genesis 16–50,* WBC (Dallas, TX: Word Books, 1994), 304.

14. Wenham, *Genesis 16–50,* 55.

15. See Heather McKay, "Jacob Makes It Across the Jabbok: An Attempt to Solve the Success/Failure Ambivalence in Israel's Self-Consciousness," *JSOT* 38 (1997): 3–13.

16. See Arnold Van Gennep, *The Rites of Passage,* trans. Monika B. Vizedom and Gabrielle L. Caffee (Chicago: University of Chicago Press, 1960), 2–3, 21.

17. Van Gennep, *Rites of Passage,* 21.

light of this concept of a rite of passage, I will examine the process of Jacob's transformation and how his experience leads to his reconciliation with Esau.

Separation

The stage of separation begins when Jacob is separated from his family because of his consistent and successful attempts to usurp the blessing intended for Esau, which results in alienation and hostility between the brothers. So Jacob departs for Haran to escape the wrath of his brother (27:41–44). Jacob's departure from Canaan is followed by a special revelation from Yahweh through a dream in Bethel, in which God promises to bless Jacob and make him great – in line with his covenant with Abraham and Isaac (28:13–15). So Jacob dedicates the place to Yahweh by setting up a pillar of stone and promises to serve God once he is able to return safely (28:20–22). Apparently for Jacob, his separation from his family is only temporary, just like the separation stage in a rite of passage.

Later, in Genesis 32–33, we can see another form of separation between Jacob and his immediate family. When he is on his way back to Canaan, he prepares to meet Esau by sending messengers ahead of him (32:3–5). This act bears some political color, for it is another subtle attempt to outwit Esau by showing that Jacob is no ordinary traveler. Jacob also tells the servants to tell Esau about his wealth (v. 5), and he creates the impression that he is traveling with and is *still with Laban* (v. 4). Here, we see how Jacob tries to deceive Esau once again by showing off his wealth and company, perhaps to intimidate his brother, whom he obsequiously calls, "my lord" (v. 5a).[18]

But when the messengers return, they report that Esau is coming to meet Jacob with four hundred strong men. This fills Jacob with fear and anxiety (32:7–8),[19] and so he devises a plan to secure the safety of his family by dividing them into two, so that if Esau attacks one half, the other half can escape (v. 8). After this, he prays to God and asks for divine intervention (vv. 9–12).[20] Then he

---

18. Jacob addresses his brother as "my lord Esau" (v. 5) because Esau is now the lord of the land that Jacob is about to cross. But the more interesting part of this encounter is the way that Jacob wants to be introduced – that he is sojourning with Laban "until now" (v. 5). The readers know that Jacob has already separated from Laban in Mizpah (32:1). Therefore, it is not true to say that he is sojourning with Laban "until now." Perhaps the statement is intended to impress Esau that Jacob has become stronger and that, aside from his own family, there are others who are with him and can come to his aid if necessary.

19. Four hundred strong men is too big a number for a simple "meet and greet." Jacob must have perceived the danger when he was informed about the number of Esau's company.

20. Perhaps Jacob is reminiscing his previous encounter with God at Bethel (28:13–15), where God makes a promise to bless him and make him into a great nation, just as Yahweh promised Abraham (12:1–3; 22:17–18).

prepares a generous gift to appease Esau, perhaps to pacify any ill feelings that he might still have against Jacob (vv. 13–21). Clearly, Jacob's purpose in offering these gifts is to appease Esau and avoid any violent confrontation (v. 21).

At this point, it is evident that the old Jacob remains – anxiously scheming, manipulating, and navigating his way around in order to escape an impending calamity. During the night, Jacob remains restless and cannot sleep, so he sends his family across the Jabbok, and then he goes back across Jabbok to camp alone (v. 22–24).[21] This is another form of separation for Jacob. Obviously, he is separated from his family and possessions. We do not know exactly why Jacob does this, but his separation from his family leads Jacob to have an encounter alone with God. This signals the second and transitional stage in a rite of passage: *liminality*.

Liminality

In a rite of passage, the initiates (the individual or community going through the rite of passage) experience a certain state of statuslessness and ambiguity as they transition from one state to another. Because a rite of passage normally begins with separation, the initiates experience a sense of loss and deprivation as they are separated from their familial identities and possessions. Once an initiate is stripped off of his or her status, property, insignia, rank, role, or position of kinship, the initiate enters the stage of *liminality*.[22] Athena Gorospe relates this story of Jacob with that of Moses (in Exodus 4) as a liminal experience.[23] She notes that both Moses and Jacob share the same kind of "structural invisibility,"[24] as both characters experience ambiguity, anonymity,

21. Wenham (*Genesis 16–50*, 295) comments how this "brief account is tantalizingly obscure, raising as many questions as it answers . . . It is not clear why Jacob should have brought his family across Jabbok and then returned to the northern side alone. Was it duty, or anxiety, or simply to inform us that there was none of his party with him when he was attacked?"

22. According to Victor Turner, "*Liminal entities* [people in state of liminality] are betwixt and between positions assigned and arrayed by law, custom, convention and ceremonial. Thus, liminality is frequently likened to death, to being in a womb, to invisibility, to darkness, to bisexuality, to the wilderness, and to an eclipse of the sun or moon." See *Ritual Process: Structure and Anti-Structure* (New York: Cornell University Press, 1991), 95.

23. Athena Gorospe, *Narrative and Identity: An Ethical Reading of Exodus 4* (Leiden: Brill, 2007), 165–168.

24. The term "structural invisibility" is from Turner, *Forest of Symbols: Aspects of Ndembu Ritual* (Ithaca, NY: Cornell University Press, 1967), 98; see also Turner, *Ritual Process*, 95, as cited by Gorospe, *Narrative and Identity*, 165.

passivity, death and growth, and continuity and discontinuity, which are common characteristics of liminal experiences.[25]

According to Franks and Meteyard, "the purpose of such a time [liminality] is to give the spiritual pilgrim an opportunity to have previous patterns of attitude and action deconstructed and disempowered so that one can more truly come to find God as the true and ultimate source of security in life."[26]

In the Bible, there are several metaphors that are associated with liminality – tomb, wilderness, and exile. These metaphors are often associated with uncertainty, deconstruction, doubt, and even death.[27] The *tomb*, which is the space between death and resurrection, implies "the need to die to the present sense of self, to the old ways of being and doing."[28] The *wilderness* suggests a place of nothingness, where one dwells outside of one's comfort zone. In the wilderness, one encounters the power and presence of God. The metaphor of *exile* refers to a place or point in time when one needs to leave one's home or country to live in a foreign land, "to be a stranger in a strange land."[29] Franks and Meteyard provide a very helpful summary of the impact of these different metaphors of liminality:

> Although each metaphor encapsulates different aspects of the transformational experience, they all point to a common reality. This involves the need to let go of, leave behind or even be forcibly expelled from old ascendant forms of self-definition and identity so that God can be found in ways never before experienced. It is thus in the place of *liminality*, when stripped of all structures of support and security, that the pilgrim and God are free to encounter each other in new and life changing ways.[30]

---

25. Gorospe, *Narrative and Identity*, 166–167. See also B. J. Oropeza, "Apostasy in the Wilderness: Paul's Message in the Corinthians in Eschatological Liminality," *JSNT* 75 (1999): 74–75.

26. Anne Franks and John Meteyard use the concept of liminality (originally employed by Richard Rohr) to describe the transition phase of one's spiritual journey in "Liminality: The Transforming Grace of In-Between Places," *The Journal of Pastoral Care and Counseling* 6, no. 3 (Fall 2007): 219.

27. Franks and Meteyard, "Liminality," 215–222.

28. Franks and Meteyard, 218.

29. Franks and Meteyard, 218–220.

30. According to Franks and Meteyard, "The purpose of such a time therefore is to give the spiritual pilgrim the opportunity to have previous patterns of attitude and action deconstructed and disempowered so that one can more truly come to find God as the true and ultimate source of security and life." See "Liminality," 220.

The Jacob narrative demonstrates all three of these metaphors in the way that Jacob is exiled from his family (27:42–28:5) and forced to live in the wilderness of Haran (29:1–30:43), while his entombment takes place during his life-threatening encounter with Yahweh in Jabbok (32:22–32). Kidner describes Jabbok as a stream or ford that flows westward from Gilead to the Jordan.[31] According to this description, the stream of Jabbok actually separates the northern territory from the south. Hence, the setting of this encounter is in itself a point of transition, or threshold, where the character of Jacob hangs in the middle of a crisis.[32] Whether Jacob's character changes or remains the same after this crisis will depend on the succeeding events.

The themes of strife, deceit, and blessing in the life of Jacob come to a climax in Jacob's encounter with a mysterious nocturnal attacker in Genesis 32–33. The attacker conceals its identity, refuses to give Jacob its name, and then abruptly disappears. Some say the attacker is Esau because of the correlation of the "face" motif (32:31; cf. 33:10). Others say it is a god or an angel from Yahweh (citing Hos 12:5). Others say that Jacob confronts his own self through a dream.[33] Others argue that this is actually a Canaanite myth and is not originally associated with Jacob or Peniel.[34] In any case, Jacob perceives this confrontation as an encounter with God himself (32:30).

Jacob's transformation occurs in the context of a struggle, after which a blessing is given. Earlier, Jacob's life is characterized by success through deceit and trickery, but this time his blessing is acquired through an intense face-to-face struggle with God. Jacob earns the right to a blessing not because he is clever, or because he is able to manipulate the circumstances, but because he is persistent and refuses to give up in spite of being overpowered by his opponent (32:26–30). Thus, we might infer that there is no transformation without confrontation. Nevertheless, while this confrontation results in blessing, it also gives Jacob *a limp*, which some interpret as God's act to humble Jacob.

Coming from a physician's perspective, Schneir Levin disagrees with the common translations of *watteqa* as "dislocated," or "put out of joint," or even "wrenched."[35] Levin notes that "tremendous violence is required for a hip to

---

31. Derek Kidner, *Genesis* (Downers Grove, IL: InterVarsity Press, 1967), 170.

32. Coats suggests that Jacob's encounter at Jabbok is an intensification of the crisis surrounding his reconciliation with Esau. See *Genesis*, 229.

33. Nathaniel Schmidt, "The Numen of Penuel," *JBL* 45 (1926): 260.

34. Steve McKenzie, "You Have Prevailed: The Function of Jacob's Encounter at Peniel in the Jacob Cycle," *RQ* 23, no. 4 (1980): 225–231.

35. Schneir Levin, "Jacob's Limp," *Judaism* 44 (1995): 325–327. Jerome A. Lund, after comparing the semantic field of *qhy* (root of *wqht* Palestinian Targumic rendering of *watteqa* in Gen 32:26), concludes in the case of Gen 32:26 that the translation of *watteqa* must be "was

dislocate."[36] Thus, he concludes that Jacob's injury is neither on the back, nor on the hip, but on the groin.[37] Taking note that the "thigh" (*yarek*) is a euphemism for the genitals, it could be a symbolism for Jacob's progeny, which is significant for the blessing he receives in seeming weakness.[38]

Henry F. Knight, on the other hand, relates Jacob's wound to his shame, fear, and remorse as he anticipates his meeting with Esau.[39] Without necessarily denying the physical wound, Knight points out that Jacob's experience that night "became neither a maudlin nor a paralyzing burden. Rather, like a limp, it was a wound that Jacob incorporated into his life and his walk with God and with others. Jacob was able to move on but not without the signs of the struggle."[40] Jacob must have realized that "prevailing is a defeat as well as a victory."[41] Hence, it may be said that Jacob's transformation is characterized not only by strength and success, but also by weakness and vulnerability.

Reincorporation

After the period of liminality, initiates in a rite of passage are brought back to their families and communities through a rite of *reincorporation* – the culmination stage in the process of transformation.[42]

One of these rites is the giving of a new name. Through the confrontation, Jacob is given a new name, "Israel," which signifies a new identity. Even though there is dispute about the etymology for "Israel," the new name shows that "a new being has been called forth."[43] However, the change is not only personal,

---

benumbed" rather than "was dislocated." See "On the Interpretation of the Palestinian Targumic Reading of WQHT in Gen 32:25," *JBL* 105 (1986): 99–103.

36. According to surgeon Rendle Short, "It takes great violence, such as a railway accident, or a fall from a height, to dislocate the hip joint, and if that happened, Jacob would have been unable to walk afterwards." See *The Bible and Modern Medicine* (London: Paternoster Press, 1953), 60. Cited by Levin, "Jacob's Limp," 326.

37. Levin, "Jacob's Limp," 327. David Fass, notes that through the experience, Jacob learns love rather than dominance ("Jacob's Limp," *Judaism* 38 [1989]: 143–150).

38. Hayim Granot, "Jacob and the Angel: Terror and Divine Providence," *JBQ* 40 (2012): 126.

39. Henry F. Knight, "Meeting Jacob at Jabbok: Wrestling with a Text – A Midrash on Genesis 32:22–32," *JES* 29 (1992): 451–460.

40. Knight, "Meeting Jacob at the Jabbok," 454.

41. Brueggemann, *Genesis*, 270.

42. A rite of re-incorporation can be expressed in several acts of physical union, such as the sharing of common meals, eating and drinking together, shaking of hands, and exchanging kisses. See Van Gennep, *Rites of Passage*, 26–40.

43. Brueggemann, *Genesis*, 268.

but also national. The change of Jacob's name to Israel extends the application of this narrative from an individual transformation story to the creation of national identity, since Israel refers not only to Jacob, but to a particular people (Gen 32:32).[44]

Reincorporation is also seen in the reconciliation scene between Jacob and Esau. When Jacob sees Esau coming with four hundred strong men, he immediately divides his household into two and puts Rachel and Joseph (his favorites) at the back, perhaps to protect them from the perceived impending attack (33:1–2).[45] Here, Jacob seems to be acting like his old self, witty and clever. Yet after arranging his family, Jacob runs ahead towards Esau, bowing seven times to the ground as he approaches (v. 3). Though bowing was a common gesture of humility in the ancient Near East, bowing seven times seems to be an exaggeration,[46] though it clearly communicates Jacob's humility before Esau.

Esau, who is depicted as a harsh and violent man in the preceding chapters of the Jacob cycle, here becomes quite gentle and accommodating towards Jacob (Gen 33:4, 12, 15). Rather than responding with arrogance or pride, Esau responds with intensifying compassion and affection for his brother (33:4). For upon seeing Jacob, "he ran," "he embraced," "he fell on Jacob's neck," and "he kissed him," so "they wept" (v. 4), creating an intense and moving scene of reconciliation. Though Esau's greeting is a common gesture between kin in the biblical context, the previous alienation between the brothers gives the gesture an added significance – Jacob is being welcomed back and reincorporated into his family.[47]

Preliminary familial greetings (33:4–7) are followed by the offering of goodwill and favor between the two brothers. The phrase, "let me find favor in your sight . . . ," is twice mentioned by Jacob (33:10, 15), both times in the context of offering and refusing to accept a favor. In verse 10, Jacob insists on giving gifts to his brother; yet in verse 15, he refuses to accept Esau's offer.

The Hebrew for favor or grace, *chen*, appears sixty-seven times in the Old Testament, referring to the positive disposition of one person towards

---

44. Coats, *Genesis*, 230. Wenham also believes that the story of Jacob's struggle at Jabbok is a prefiguration of Israel's national identity (*Genesis 16–50*, 294).

45. This is perhaps the narrator's foreshadowing of Jacob's favoritism towards Rachel and Joseph, which will later become evident in the Joseph cycle (Gen 37:1–50:26).

46. According to Wenham, this echoes the blessing that was intended for Esau but was stolen by Jacob (Gen 27:29). See *Genesis 16–50*, 298.

47. A rite of re-incorporation can be expressed in several acts of physical union, such as the sharing of common meals, eating and drinking together, shaking of hands, and exchanging kisses. See Van Gennep, *Rites of Passage*, 26–40.

another.[48] Usually, it is used to ask for a favor from someone, but in this context, Jacob is not requesting anything from Esau, but rather offering something to him. By accepting the gifts, Esau indicates that Jacob is being received with favor or grace (*chen*). This does not mean that Esau's forgiveness is contingent on Jacob giving him gifts, since Esau is actually reluctant to accept the gifts, not wanting to take advantage of Jacob's vulnerability.

In relation to the overall Jacob narrative cycle, there are several significant reversals at this point. At the beginning, Jacob takes the birthright and blessings from Esau, who threatens to kill Jacob the moment that their father dies (Gen 27:36, 41). However, in this scene, their relationship undergoes a radical shift. If earlier, Jacob wanted to take whatever his brother had, here Jacob refuses to take anything from his brother – not even a protective escort. Instead, Jacob insists on giving what he has to his brother.

Esau, on the other hand, reluctantly receives gifts from his brother, who previously stole his blessings – a reversal that is further emphasized when Jacob shifts the term from gifts (*minchah* in v. 10) to blessings (*b'rekah* in v. 11). This shift indicates that Jacob is now seeking to return the blessings which he stole from Esau.[49] Another reversal is that Esau's threat to kill Jacob is replaced by an offer of protection (33:12, 15). Thus, their meeting concludes with Esau receiving the blessings, while Jacob preserves his own life and that of his family.

This reconciliation story is a powerful reminder for the descendants of both Jacob and Esau – Israel and Edom – that whatever differences or conflicts their ancestors may have had against each other in the past, they have already been resolved in this peaceful reconciliation. In other words, the offense or debt of Jacob against Esau is already paid. Because Jacob returns the stolen blessings, there should be no enmity between their families.

The reconciliation between the brothers would not have been possible if Jacob had not encountered Yahweh and been transformed into a blessed and humble man. Even more, the transformation of Esau's character alerts readers to the importance of transformation in the process of reconciliation.[50]

The story of Jacob's reconciliation with Esau gives us a very powerful model in resolving conflicts, as it depicts the complex processes involved in reconciliation. While reconciliation is never easy, Jacob's story shows that

---

48. D. N. Freedman, J. R. Lundbom, and H. J. Fabry, "*ḥānan*," in *TDOT* 5:24.

49. Victor P. Hamilton, *The Book of Genesis* (Grand Rapids: Eerdmans, 1995), 346.

50. Alfred Agyenta states, "[F]undamentally, reconciliation is a matter of attitudinal change (*metanoia*), especially a change from the desire to eliminate or dispossess each other to mutual respect and collaboration between former rivals." See "When Reconciliation Means More than 'Re-Membering' of Former Enemies," *Ephemerides Theologicae Lovanienses* 83, no. 1 (2007): 132.

it is possible. Jacob's separation from his family, his movement to a state of liminality, and his final reincorporation can be ritualized to aid in facilitating peaceful reconciliation.

From this narrative, we also learn that reconciliation is not a single and one-time event, but rather a product of a difficult struggle, which results in the transformation of the concerned parties. Reconciliation would not be possible if Jacob refused to embrace his struggles and confront his perceived opponents. Jacob goes through the difficult process of moving away from his family and being in a place of uncertainty before he is reunited with his family. Here, we can learn that if we are really serious about reconciliation, we must be willing to go through the same difficult process of transformation.

Appropriating "the Face of God" Motif in Resolving Conflicts

In the Old Testament way of thinking, it is generally believed that nobody can survive a face-to-face encounter with the divine being, since God is so magnificent and awesome that anyone who sees his face will die (Exod 33:20; Isa 6:5). However, in this story, Jacob not only sees God's face, but actually has an intense all-night physical struggle with *Elohim* (32:30). More significantly, God's character in the story shows some vulnerability, since God allows Jacob to coerce him into submitting to Jacob's demand for a blessing (32:26–29).[51]

Thus, Jacob's success over the unidentified man is a "victory," and yet this victory would not be possible if God did not spare him (v. 30). Jacob's "success" is an undeserved blessing, especially when Jacob realizes that his life is preserved even though his mysterious opponent, who strikes and wounds Jacob, is much stronger (v. 25). In this encounter, Jacob must realize that his success is not because of his own strength, but rather because God mercifully spares him. This realization, in the context of a near-death experience, gives Jacob a sense of humility and gratitude before God, who rescues him.

The phrase, "face of God," appears twice in this narrative. It is first mentioned in Jacob's confrontation with an unidentified attacker (32:31). Later, it is echoed in his reconciliation with Esau. The concept carries a very strong theological as well as ethical message about looking at "the face of the other" as

---

51. Gerhard Von Rad, *Genesis: A Commentary* (Philadelphia, PA: Westminster Press, 1972), 322. The attacker even explains that the meaning of the name, "Israel," is about Jacob prevailing in his struggles with both man and God (32:28).

"the face of God."[52] In this narrative, Jacob realizes that his nocturnal attacker, whose face and name remain a mystery, is, in fact, God.

Later, Jacob declares that when he looks upon the face of his brother – his former enemy – it resembles the face of God (33:10). This challenges us to look at the face of a stranger, even an enemy, as the very face of God, which moves us to consider other people's worth and dignity as important as our own. This expresses the greatest commandment, which is "to love your neighbor as yourself" (Lev 19:18b). In the New Testament, Jesus extends this commandment to loving not only the ones who are good to us, but also to loving our enemies (Matt 5:44; Luke 6:27).

Through this reflection, I would like to highlight two crucial factors in developing a model for resolving conflicts. First, we must have the humility to admit our insecurities and vulnerabilities in the face of adversity. In the Old Testament, humility is connected with the task of upholding God's justice and love (Mic 6:8). In the New Testament, Paul defines humility as regarding "others as better than [one's] self." We are not to look after our own selfish interests, but to prioritize the interests of others (Phil 2:3–4).

We need to be humble in order to recognize the value and worth of others. Unless we realize our finite existence, we cannot genuinely love others. In resolving conflicts, we must not look after our own interests, but rather to the interests of others. We can only do this if we treat others the way God sees and treats them – as created in God's image – with mutual respect and value, even when this is a struggle.[53] Elias Chacour, a Catholic priest, writes:

> The true icon is your neighbor, the human being who has been created in the image and with the likeness of God. How beautiful it is when our eyes are transfigured and we see that our neighbor is the icon of God . . . How serious it is when we hate the image of God, whoever that may be . . . How serious it is when we cannot go and say, 'I am sorry about the icon of God who was hurt by my behavior.' We all need to be transfigured so we can recognize the glory of God in one another.[54]

---

52. See Immanuel Levinas, "Exteriority and the Face," in *Totality and Infinity: An Essay on Exteriority,* trans. Alphonso Lingis (Boston: Martinus Nijhoff Publishers, 1979).

53. Clare Amos comments, "It is only if we are prepared to continue our struggle with God that we can see our 'brothers' in their true light, as God sees them. Conversely, it is when we wrestle for a more authentic relationship with our brothers and sisters we discover that we are given God's blessing." See "The Genesis of Reconciliation: The Reconciliation of Genesis," in *Mission Studies* 23, no. 1 (2006): 21.

54. Cited by Amos, "Genesis of Reconciliation," 22.

When we humbly admit our own weaknesses and vulnerability, while acknowledging the importance of the Other as the manifestation of the face of God, we will be able to extend to the Other the blessings we receive from God. This is the second crucial factor in conflict resolution: being responsible towards others and seeking to bless them unconditionally, just as Jacob blesses Esau without asking for something in return.

According to Emmanuel Levinas, true responsibility is being responsible to the Other, seeing the Other's face as our own, depending on the Other as much as he or she is dependent on us. However, to care for the Other is a personal responsibility, whether it is reciprocated or not. Levinas says, "I am responsible for the *Other* without waiting for reciprocity, even if I were to die for it."[55]

In the Jacob narrative, reconciliation would not be possible if Jacob were to refuse to give Esau his blessings and vice versa. However, the blessings that the brothers give to and receive from each other are not demanded from them; rather, they are spontaneous and voluntary. In the same way, this is how Jesus wants his disciples to treat their enemies. In Luke 6:27–31, Jesus says,

> [27]"But I say to you that listen, Love your enemies, do good to those who hate you, [28]bless those who curse you, pray for those who abuse you. [29]If anyone strikes you on the cheek, offer the other also; and from anyone who takes away your coat do not withhold even your shirt. [30]Give to everyone who begs from you; and if anyone takes away your goods, do not ask for them again. [31]Do to others as you would have them do to you." (Luke 6:27–31, NRSV)[56]

Notice here how Jesus commands his disciples to love their enemies not only in words, but also through acts of kindness, such as blessing, praying, offering a cheek to be slapped, giving away one's shirt, and sharing with everyone who begs. Ultimately, Jesus says, "Do to others as you would have them do to you" (Luke 6:31), thereby radicalizing the golden rule by telling his disciples that love must be genuine and intentional, demonstrated through unconditional acts of goodness without demanding anything in return. In verse 35, Jesus reiterates the phrase, "love your enemies," in connection with

---

55. Nemo, "Ethics and Identity," 196, emphasis mine.

56. Some philosophers might see this as an aberration of the ethics of reciprocity, which is crucial to the implementation of justice in all spheres of society. Others, such as Paul Ricoeur, notice the juxtaposition of the command, "Love your enemies," with that of, "Do to others as what you would have them do to you," as "supra-ethical," creating genuine reciprocity that is devoid of the self-interested motives expressed in "superabundant generosity." See Alan Kirk, "Love Your Enemies, The Golden Rule and Ancient Reciprocity (Luke 6:27–35)," in *JBL* 122 no. 4 (2003): 670.

affirming his disciples' identity as children of God. Jesus is telling his disciples that when they love their enemies unconditionally and do good things to those who mistreat them, they will be likened to God himself, who is good to those who are ungrateful and wicked. In other words, they are better people.

This teaching is also echoed by Paul in Romans 12:9–21, where he exhorts believers to "be devoted to one another in love" as a way of "serving the Lord" (vv. 10–11) in order to bless those who persecute them, empathize with others, and live in harmony with them (vv. 14–16). Then Paul quotes Proverbs 25:21–22: "If your enemies are hungry, feed them; if they are thirsty, give them something to drink; for by doing this you will heap burning coals on their heads" (Rom 12:20, NRSV). The most striking exhortation here is, "Do not be overcome by evil, but overcome evil with good" (v. 21). In this verse, Paul teaches believers that the path of imitating Jesus Christ and following his teachings is to overcome others – especially our enemies – not by repaying evil with evil, but rather by repaying evil with good. In this way, peace is assured by breaking the cycle of violence, so that it cannot spread, so that conflicts might be resolved through unconditional love and generosity – even to our enemies.

Conclusion

The reconciliation narrative between Jacob and Esau is but one of the many stories in the Bible that can serve as a model of restoration for both interior and exterior conflicts. Jacob's experience of *liminality* facilitates his transformation, for it brings about his awareness of his limitations and weaknesses before God. Conversely, it gives him a sense of humility prior to and during his encounter with Esau, whom he perceives as a reflection of God's image and likeness. Jacob's awareness of his weakness prepares him to bless his brother (his former enemy) without asking for anything in return. Jacob's actions demonstrate what it means to love our enemy genuinely. Indeed, this story is a powerful tool for instructing the descendants of Israel and Edom concerning their proper treatment of one another – not as enemies, but as brothers.

Today, we are challenged to appropriate this story into our own stories of discord and disharmony, selfishness, arrogance, and pride. Jacob's story challenges us to embrace our vulnerabilities and weaknesses before God and before our fellow human beings so that we might demonstrate genuine respect, unconditional love, and service to others, resolving our conflicts by reciprocating evil with good, in the same way that light overcomes the darkness.

Section II

The Ways of Peace

4

Issues in Israeli and Palestinian Reconciliation Encounters

Salim J. Munayer

Musalaha is a nonprofit organization that promotes reconciliation between Israelis and Palestinians. We advocate and facilitate reconciliation encounters among Palestinian and Israeli believers based on the life and teaching of Jesus. Just as Jesus reached out beyond his own ethnic community, we seek to impact our societies with his message of reconciliation through bridge building efforts between Muslims, Christians, and Jews, according to the common values and reconciliation principles contained within all three Abrahamic faiths. In this essay, we highlight the challenges we face, why they exist, and what we can we do about them.

Obstacles to Reconciliation

In our work, we encounter many obstacles to reconciliation. These obstacles take a variety of forms and are not unique to the Israeli-Palestinian conflict. However, to better understand both the variety of obstacles and the work we do, we will discuss them in the context of this particular conflict. Obstacles can be physical, ideological, emotional, or psychological, and they often overlap. Encountering these obstacles may be shocking for someone new to reconciliation encounters, but over time, participants will learn to recognize and successfully address them.[1]

Finding a Neutral Forum

One of the major physical obstacles to reconciliation is finding a forum where relationships and trust can develop successfully. In our society, there is a clear division between Israelis and Palestinians, which is manifested by a myriad of checkpoints, walls, and fences. This divide also exists between Israeli Jews and Israeli-Palestinians due to significant prejudice, cultural division, differing opportunities available, and the tendency for these groups to live in different neighborhoods. Furthermore, finding a space where both Palestinians and Israelis can come together is a difficult logistical issue. Israelis cannot go into the West Bank, and Palestinians over the age of sixteen cannot come into Israel unless they receive special permission.

Israeli Jews are not allowed to enter the West Bank by military ruling and Palestinians from the West Bank are not allowed to enter Israel except during brief times of the year when they have permits. Even if both sides were freely able to visit one another, Palestinians feel uncomfortable in Israel where soldiers and security with guns are ever-present, where Hebrew is the dominant language, and where they feel largely unwelcome. Likewise, Israelis feel uncomfortable entering Palestinian areas where signs are in Arabic and they perceive they might be unsafe.

There are a few areas along the borders where both Israelis and Palestinians can legally meet, and we do use these sites. However, to arrive at these locations, Israelis and Palestinians pass through checkpoints, soldiers, and other physical manifestations of the conflict that emphasize the imbalance of power.

When looking for a place to meet, we attempt to find a neutral location, where both sides feel equally comfortable or uncomfortable. If we take a group to an Arabic speaking country, the Palestinian participants are naturally more comfortable. If we take a group to a European country that is more Western and similar to Israeli society, Israeli participants often feel more in their element than Palestinian participants. The most neutral ground we have been able to find is the desert. We generally go to Jordan for our desert encounters, where we are removed from civilization and physical reminders of our conflict, such

---

1. This paper relies heavily on Musalaha's publication, Salim Munayer, *Musalaha: A Curriculum of Reconciliation* (Jerusalem: Musalaha Ministry of Reconciliation, 2011), and sections are taken verbatim from this publication.

as weapons, soldiers, and checkpoints. Consequently, this is the best neutral location we have found for relationship building.

Imbalance of Power

Another physical obstacle to reconciliation is the severe imbalance of power between Israelis and Palestinians. Israel has a state, a strong military, and is in control of the country as well as the lives of Palestinians. Palestinians have no state, no military, and their political situation and daily lives are subject to Israeli control. Through our encounters, we see how this imbalance manifests itself in our group identities, and we become more aware of how our culture and education reinforce this imbalance of power. One of the challenges in bringing people together is attempting to counteract this.

Emotional Obstacles

Physical barriers to reconciliation are often the easiest to recognize, but conflict among groups is almost always much more complex and dynamic than may first appear. Some of the most difficult obstacles to contend with are those within ourselves, namely our emotional obstacles. Sometimes participants are aware of their emotional obstacles, but oftentimes they become aware of them through their encounter with the other. On occasion, people who have been invited to Musalaha have a suspicion of the other people, their intent, or even of Musalaha. Sometimes the Israeli side is suspicious that Musalaha is pro-Palestinian; sometimes the Palestinian side is suspicious that Musalaha is pro-Israeli. Dealing with people's initial suspicion of each other or Musalaha is one of the first issues we encounter with new recruits and participants. After encountering the other side, suspicions may still exist, but gradually, as participants get to know one another, the suspicion dissipates.

Psychological Obstacles

Earlier we discussed the importance of having a forum to foster dialogue and relationship building. But even when we have a neutral forum, psychological obstacles can make it difficult to develop relationships. Many times, we are unaware of our psychological obstacles and take offense when accused of having them. There are a number of psychological obstacles we generally face while recruiting or during the process of reconciliation. In the following discussion, we will focus on a few in particular and delineate the significance of each: the divide between "us" and "them," moral superiority, dehumanization and demonization, victimization and self-fulfilling prophecy.

Us versus them, or "othering" occurs when we use social differences to distinguish ourselves from someone else, and this becomes the basis for viewing ourselves or our social group more positively than another social group. The "us" versus "them" dynamic emerges when in-group self-regard develops, which leads to competition and comparison, and eventually to out-group hate. It becomes easy to stereotype the "other," which allows "us" to justify doing anything to "them."[2] Second, people have needs, both individually and collectively. Many of these needs are connected to identity and have to do with our collective beliefs, values, culture, history, and spirituality. When we feel that any of our personal or group needs are denied, we fight for them. This is a basic human reaction and leads to the development of intergroup conflict. This is especially true for groups who are oppressed. This "us" versus "them" mentality is often tied to what we call "moral superiority." *Moral superiority* occurs when participants feel that their people or their actions are right because they have better moral values than those who are different.

Two related psychological obstacles to reconciliation are *dehumanization* and *demonization*. Dehumanization occurs when members of a certain group accuse another of being inferior to them and emphasize this through their words or actions. This can happen on an individual and group level as well as a state level, such as when a state accuses a minority group or another state of being inferior and consequently takes discriminatory action against them. Demonization occurs when groups or individuals are characterized as being evil. In our conflict, both Israelis and Palestinians have been guilty of dehumanizing and demonizing the other side.

Victimization is another obstacle, which occurs when someone is victimized, punished unjustly, or cheated. A specific example of victimization in our conflict would be that of a refugee who has lost his/her land. In 1948, many Palestinians fled or were driven from their villages during the course of a battle, hoping to return once the situation quieted. By not allowing these refugees to return, they were victimized.

---

2. This dynamic is covered by John Paul Lederach, *Building Peace, Sustainable Reconciliation in Divided Societies* (Washington, DC: United States Institute of Peace Press, 1997), 13. Also, Marilynn B. Brewer, "Ingroup Identification and Intergroup Conflict, When Does Ingroup Love Become Outgroup Hate?" in *Social Identity, Intergroup Conflict, and Conflict Reduction*, eds. Richard D. Ashmore, Lee Jussim and David Wilder (Oxford: Oxford University Press, 2001), 24–30.

When assumptions and stereotypes have been maintained long enough, it is easy for a *self-fulfilling prophecy* to emerge, which is when someone predicts a certain negative outcome and is so convinced that it will be negative that they do not allow a positive outcome to occur. For example, if an Israeli believes that all Palestinians hate all Israelis, and therefore we should take harsh measures against them and keep them away from us, many Palestinians will likely come to hate Israelis as a result of the measures taken. In our work, we often have to challenge skepticism that there is no point in dialogue, no point in meeting, that we will never agree, and that all efforts are destined to fail. People who come to our meetings with this mentality get scared and leave at the first point of disagreement, believing that their prophecy has come to pass. Yet when participants are willing to listen to one another's differences and begin to work through them together, they will see the benefits in meeting, find points of agreement, and learn to respect the points on which they disagree.

Addressing Conflict Too Quickly

During initial encounters, it is common for some participants to rush into discussing the bigger and more sensitive issues of the conflict. In our experience, we have found that dealing with conflictual issues too quickly can cause participants to get hurt and withdraw without having a chance to develop relationships. Thus it is best to establish relationships and develop trust between the participants before discussing more sensitive issues. Some issues should be addressed in later stages of the journey of reconciliation. We try and facilitate discussion of these issues throughout the stages of reconciliation.

Temptation to Maintain Status Quo

Another temptation that we frequently encounter in our work is the impulse to ignore reality and maintain the status quo. Potential participants sometimes fear that coming to Musalaha and engaging in dialogue or reconciliation somehow ignores their own grievances and the status quo in the process. This is particularly important for many Palestinian participants, who fear that reconciling with Israelis is an acceptance of the Israeli occupation. We assure both groups that Musalaha does not stand for the status quo, but that change can only happen when we meet each other and work together.

Identifying the Roots of Intractable Conflict

Thus far, we have examined obstacles to reconciliation. Now we will focus specifically on intractable conflict, using Israel-Palestine as a clear example. In the final section, we will discuss the stages of reconciliation that are part of our work at Musalaha.

Conflict is inevitable. The question is not whether we will experience conflict, but rather how we will choose to manage the conflicts we will inevitably encounter. We can most easily define conflict as a disagreement between people that can have various forms of expression. The scale of the conflict may vary (an argument with your spouse versus a war between two countries), and the form of the conflict may be more or less intense (a war of words versus a war of bullets and bombs), but the element of disagreement is always present.

When an intergroup conflict continues for a long time and is seemingly impossible to resolve, it has become *intractable*. All conflicts have the potential to develop along very destructive and dangerous lines, and intractable or protracted conflicts are most likely to take on these characteristics. The longer these conflicts last, the more likely it is that they will become violent, and the harder it will be to resolve them. There are a number of qualities that seem common to all intractable conflicts, even though each conflict is unique. By identifying these qualities, we can better understand why intractable conflicts seem so difficult to overcome, and then come up with methods to meet these challenges head-on.

One of the most fundamental reasons for intergroup conflict is competition over resources. This competition is linked with the denial of human needs. When a competing group denies us something that we as a group need, conflict is unavoidable. Usually, the scarcer the resources are, the more intense and protracted the conflict will be. Also, when the competition is over basic resources, the conflict is very likely to become intractable. Basic needs might be food, water, land, or something less tangible, such as recognition, legitimacy, or historical narrative.

In the context of the Israeli-Palestinian conflict, competition is very pronounced. At its most basic level, the conflict is over tangible resources, such as land and water. The conflict centers around contesting claims about who will control the land, who will own it, who will live in it, and who will have access to the limited supply of water which will sustain life. This fierce competition is also over intangible resources, such as the support of the international community, recognition of the right to self-determination, and legitimacy as a people based on history.

Another cause for intractable conflict is the development of a zero-sum mentality by the two competing sides, a perspective that leads people to think only in terms of black and white. There is no room for gray, no middle ground, only an "either/or" perspective, which is a natural outcome from the competition over resources. We will fight for physical and intangible resources with much more conviction if we really believe that it is a fight to the death and that our survival depends on it. Either "we" win, or "they" win. Because the resources are limited, there is no other possible outcome.

This "either/or" mentality keeps the Israeli-Palestinian conflict from being resolved, since both sides view legitimacy and identity as mutually exclusive. In this conflict, each identity gains some of its strength and legitimacy from negating and delegitimizing the other: "Either we are or they are. *They* can acquire national identity and rights only at the expense of *our* identity and rights."[3] For many Israelis, admitting that the Palestinian people exist poses a threat, and the same is true for many Palestinians, who claim that "Jewishness" refers only to a religion, not a people with a historical connection to the land. In both cases, Israelis and Palestinians feel threatened by the identity of the other side, because if their identity is recognized, then their claim to the land must also be recognized. Within a zero-sum mentality, there is no room for competing claims, no room for sharing.

The path that leads to intractable conflict usually steers both sides towards stereotyping and dehumanizing the other side. Once we frame the conflict in terms of a competition over scarce resources and truly believe that our survival as a group depends on overcoming others, it is easy to make general statements that stereotype the other side. We begin by telling ourselves, "they are treacherous, we are trustworthy; they want war, we want peace," and eventually we really believe it. Through this process, we often reach the dangerous point of dehumanizing the other side, such as saying (or thinking), "they are monsters," which justifies almost any act of violence against them.

Israelis and Palestinians have routinely viewed each other with suspicion and hatred, through the lenses of stereotypes and generalizations. This process has had tragic consequences, as both sides have not only killed civilians among their enemies but have also justified their actions by dehumanizing the other

---

3. Herbert C. Kelman, "The Role of National Identity in Conflict Resolution: Experiences from Israeli-Palestinian Problem-Solving Workshops," in *Social Identity, Intergroup Conflict, and Conflict Reduction*, eds. Richard D. Ashmore, Lee Jussim, and David Wilder (Oxford: Oxford University Press, 2001), 192.

side. Once this line is crossed, "Behaviors that would be unacceptable or outrageous if directed towards those 'like oneself' are now permitted towards those who are 'so different'; the moral insensitivity of one side triggers and justifies the same from the other."[4]

In most cases, intractable conflicts occur between two groups who live very close to each other. It is much easier to stir up hatred and anger towards an enemy that lives close by than for an enemy that lives far away. It is easy to point to them and "show" how they are literally stealing our jobs, land, culture, or any other contested resource. This is why proximity is often a factor in intractable conflicts, because it facilitates a cycle of violence and retaliation that would not be possible if the two sides lived farther away from each other. This dynamic also increases the likelihood of an escalation of violence, since each violent act is a reaction to violence itself.

Proximity has been a major factor in the Israeli-Palestinian conflict, since both sides live only a few kilometers away and, in many cases, just a few streets away or even next door. Whenever there is an act of violence, it is always followed by an act of violence by the other side, making peace negotiations difficult, and making any ceasefire or treaty very fragile and easy to ignore or break. Counter-violence in response to violence eventually becomes, in and of itself, the cause for perpetuating conflict. Theorists call this "reciprocal causation," and the cycle is especially present between groups with decades, or even generations, of mutual, historical animosity.

Every conflict, but especially intractable conflicts, develop historical narratives and "sacred truths" on both sides. This natural development occurs among all groups, since their collective experience binds them together. In conflict situations, especially intractable ones, both sides have conflicting historical narratives, which are essential to their identity and to the legitimacy of their cause. The ways that we understand and frame our past says a lot about our self-perception and self-image as a group. In conflict, both sides usually portray themselves as the innocent victim and the other side as the aggressor. The narrative we tell ourselves becomes sacred, almost myth-like in its significance to our legitimacy. Any attempt to question or challenge this narrative can be very painful and is usually met with stiff resistance. The phenomenon of competing historical narratives can become a very real obstacle to reconciliation in intractable conflicts, because the longer the conflict continues, the further entrenched the historical narratives become.

---

4. David Augsburger, *Conflict Mediation Across Cultures: Pathways and Patterns* (Louisville, KY: Westminster/John Knox Press, 1992), 51.

Conflicting historical narratives are at the heart of the Israeli-Palestinian conflict. It is impossible to imagine a form of Israeli identity and legitimacy that ignores the Holocaust, just as it is unthinkable to imagine Palestinian identity without the *Nakba*.[5] For both sides, portraying themselves as the sole victim in the conflict justifies any violence they commit against the other side. An individual's personal experience is ignored, especially positive interaction with the "other," because it does not reinforce the group's historical narrative, which takes precedence. In the Israeli-Palestinian context, Israelis say, "we were kicked out by the Romans," and Palestinians say, "we were kicked out in 1948." Also, newcomers are viewed as invaders and contrasted with native or indigenous people. This also has relevance to the Israeli-Palestinian conflict, since both sides view themselves as the native or indigenous people and the other side as the invaders.

Stages of Reconciliation

A Forum for Reconciliation: The Desert Encounter

One of the unique features of our approach to reconciliation is that when we begin the process of reconciliation between Israelis and Palestinians, particularly with youth, young adults, and young leaders, we go to the desert. As discussed in "Obstacles to Reconciliation" above, it is difficult to find a neutral location to meet because Israel and Palestine are divided by checkpoints, walls, fences, and significant prejudice.

The desert is absent of Arabic or Hebrew signs, soldiers and guns, and other symbols of the imbalance of power. In the desert, we meet on equal ground, which accelerates the process of relationship and trust building. Furthermore, in the desert, we are dependent on one another for survival. We need to stay close together for safety and shelter, and we are in a place where we can connect with nature and one another in a way that is impossible in our hometowns. This allows us to connect on a deeper level and quickly strengthen relationships.

In our experience, when Israelis and Palestinians first come together, they are excited and enthusiastic, but their feelings are tempered by caution and hesitation. Both during and after a Musalaha encounter, we see an increase in the social acceptance of the other, primarily on an interpersonal level, but also on an intergroup level. We have noticed that in our years of working in

---

5. For more information on the *Nakba* – the catastrophic events around the 1948 declaration of the State of Israel – please see Salim Munayer and Lisa Loden, *Through My Enemy's Eyes* (Milton Keynes, UK: Paternoster, 2014), especially 11–14.

reconciliation there tend to be repeating patterns and dynamics, and we refer to these as the stages of reconciliation.

Stage One: Beginning Relationships

In the desert, we focus on our commonalities and, in facilitated discussions, allow participants to discuss their differences. In the desert, we accompany participants through the first stage of the reconciliation journey, which is called "beginning relationships." During this stage, we teach about conflict, the stages of reconciliation, biblical principles of reconciliation, and listening. The journey of reconciliation is not only fulfilling and meaningful, but also painful and exacting, and so it is important for participants to know that the feelings of hesitation, caution, excitement, fear, and pain are all part of the process, and that this process is normal and natural.

After initial encounters, Israelis and Palestinians return home to their separate societies. It is difficult for them to continue their face-to-face relationships, since it is nearly impossible for them to meet each other. Israelis are not allowed to enter the Palestinian Authority, and many Palestinians are only given permission to enter Israel for one or two short periods every year.

Research has shown that bringing Israelis and Palestinians together for a meaningful encounter reduces social distance and encourages acceptance of the other. However, our research shows that the positive effects of a one-time encounter cannot be sustained without ongoing face-to-face meetings and an encouragement to maintain relationships. Thus, Musalaha seeks to maintain the positive momentum from the initial encounters between Israelis and Palestinians. Moreover, rather than bringing people together for one event, we encourage people to journey towards reconciliation together by providing follow-up encounters. These follow-ups provide opportunities for participants to build their interpersonal relationships while also participating in intergroup activities.

Stage Two: Opening Up

The second stage of the reconciliation journey is called "opening up." During this stage, we emphasize the importance of listening to one another and continue to strengthen relationships through trust-building activities. We teach topics such as identity, approaches to conflict, history and narrative, obstacles to reconciliation, and theological differences. Because participants have had time to develop relationships and are aware of their commonalities, they feel more comfortable expressing their differences.

Stage Three: Withdrawal

Musalaha and other organizations have noted that after the initial positive contact with the other side, there is a third stage in the reconciliation journey called "withdrawal," where participants seem to step back. The reason for this is generally due to the issues raised during stage two, which often challenge participants' perceptions of the conflict, people, or identity. Identity is one of the first casualties of painful conflict, and some sort of withdrawal is simply part of the process. I describe this stage in one document as the following: "The goal is not to avoid pain, but rather to persist in the never-ending work of self-definition and negotiation required to transform the differences that exist in any relationship from liabilities into assets."[6] Although participants are informed of this stage in the initial encounter, it is always a shock to be challenged and then to feel the need to step back.

During this period of withdrawal, participants often reflect on identity independently of one another and also as a group. We discuss topics such as power, forgiveness, and dealing with trauma.

Stage Four: Validating One's Identity

In stage four, we encourage participants to be aware of and accept the feelings they experienced in stage three, where their individual self-esteem and group confidence were challenged. We discuss topics such as reclaiming identity and remembering rightly. We also affirm participants' respective identities, since denying one's identity will not lead to genuine reconciliation.

During this pivotal stage, participants decide either to continue with the journey of reconciliation or to back out completely. Some choose to retreat to their own theological, political, and/or cultural positions and prejudices. Those who continue with the reconciliation journey often make a conscious decision to return with a new openness and vulnerability in spite of the challenges.

---

6. Salim Munayer, *Musalaha: A Curriculum of Reconciliation* (Jerusalem: Musalaha Ministry of Reconciliation, 2014), 23.

Stage Five: Committing and Returning

In stage five, "committing and returning," participants commit to the process and return to taking risks in order to deepen relationships. In this stage, participants are able to listen to each other's grievances in the context of relationship, and so can listen without becoming defensive. Due to the maturity that has developed throughout the process, they are able to understand that both sides have legitimate grievances and to accept one another without feeling threatened. Participants are also willing to recognize the shortcomings of their own people and how their side has contributed to the breakdown of relationship and violence in the conflict. In this stage, trust is restored between participants, and moving forward becomes more natural and less painful.

In intractable conflicts, it is easy to become discouraged with the lack of progress in our societies, and so we offer teaching on dealing with discouragement. During this stage, we also introduce the important and essential issue of justice. As a faith-based organization, we address justice from a biblical perspective and offer teaching on a theology of reconciliation. One verse that guides our teaching is, "Mercy and truth have met together; righteousness and peace have kissed."[7] Musalaha's approach is that justice can only be effective when each of these four elements is present – mercy, truth, justice (righteousness), and peace. Justice without mercy leads to further injustice. We cannot achieve justice without addressing the truth. And there is no justice if it does not bring peace.

Stage Six: Taking Steps

As a result of mutual recognition, commitment to one another and to reconciliation, participants journey to the sixth stage, "taking steps," where they seek to restore the relationship and rectify damage committed by their respective peoples. During this stage, Israelis and Palestinians confess their part in the conflict, request forgiveness, and take action together and within their respective communities. This manifests itself through advocacy, joint projects, and continued involvement in the reconciliation process.

In this final stage, participants who have been perpetrators of violence or who have held onto bitterness as a result of the conflict often feel liberation from guilt. Participants who have been victims feel free to let go of blame. Since the issues have been considered and addressed within the context of relationship,

---

7. Ps 85:10. New King James Version (NKJV). Copyright © 1982 by Thomas Nelson, Inc. Used by permission. All rights reserved.

both sides feel comfortable returning to their societies to begin advocating the reconciliation process they have completed. Participants become leaders, who guide others through the reconciliation journey.

In order to equip participants with the knowledge and tools necessary to bring these principles back to their own societies, we offer teaching on justice and reconciliation, group facilitation, and a Christian perspective on personal and societal transformation. Participants realize that the process is only just beginning as they work together to bring this message of reconciliation to their people.

As participants become leaders, they continually go through the stages of reconciliation, and each time the meaning deepens. The issues that were painful the first time become less painful, and one sign of maturity is that the withdrawal period becomes shorter with time. New participants can only fully appreciate what they have gone through in hindsight, since the pain is always shocking, difficult, and challenging. As participants go through the process again and again, they become more attuned to what is happening.

Conclusion

While conflict is a prominent feature of our lives, and the obstacles to reconciliation are numerous, we can address conflicts by building relationships and engaging in reconciliation. Musalaha's goal is to influence participants to be advocates for one another, agents of change within their own societies, and to encourage participants to be leaders within their respective communities.

5

Peacebuilding from Below in a Multicultural Setting

A Case Study of a Space for Peace and Its Challenges to the Evangelical Faith Community

Fermin P. Manalo Jr.

Armed conflicts cause enormous and far-reaching social, economic, political, and psychological consequences to civilian populations and institutions. Thus, resolving armed conflicts and addressing their root causes to bring about sustained peace should be a concern of all citizens. However, the power and responsibility to address armed conflicts is traditionally and exclusively assumed by the state. In this approach, which is referred to as "elite pact-making"[1] or "state-centric peacemaking,"[2] the state and the armed opposition decide on the terms of the peace settlement based on their notions of peace and security.

This state-centric approach generally excludes the significant participation of ordinary citizens, especially those who have directly experienced the

---

1. Catherine Barnes, "Democratizing Peacemaking Processes: Strategies and Dilemmas for Public Participation," *Accord* 13 (2002): 7.

2. Hiroshi Oda, "Peacebuilding from Below: Theoretical and Methodological Considerations Toward an Anthropological Study on Peace," *Journal of the Graduate School of Letters* 2, no. 1 (2007): 6, http://eprints.lib.hokudai.ac.jp/dspace/bitstream/2115/20475/1/ODA.pdf.

consequences of armed conflicts. Their peacebuilding experiences, no matter how rich, are rarely taken into account. In many cases, they are merely regarded as the recipients of aids and services to help them cope with the effects of conflict.

During the past two decades, however, peace and conflict studies have given significant attention to citizen initiatives that influence national-level peace processes and facilitate community-level peace. These initiatives represent a paradigm shift in addressing armed conflicts, moving from national security to human security.[3] This new paradigm emphasizes principles such as justice, equity, human rights, reconciliation, inclusiveness, community participation, and sustainable development. These initiatives are further legitimized by increasing support from the United Nations (UN) and international development organizations.

This study will highlight peacebuilding efforts that have been initiated by communities caught in large-scale armed conflicts by tracing efforts to restore shattered relationships among three distinct group of peoples in Mindanao, the southern island of the Philippines – Muslims, Christians, and *Lumads* (non-Muslim indigenous peoples in Mindanao). The study will examine attempts by these communities to secure and rebuild themselves by influencing the behavior of the protagonists.[4] The study will also highlight the role of a faith-based institution in facilitating these processes. By applying a community development framework in situations of massive violence, the study will draw lessons that can contribute to the body of knowledge on Peacebuilding from Below. Finally, it will distill implications for those in the evangelical faith community who plan to participate in peacebuilding as a form of witness.

Conceptual Terrain

Peacebuilding

The concept of peacebuilding was first introduced by Johan Galtung, the

---

3. The traditional concept of security or national security is focused on securing the state from external threat or any military aggression. It is designed to promote the demands ascribed to the state and to subordinate all other interests to those of the state. It makes the state the primary actor on any matter pertaining to issues of security. As a paradigm shift, human security focuses on securing individuals and communities from harm or vulnerabilities caused by poverty, hunger, disease, repression, exclusion, disasters, and a multitude of threats that cut across different aspects of human life. Human security implies a need to interface national security with development and human rights, obligating states to prioritize the protection of these securities and giving citizens decisive participation. See "United Nations Trust Fund for Human Security," *Human Security in Theory and Practice* (New York: UNTFHS, 2009).

4. Part of this article is revised from Fermin Manalo Jr., "Community Development Animating Peacebuilding from Below: The Case of *GiNaPaLaDTaKa* Space for Peace in Pikit, North Cotabato," *Philippine Journal of Social Development* 5 (2013):112–142.

"father" of peace and conflict studies, who conceptualized and differentiated peacebuilding from peacekeeping and peacemaking. Peacekeeping and peacemaking, which were the major approaches used in addressing earlier social conflicts, are associated with a statist approach. However, Galtung reconceptualized peace differently.

> peace has a structure different from, perhaps over and above, peacekeeping and ad hoc peacemaking . . . The mechanisms that peace is based on should be built into the structure and be present as a reservoir for the system itself to draw up . . . More specifically, structures must be found that remove causes of wars and offer alternatives to war in situations where wars might occur.[5]

This notion of peace aims to address the root causes of violence, where the outcome is a condition called *positive peace*.[6] *Positive peace* pertains to situations that result from addressing structural violence and other roots of social conflicts. It is differentiated from *negative peace*, which pertains to the absence of war, direct violence, or aggression.

Former UN Secretary General Boutros-Ghali put peacebuilding into the official language of international diplomacy, defining it as a post-conflict framework that seeks to "identify and support structures which will tend to strengthen and solidify peace in order to avoid a relapse into conflict."[7]

John Paul Lederach, drawing from his long academic work and field experience, went beyond the international development's definition and emphasized peacebuilding as "a comprehensive concept that encompasses, generates and sustains the full array of processes, approaches, and stages needed to transform conflict towards more sustainable, peaceful relationships."[8] It focuses on addressing "structural issues, social dynamics of relationship building, and the development of supportive infrastructure for peace."[9]

Miall summarizes Lederach's concept of peacebuilding as:

---

5. Johan Galtung, "Three Approaches to Peace: Peacekeeping, Peacemaking, and Peacebuilding," in *Peace, War and Defense: Essays in Peace Research*, vol. 2, ed. Johan Galtung (Copenhagen: Christian Ejlers, 1976), 297–298.

6. See Johan Galtung, "Positive and Negative Peace," in *Peace and Conflict Studies: A Reader*, ed. C. P. Webel and J. Johansen (London: Routledge, 2012), 75–80.

7. Boutros Boutros-Ghali, *An Agenda for Peace: Preventive Diplomacy, Peacemaking and Peace-keeping: Report of the Secretary-General*, 17 June 1992, United Nations, http://www.un-documents.net/a47-277.htm.

8. John Paul Lederach, *Building Peace: Sustainable Reconciliation in Divided Societies* (Washington, DC: United States Institute of Peace Press, 1997), 20.

9. Lederach, *Building Peace*, 21.

a long-term transformation of a war system into a peace system, inspired by a quest for the values of peace and justice, truth and mercy. The key dimensions of this process are changes in the personal, structural, relational and cultural aspects of conflict, brought about over different time-periods (short-, mid- and long-term) and affecting different system levels at different times.[10]

It is seen as a process of "engaging with and transforming relationships, interests, discourses, and if necessary, the very constitution of society that supports the continuation of violent conflicts."[11] It is envisioned as creating just power relations and "new social meanings that do not reproduce those social patterns and regimes of truth that were predominant before and during the acute stage of conflict."[12] This process is undergirded by values such as human rights, justice, equality, self-determination, ecological integrity, equitable economy, and sustainable development.[13]

Peacebuilding from Below

In order to emphasize the ideological and developmental dimensions of peacebuilding (i.e. participatory and bottom-up), as opposed to the more exclusive and top-down state-centrist approach, this study advocates *peacebuilding from below*. This approach recognizes the *legitimacy* of non-state actors – especially those whom Lederach refers to as the middle and grassroots civil society organizations, traditional institutions, and grassroots communities – and considers these actors as the *primary animating factors*.[14] This recognition is based on the assumption that the depth and breadth of war and related violence are felt most by local communities, although with differing extents based on their gender and other social positions.[15] Thus non-

---

10. Hugh Miall, "Conflict Transformation: A Multidimensional Task" in *Berghof Handbook for Conflict Transformation*, eds. Alexander Austin and N. Ropers (Berlin: Berghof Research Center for Constructive Conflict Management, 2001), 6.

11. Miall, "Conflict Transformation," 4.

12. Marina Skrabalo, "Documenting the Impact of Community Peacebuilding Practices in the Post Yugoslav Region as a Basis for Policy Framework Development," Project paper (Centre for Peace Studies, Zagreb, Croatia, 2003), 5, http://www.policy.hu/skrabalo/rp.html.

13. David P. Barash and Charles Webel, *Peace and Conflict Studies* (Thousand Oaks, CA: Sage Publications, 2002).

14. See Oda, "Peacebuilding from Below"; Oliver Ramsbotham, Tom Woodhouse, and Hugh Miall, *Contemporary Conflict Resolution: The Prevention, Management and Transformation of Deadly Conflicts* (Cambridge, UK: Polity Press, 2011).

15. Celia McKeon, *From the Ground Up: Exploring Dichotomies in Grassroots Peacebuilding*, 2003, http://www.c-r.org/downloads/FromTheGroundUp_200310_ENG.pdf.

state actors are in the best position to recommend ways to resolve the violent conflicts. Earl Conteh-Morgan, using a human security lens, envisions the lived experiences and perspectives of local communities as central to the agenda of national-level peacebuilding.[16]

As a social political process, peacebuilding from below aims to create a social, cultural, and economic foundation for sustained peace and to influence national-level peace processes and policy making. This approach seeks to strengthen citizen-based peacebuilding and to open public political spaces in order for civil society institutions to flourish.

The logic and nature of peacebuilding from below is best captured in Lederach's *Pyramid of Actors and Approaches*,[17] which is illustrated below:

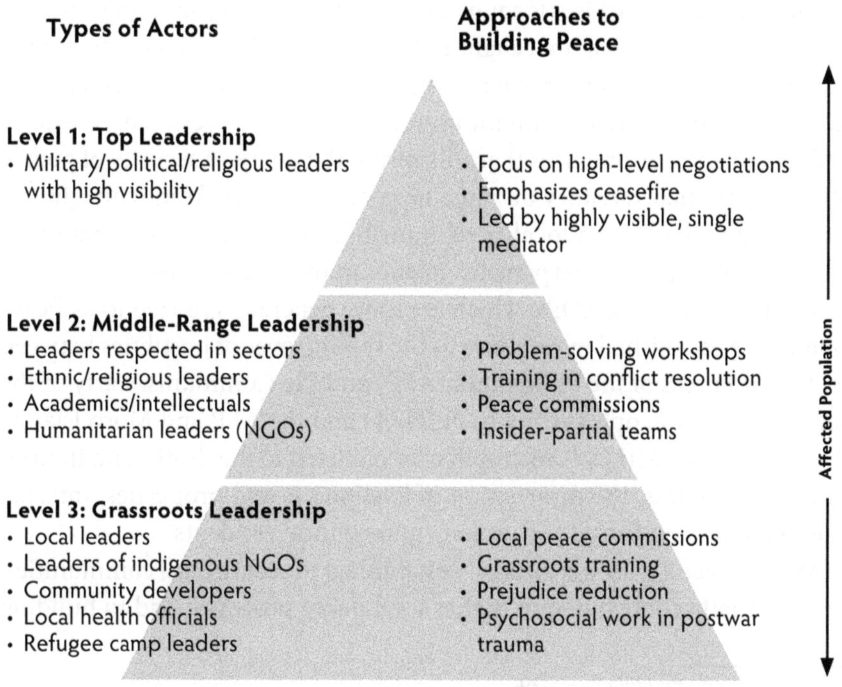

Types of Actors   **Approaches to Building Peace**

Level 1: Top Leadership
- Military/political/religious leaders with high visibility

- Focus on high-level negotiations
- Emphasizes ceasefire
- Led by highly visible, single mediator

Level 2: Middle-Range Leadership
- Leaders respected in sectors
- Ethnic/religious leaders
- Academics/intellectuals
- Humanitarian leaders (NGOs)

- Problem-solving workshops
- Training in conflict resolution
- Peace commissions
- Insider-partial teams

Level 3: Grassroots Leadership
- Local leaders
- Leaders of indigenous NGOs
- Community developers
- Local health officials
- Refugee camp leaders

- Local peace commissions
- Grassroots training
- Prejudice reduction
- Psychosocial work in postwar trauma

Affected Population

Figure 1. Lederach's Pyramid of Actors and Approaches

---

16. Earl Conteh-Morgan, "Peacebuilding and Human Security: A Constructivist Perspective," *International Journal of Peace Studies* 10, no. 1 (2005): 69–86, http://www.gmu.edu/programs/icar/ijps/vol10_1/Conteh-Morgan_101IJPS.pdf.

17. Derived from Paul Lederach, *Building Peace: Sustainable Reconciliation in Divided Societies* (Washington, DC: United States Institute of Peace Press, 1997), 39, as cited by Michelle Maiese, "Levels of Action," in *Beyond Intractability*, eds. Guy Burgess and Heidi Burgess, Conflict Information Consortium, University of Colorado, Boulder, June 2003, https://www.beyondintractability.org/essay/hierarchical_intervention_levels.

This pyramid presents the levels by which violent conflict affects populations and the corresponding actors and leaders as well as the roles each plays in building peace. The pyramid suggests how peacebuilding efforts by the grassroots and civil society can influence higher level (state-centric) peace processes and policies by building on local capacities and the accumulated knowledge of local communities while strengthening local institutions. More than formal negotiations, peacebuilding from below can help rebuild societies that are caught in destructive cycles of violence and facilitate sustainable peace.[18]

Zone of Peace

A zone of peace (ZOP) is a form of citizen-initiated peacebuilding through which communities that are caught in the midst of violent conflicts declare their areas as *off limits* to combat activities by the contending armed forces.[19] The community negotiates with the armed forces to observe certain norms of conduct, policies, or practices that will ensure the safety or security of people within a particular territory or zone. Its goals can range from managing or controlling violence in a locality to contributing to the transformation of conditions that cause or perpetuate violence in the larger society.[20]

In the Philippines, ZOPs, which are more generally referred to as Peace Zones, were established in response to the spilling over of hostilities between the Armed Forces of the Philippines (AFP) and the Communist Party of the Philippines-New People's Army (CPP/NPA) and the AFP and Moro Islamic Liberation Front (MILF).[21] Such spill over often led to the deaths and injuries of non-combatants, the destruction of livelihoods and properties, internal displacements, and forced recruitment among local residents.

While Peace Zones were initially established to secure local communities, they eventually contributed to higher level peace processes and to building

---

18. Lederach, *Building Peace*, 39.

19. Christopher Mitchell, "The Theory and Practice of Sanctuary: From Asylia to Local Zones of Peace," in *Zones of Peace*, ed. Landon E. Hancock and Christopher Mitchell (Bloomfield, CT: Kumarian Press, 2007), 1–28.

20. Landon E. Hancock and Pushpa Iyer, "The Nature, Structure, and Variety of Peace Zones," in *Zones of Peace*, ed. Landon E. Hancock and Christopher Mitchell (Bloomfield, CT: Kumarian Press, 2007), 29–50.

21. Kevin Avruch and Roberto S. Jose, "Peace Zones in the Philippines," in *Zones of Peace*, 51–69; Miriam Coronel-Ferrer, "Civil Society Institutional Response: Peaceful Intervention to Resolve Armed Conflicts," *Policy Notes* 3 (2006): 1–10. See also Soliman M. Santos, *Peace Zones in the Philippines: Concept, Policy, and Instruments* (Quezon City: Gaston Z. Ortigas Peace Institute, 2005).

a peace constituency.[22] From two decades of experience – the mid-1980s to 2005 – the definition of Peace Zone evolved into the following:

> a people initiated, community-based arrangement in a local geographical area which residents themselves declare to be off-limits to armed conflict primarily to protect the civilians, livelihood and property there and also to contribute to the more comprehensive peace process.[23]

The Case of *GiNaPaLaDTaKa* Space for Peace

Research Method

The research used the case study method, focusing on seven barangays (political administrative villages) that comprise the *GiNaPaLaDTaKa* Space for Peace project – *Gi*natilan, *Na*lapaan, *Pa*nicupan, *La*gunde, *Da*lengaoen, *Ta*kepan, and *Ka*lakakan – in Pikit, North Cotabato, Central Mindanao, Philippines. *GiNaPaLaDTaKa*, the acronym consisting of the first syllables of the barangays, literally means, "I bless You."[24] The study relied on secondary sources, field observations, and semi-structured interviews with persons who were involved with or are knowledgeable about *GiNaPaLaDTaKa*.[25] Most primary data was gathered during a field visit in the *GiNaPaLaDTaKa* areas and nearby towns of North Cotabato by the author and his "Community-based Conflict Resolution and Peacebuilding Strategies" class at the University of the Philippines in February 2013.

History of Peaceful Relationship

The seven barangays are populated by people of various ethnic and religious backgrounds, such as the Maguindanaoans (Muslims), Bisaya and Ilocanos (Christians), and Manobos (*Lumads*). The Maguindanaoans comprise

---

22. Santos, *Peace Zones in the Philippines*, 18–19.

23. Santos, *Peace Zones in the Philippines*, 10.

24. Ernesto A. Anasarias, "Children as Zones of Peace: Child Centered Organizing and Development in Conflict-Affected Communities in Pikit, North Cotabato" (master's thesis, University of the Philippines, 2008), 103.

25. Interview by author with: E. Anasarias, Executive Director, Balay Rehabilitation Center, Quezon City, February and May 2013; G. Gamboa, Peace Education Coordinator, Oblates Missionary Foundation-Inter-Religious Dialogue Program (OMF-IRD), Immaculate Conception Parish, Pikit, North Cotabato, 22 February 2013; and Leaders of *GiNaPaLaDTaKa* Barangays, Bgy. Takepan, Pikit, North Cotabato, 22 February 2013.

85 percent of the population. The total population of the seven barangays was estimated at ten thousand in 2008. It represents 15 percent of the total Pikit population.

The municipality of Pikit in North Cotabato, Central Mindanao, where the seven barangays are located, was founded in 1913 by the American colonial regime as a colony for Cebuanos who migrated to Mindanao. It was later made a resettlement for farmers of Luzon and Visayas prior to World War II. It is located seventy-two kilometers west of Cotabato City. Pikit is a Maguindanaoan word for "connected hills."[26]

Historically, the Muslims, Christians, and *Lumads* in Pikit shared a long history of peaceful relationship.[27] They enjoyed neighborly relationships and accepted religious differences. There was a local kinship that was not based entirely on genealogy but on affinity and cultural bonding. Intermarriage was common among the three groups.

Community Life Shattered

In the late 1960s, Pikit experienced atrocities that were perpetrated by paramilitary groups, such as the *Ilaga, Blackshirts/Barracudas*. The *Ilaga* was formed by a segment of the Christian population to fight the Muslims in response to the Mindanao Independence Movement. The *Blackshirts/ Barracudas* were formed by a segment of the Muslim population to retaliate against the *Ilaga*. Both groups preyed on the civilian population and were used by local and national politicians for their personal ends.[28] The atrocities shattered the harmonious ties between the Muslims and Christians in Pikit and nearby towns. Memories of the atrocities were passed on to succeeding generations, creating deep-seated distrust and prejudice.

From the 1970s onward, Pikit was an arena of fierce clashes between the government's Armed Forces of the Philippines (AFP) and the secessionist

---

26. Anasarias, "Children as Zones of Peace," 80.

27. Pushpa Iyer, "Peace Zones of Mindanao, Philippines: Civil Society Efforts to End Violence" (case study, CDA Collaborative Learning Projects, 2004), http://cdacollaborative. org/wordpress/wp-content/uploads/2016/01/Peace-Zones-of-Mindanao-Philippines-Civil-Society-Efforts-to-End-Violence.pdf.

28. Karl Gaspar, Elpidio A. Lapad, and Ailynne J. Maravillas, *Mapagkamalinawon: A Reader for the Mindanawon Peace Advocate* (Davao City: Alternate Forum for Research in Mindanao and Catholic Relief Services, 2002); Stuart Kaufman, "Symbolic Politics and Ethnic War in the Philippines" (lecture presented at the International Studies Association 48th Annual Convention, Chicago, IL, March 2007); Amado L. Picardal, "Christian-Muslim Dialogue in Mindanao," *Asian Christian Review* 2 (2008): 54–72, http://www.asianchristianreview.org/acr_pdf/acr_pdf_0202-03_08picardal.pdf.

forces, such as the Moro National Liberation Front (MNLF) and later the Moro Islamic Liberation Front (MILF). But the present residents remember most the three intense and large-scale fights between the MILF and the AFP in 1997, 2000, and 2003, which caused death, destruction, and the repeated evacuation of the communities. The most massive conflict was in 2000 during the all-out war against the MILF waged by Joseph Estrada, the Philippines president at the time, which displaced about sixty thousand, or about 60 percent of the population of Pikit. Forty percent were children.[29] The residents sought shelter in the town center and nearby towns, where they stayed an average of six months, depending on the security conditions in their communities.

From Conflict Sensitive Relief and Rehabilitation to Community-Based Peacebuilding

In response to the humanitarian crisis spawned by the 1997 hostilities, the Immaculate Conception (IMC) Parish of Pikit under Father Bert Layson, OMI, and the Oblates Missionary Foundation-Inter-Religious Dialogue (OMF-IRD) organized relief operations among the displaced residents. Rehabilitation work was conducted as soon as the "*bakwits*" (which is derived from the word "evacuate") returned to their communities.

The rehabilitation effort was initially hampered by the Muslim's mistrust, since it was initiated by a Christian institution, and the Christian parishioners refused to use congregational funds for Muslims. After a "passionate debate and soul searching," the congregation, moved by their understanding of Jesus's teaching, decided to help.[30] The OMF-IRD then engaged in confidence-building processes for Christians and Muslims, seeking to ensure that all efforts were conflict sensitive. The effort eventually paid off, with both Muslims and Christians working together. The initiative also reached out to the Manobo (*Lumads*), who have been exploited by both Christians and Muslims.

During Estrada's all-out war against the MILF, the rehabilitation work included disaster risk reduction, human rights education, and psychosocial measures to address "invisible damages," such as anger, hatred, prejudice, and trauma, which – if left unaddressed – might result in more violence. At the same time, the OMF-IRD negotiated with the AFP and MILF to enter into a

---

29. Anasarias, "Children as Zones of Peace," 79.

30. Roberto C. Layson, "Peacetalk: It's Because We Are Different That We Have So Much to Share," *MindaNews*, 9 June 2014, http://www.mindanews.com/mindaviews/2014/06/peacetalk-its-because-we-are-different-that-we-have-so-much-to-share/.

ceasefire between them. It also lobbied local government units to support the rehabilitation work.

Culture of Peace as Means for Rebuilding the Community

In order to facilitate the restoration and rebuilding of shattered community life within the seven barangays in Pikit, the OMF-IRD embarked on a Culture of Peace (COP) program along with rehabilitation. The COP is based on *Panagtagbo sa Kalinaw* (a Cebuano term that means "Encounter/Dialogue for Peace") and is a "Basic Orientation Manual Towards a Culture of Peace for Communities of Mindanao."[31] The COP aims to facilitate the restoration of trust, cooperation, and a sense of community among the Muslims, Christians (settlers and Christianized indigenous peoples), and *Lumads*. Collectively, these three groups, which comprise the population of Mindanao, are referred to as tri-people.[32] The COP is founded on multiculturalism, non-discrimination, solidarity, and participation.[33]

At the core of COP is peace education, which aims to enable participants to: a) develop a common understanding of the tri-people history of Mindanao and how historical conflict divided them, b) craft a shared vision of peace, and c) resolve to become agents of peace in their communities. The course includes the following topics: the history of Mindanao, prejudice reduction and understanding, conflict management and resolution; negotiation and communication, inter-religious dialogue, the role of religion in conflict and peace, and peace values. The COP sessions invoke the long history of kinship that bound the three groups until the 1960s and explores how that kinship can be developed and enhanced to restore peaceful relationships and vibrant community life.[34]

Two important elements of the COP process are healing and reconciliation among the participants, who have been severely affected both psychologically and spiritually by the hostilities. Father Layson describes how the COP facilitates this:

> . . . the participants sit in a circle in a victim-offender setting and where each participant is given the chance to speak his or her

---

31. Antonio J. Ledesma, *Panagtagbo sa Kalinaw: A Basic Orientation Manual Towards a Culture of Peace for Mindanao Communities* (Manila: UNICEF, 1998).

32. This term is being used to denote a multicultural/multi-ethnic approach to peace and development in Mindanao.

33. Anasarias, "Children as Zones of Peace."

34. Interview by author with E. Anasarias, 22 February 2013.

painful experience of the past while the rest listens with empathy. The process is usually highly charged with emotion. Then, the whole process ends up with the participants reconciling with each other and making peace with one another . . . The heart of peace is the peace of heart."[35]

Leaders from affected communities in Pikit and trainers from the parish were the first to attend the COP course. They, in turn, facilitated the course among adults, children, and even among soldiers, rebels, and barangay officials. Professionals, such as school teachers, were also trained to include COP in the curriculum.

Outcomes of Culture of Peace Program

Restoration of Community Life and Forging a Common Vision of Peace
The COP led to the restoration of trust and friendly relationships among the tri-people. Respect for each other's religion/beliefs and other cultural distinctiveness now prevails. In order to address inter-people and intra-people disputes, the COP helped to install appropriate conflict management/resolution and adjudication systems that complement the official barangay dispute resolution process.[36]

The restoration of tri-people harmony is expressed in the "People's Declaration: GiNaPaLaDTaKa Space for Peace and Children as Zones of Peace," a 2004 document that articulates the shared vision of peace and prosperity:

> *Pangarap namin na wala nang mang-aapi at walang maaapi. Maibabalik ang magandang pagkakakilanlan at pagtitiwala sa isa't isa. Maghahari ang pagmamahalan, pagpapatawad at pagtanggap sa mga pagkakamali. Magiging makatotohanan ang bawat isa sa kani-kaniyang paniniwala, kultura't, relihiyon.* [37]

> (We dream of a life where there will be no more oppressors and oppressed. We aspire to restore our trust towards one another. We seek to rebuild our community life where love reigns, and where there is forgiveness and recognition of mistakes. We strive to build

---

35. Layson, "Peacetalk," 9 June 2014.

36. Interview by author with: E. Anasarias, G. Gamboa, and Leaders of *GiNaPaLaDTaKa*, 22 February 2013.

37. "People's Declaration: GiNaPaLaDTaKa Space for Peace and Children as Zones of Peace," https://balayph.net/multimedia/videos?start=8.

our community on good moral principles where one is faithful to one's religion and culture.)[38]

Building a Space for Peace to Institutionalize the Culture of Peace

Another major outcome of the COP was the establishment of a collective peace zone (commonly referred to by NGOs as a *Space for Peace,* which will be the term used here). In creating a Space for Peace, the communities appealed to the AFP, MILF, and all armed groups to respect the areas as off limits to any combat activities. Inside the Space for Peace, members of any armed group could pass through or even become part of the community and participate in the maintenance of peace. But they could not undertake any hostile or combat-related activity inside the Space for Peace.

The main principle behind the Space for Peace is to create a "space where displaced people could return and rebuild their community."[39] Such space is meant to guarantee a sense of safety for children to go to school, for people to attend to their livelihoods, and for NGOs to assist in rebuilding, in order to ensure physical, social, and psychological security.

Father Bert Layson began facilitating the Space for Peace in 2000 in Barangay Nalapaan. During the heavy clashes in Pikit in 2003, the contending forces respected the Space for Peace. While most of Pikit was turned into a battlefield and about two-thirds of the population evacuated, Nalapaan was spared. Evacuation was minimized, although the residents remained alert and vigilant, establishing systems for monitoring the security situation and negotiating with any armed group attempting to do combat-related activities in the community. To further reinforce the peace initiative in Nalapaan, international organizations and the national government provided livelihood and infrastructure supports.

Inspired by the gains of Nalapaan's Space for Peace, six nearby barangays most severely affected by the war – Ginatilan, Panicupan, Lagunde, Dalengaoen, Takepan, and Kalakakan – decided to form a collective Space for Peace called *GiNaPaLaDTaKa,* which was formally launched on November 29, 2004 in Barangay Takepan through a formal declaration of peace and unity. Representatives of the MILF, the Philippine Army, the Office of the Presidential Adviser on the Peace Process, and various NGOs, church organizations, and media attended the ceremony. The initiative received support from several civil

---

38. Peter Berliner, Ernesto Anasarias, and Elena de Casas Soberón, "Religious Diversity as Peacebuilding: The Space for Peace," *Journal of Religion, Conflict, and Peace* 4, no. 1 (2010): 5.

39. Santos, *Peace Zones in the Philippines,* 7.

society organizations and was officially endorsed by the municipal government of Pikit.

The declaration, which is entitled "People's Declaration: GiNaPaLaDTaKa Space for Peace and Children as Zones of Peace," expresses the communities' aspirations for peace. It traces the history and dynamics of peaceful community life and how that was shattered by the clashes. The declaration enumerates the economic, political, social, and cultural sufferings that they experienced as a result of the violent episodes. In declaring a "Space for Peace and Children as Zones of Peace," the communities called on various armed groups, local and national government officials, NGOs, media, and religious organizations to support their aspirations for peace. The declaration concludes with the vision of peace and prosperity quoted above.

The *GiNaPaLaDTaKa* Space for Peace was led by a council for peace, which consisted of representatives from each barangay as well as a tri-people representation. The Council held consultations – on the household level – on the communities' vision of peace, negotiated with the AFP and MILF to respect the Space for Peace, and led the campaign for support from the general public. Through the council, the communities participated in campaigns to influence the conduct and agenda of the ongoing peace negotiations between the Philippine Government and the MILF.

Religion/Spirituality as a Crucial Resource in Building a Space for Peace
The COP serves as the framework and fulcrum for peacebuilding in *GiNaPaLaDTaKa* to help restore and strengthen the sense of community that binds the people together even during violent episodes. The communities anchor their hope for a tri-people community of peace by accepting each other's religious distinctiveness while drawing from a common resource for peace. This hope is expressed explicitly in the 2004 People's Declaration:

> *Kasama ang Diyos, si Allah, at Magbabaya, nawa'y ang pagsisikap na ito ay magbunga ng kabutihan para sa ating lahat, ngayon at sa susunod pang mga henerasyon.*[40]

> (With the blessings of God/Allah/Magbabaya, we hope that this endeavor will bear fruit for the good of all, today, and in the next generation of tri-people in Mindanao.)

---

40. As cited in Berliner, Anasarias, and de Casas Soberón, "Religious Diversity as Peacebuilding," 5.

Respect for religious distinctions and various expressions of spirituality serves as the core element for building and sustaining the Culture of Peace in *GiNaPaLaDTaKa*.[41] One of the first things the residents did upon returning from evacuation was to begin rebuilding sacred places, which points to the centrality of religion/spirituality in their lives.

Organizing Children as Zones of Peace

Almost half of the affected population in Pikit were children and youth (eighteen years and under). In order to provide these children and youth with "physical, emotional, social, cultural and developmental space within the Space for Peace,"[42] the Balay Rehabilitation Center developed a *Children as Zones of Peace* (CZOP) program. By offering protection, trauma healing, reconciliation, and development, the CZOP enabled children and youth to articulate their views about violence and their aspirations for a peaceful life. The program equipped them with ideals and capabilities to participate in the communities' peacebuilding efforts by implementing peace education through COP seminars and interfaith dialogues. Through the CZOP, youth and children effectively participated in crafting the *GiNaPaLaDTaKa's* peace agenda as embodied in the 2004 People's Declaration.

Participation in the Peace Process

During this case study in 2013, the *GiNaPaLaDTaKa* Space for Peace was being sustained, and plans were underway among partner NGOs, such as the Balay Rehabilitation Center, to facilitate community-led peacebuilding in nearby communities. Special task forces composed of *Bantay Ceasefire* (community volunteers who monitor compliance with ceasefire agreement between the government and MILF) regularly monitored behavior and negotiated with any armed groups seeking to pass through the area.

GiNaPaLaDTaKa leaders participated in bottom up efforts by civil society organizations in Mindanao to influence the conduct and agenda of the peace negotiation between the Philippine Government and the MILF. This participation was very pronounced during the campaign to resume the ceasefire and peace talks and to include a civilian protection mechanism in the peace agenda.

---

41. Berliner, Anasarias, and de Casas Soberón, "Religious Diversity as Peacebuilding."
42. Anasarias, "Children as Zones of Peace," 148.

Insights on Peacebuilding as a Community-Based Initiative

The *GiNaPaLaDTaKa* Space for Peace bears all the features of a community-based initiative. First, it covers a particular geographic territory. Second, it was initiated, declared, and is sustained by the residents of the community with assistance from intermediary institutions, such as NGOs and church-based organizations. Third, it was motivated by a vision of peace that grew out of conviction, consultation, and consensus among the communities. Lastly, it was formally launched with a written declaration or resolution that contained specific conditions and for implementing structures within the community.[43]

The *GiNaPaLaDTaKa* vision of peace is not confined to its own localities, but seeks to reach the whole of Mindanao society. It is anchored on the community's reconstruction and collective understanding of their history and the context of their conflict, their present condition, and the meaningful connections between their past and the present.

By employing community development principles and strategies, we can identify and interpret the processes that animate *GiNaPaLaDTaKa* as a community-based initiative in order to propose ways of applying these principles and strategies in other situations of massive violence.

In the following five sections, I will offer insights on community-based peacebuilding from below based on the *GiNaPaLaDTaKa* experience. Using community development as a lens, I will explore the principles, strategies, and cultural resources that animate such experiences.

Development Education in the Context of Peacebuilding

Generally, development education (DE) consists of three elements: 1) the formation of an awareness of one's value and entitlements, 2) the development of critical awareness, and 3) the building of knowledge and skills necessary for managing development efforts.

In a peacebuilding context, DE will be crucial in enabling communities to understand their entitlement to a life of security and peace as well as the right to participate in all decisions that impact their lives. As such, *a rights-based approach* will be very helpful, in instilling an awareness among communities of the internationally guaranteed rights in situations of armed conflicts and emergencies and the duties of the State in upholding these rights.

---

43. Following the definition of Avruch and Jose, "Peace Zones in the Philippines," *Zones of Peace,* and by multi-sectoral peace advocates, as cited by Santos, *Peace Zones in the Philippines,* 24.

However, it is worth noting how the *GiNaPaLaDTaKa* communities invoked this right to protection and security from both the AFP and MILF forces in their 2004 People's Declaration. Rather than using a "power persuasion approach and coercive diplomacy,"[44] the communities reframed their appeal by presenting the *GiNaPalaDTaKa* initiative as a way of strengthening the peace process, which both parties supported. In effect, their appeal resonated with the peace process' framework of redressing long suffering, restoring livelihoods, rebuilding relationships, and building a peaceful environment. The People's Declaration was framed in a manner that regarded the combatant forces as major stakeholders of peace.

A second critical component of DE is to enhance a community's capacity to analyze the causes, dynamics, and consequences of armed conflicts and how they are intertwined with social conditions, such as poverty. In the case of *GiNaPaLaDTaKa*, this component was the foundation of the COP program, which included the tri-people's perceptions of the conflict, the historical roots of the conflict, and a social analysis of the broader issues underlying the conflict.

A third critical component of DE is to build the knowledge and skills of community peace educators and COP facilitators. This will include facilitating trauma awareness and healing, community reconciliation, development of peace enhancing values, and building skills on mediation, negotiation, advocacy, and planning.

The tri-people approach to peace education proved to be a key element of DE in *GiNaPaLaDTaKa,* creating an atmosphere for listening in order to gain a common understanding of the conflict and craft of a common vision for a peaceful future. The emphasis on shared values and culture, especially religion and kinship, served as a platform for attaining the shared vision.

Community Organizing in the Context of Peacebuilding

Community organizing provides the structure or platform through which a community can collectively analyze their conflict condition, craft a vision of peace, and work towards realizing such vision. Through this structure, which is culturally appropriate, the community can work out both day-to-day and long-term ameliorative actions.

Being organized and widely recognized can help a community demand participation in decision-making negotiations that might affect their security and welfare. The *GiNaPaLaDTaKa* communities capitalized on their widespread

---

44. Anasarias, "Children as Zones of Peace," 60.

recognition to gain more support from the church, media, NGOs, and the local government unit. By being organized, the *GiNaPaLaDTaKa* galvanized consensus building on their long-term vision of peace and helped to formulate and implement policies that sought to minimize vulnerabilities and rebuild shattered relationships. The tri-people composition of the council of peace helped to ensure compliance by both residents and the armed groups, with the norms set within each community. For example, members of each group dealt with security issues on their own (e.g. Muslims dealt with Muslims, Christians with Christians, and *Lumads* with *Lumads*). By organizing and networking, the *GiNaPaLaDTaKa* communities and their civil partners were able to form a moral and political presence that the military and political forces found difficult to ignore.

Community-Based Resource Management in the Context of Peacebuilding

Community-based resource management enables a community to conduct an inventory of peace resources that are available within or outside the community. These resources are used to address the consequences of conflicts and violence, build community solidarity, and achieve sustainable peace.

In the *GiNaPaLaDTaKa*, community-based resource management was evident in the way that the various communities appreciated, harnessed, and utilized internal and external resources for building a COP. The internal resources were resilience, cultural and spiritual values, kinship ties, memory of neighborly relations, and other forms of community cooperation. External resources included the support of the church and NGOs. Other resources included processes for dialoguing and mediation, problem solving, advocacy, reconstructing history, strategic linkages, and material support.

The churches and mosques, which were tangible assets, provided the non-tangible resource of hope. As mentioned above, one of the first things the community members did upon returning to their communities from evacuation was to repair or restore their places of worship.

In conclusion, the whole process of building a COP rested on being able to restore and strengthen a very important community resource – *social capital,* which generally refers to "institutions, relationships, attitudes, and values that govern interactions among people and contribute to economic and social development."[45] In a peacebuilding context, social capital refers to "valuable

---

45. Christiaan Grootaert and Thierry van Bastelaer, "Social Capital: From Definition to Measurement," in *Understanding and Measuring Social Capital: Multidisciplinary Tools for Practitioners*, ed. Christiaan Grootaert and Thierry van Bastelaer (Washington, DC: The World

social networks that one has, and which one can tap on the basis of reciprocity" for addressing violence and working for peace.[46]

Advocacy in the Context of Peacebuilding

Through advocacy, the community influences public opinion and effects a policy environment that is favorable to its peace initiatives. In *GiNaPaLaDTaKa*, advocacy focused on bringing the communities' experience of violence and the merit of building a Space for Peace to the attention of local and national government policy makers. Beyond this, *GiNaPaLaDTaKa* also participated in the peace movement's efforts to influence the peace negotiations between the Philippine government and the MILF, particularly the resumption of a ceasefire and the inclusion of civilian protection in the negotiation agenda.

The effort to influence the content and conduct of the peace negotiations resonates with Lederach's Pyramid (see Figure 1). The *GiNaPaLaDTaKa* communities correspond with the grassroots leaders' level. With support from church organizations and NGOs (the middle level in Lederach's Pyramid), they sought to reach the upper leadership, such as the government and MILF negotiators and principals. The middle group also helped equip community members to monitor compliance with the terms of ceasefire between the government and the MILF.

The inclusion of *Children as Zones of Peace* in the People's Declaration added advocacy strength to the appeal of the Space for Peace by presenting the warring parties with the dilemma of locating children in their "politico-military scheme."[47]

Sustainability Issues

A community's ability to maintain a solid front and effectively expand to nearby areas will help engender respect for the peace zone. This has to do with the concept of inviolability, which is the assurance that the norms that comprise a peace zone will be respected by the combatant forces, other armed groups, and the civilian population within the zone. Isolation increases a peace zone's

---

Bank, 2002), 2.

46. Miriam Coronel-Ferrer, *Framework and Synthesis of Lessons Learned in Civil-Society Peacebuilding*, vol. 1 of Learning Experiences Study on Civil-Society Peace Building in the Philippines (Quezon City: UP Center for Integrative and Development Studies in partnership with the United Nations Development Programme, 2005), 60–61.

47. Anasarias, "Children as Zones of Peace," 220.

violability and leads to marginalization. Respecting a peace zone can either be a short-lived tactical initiative of a ground commander or a long-term policy from the highest political or military leadership. If a community is only concerned with its own security interests, it might lose support from peace advocacy groups, especially those that are critical of peace zones for "fostering piecemeal and even parochial concepts of peace."[48]

In this regard, the ultimate challenge for *GiNaPaLaDTaKa* is to expand the principles and practice of the Space for Peace to the widest and broadest geographic and social regions so that it can become a significant peace advocacy movement.[49] To this end, *GiNaPaLaDTaKa* needs sustained support from influential groups, such as civil society organizations, media, church, and international bodies, in order to keep pressure on the MILF and AFP to uphold community-initiated peace efforts. Moreover, the energy and gains from *GiNaPaLaDTaKa* need to be directed towards the long-term transformation of Mindanao and the foundation of national-level peacebuilding.

To achieve this goal, the *GiNaPaLaDTaKa* communities will need to build their gains on the three pillars of exercising community governance: community leadership, community empowerment, and community ownership.[50] *Community leadership* focuses on the formulation and dissemination of a vision of peace that ensures the broadest participation of community members. *Community empowerment* focuses on exercising significant access to or control over resources that are crucial to the communities' survival and development. *Community ownership* focuses on institutionalizing inclusiveness (such as that achieved among the tri-people) and a sense of responsibility and accountability over development programs.

---

48. Santos, *Peace Zones in the Philippines*, 18.

49. Here the application of Lederach's Pyramid becomes relevant. The *GiNaPaLaDTaKa* experience presents opportunities to explore the principles and strategies by which collaboration between middle-level and grassroots leaders can create a viable movement, which can influence peace negotiations and national-level peacebuilding policy and programs. Lederach provides the capacity building processes that are appropriate for each level.

50. Oscar P. Ferrer, "Community Governance: Understanding Community Processes and Initiatives: Four Case Studies on Local Initiatives in Public Administration and Governance" (PhD diss., University of the Philippines, 2006). *Community governance* refers to being able to exercise a decisive role in the management of community resources, the formulation of norms and policies, as well as envisioning and realizing a desired development path.

The Role of Faith-Based Organizations

While the *GiNaPaLaDTaKa* testifies how an empowered community can secure and rebuild itself, the IMC Parish and OMF-IRD (as an intermediary/middle-level organization) played an animating role. Their relief work and culturally sensitive rehabilitation and psychosocial interventions facilitated healing and reconciliation, creating a culture of peace that bound people together. By deliberately building the capacity of local facilitators and organizers within the community, they helped to sustain the peace process.

One can easily attribute the nature and direction of the work of the IMC and OMF-IRD to their spirituality and their understanding of healing and reconciliation as prominent elements of the social teachings of the church. The parish's decision to be involved with and allot congregational resources to help Muslims attests to what Father Layson describes as a "process of transformation," where the decisive factor was a keen understanding of the demands of their Christian belief.

> The all-out war in 2000 which displaced over a million civilians in Mindanao brought the church in Pikit through a painful process of transformation. The parish at that time was divided whether or not to extend humanitarian assistance to Muslim evacuees. It was only after a passionate debate and soul-searching by the members of the Parish Pastoral Council that the parish decided to break the walls of apathy and mediocrity remembering the command of Jesus in the Gospel that tells them to "Love your neighbor as yourself," and the exhortation of Jesus that "whatever you do to the least of my brothers, you do it unto me."[51]

This spirituality transcends sectarianism and exclusivism, which became evident in the way the relief and rehabilitation works were deliberately designed with Muslims and Christians cooperating with each other and feeling the pain of suffering together. Father Layson describes all that the volunteers shared together during this time:

> The parish then organized the Disaster Response Team (DRT) composed mainly of young Muslim and Christian volunteers. Whether under the scorching heat of the sun or the pouring rain and amidst bullet fires, these young volunteers distributed food to thousands of starving evacuees in various evacuation centers.

---

51. Layson, "Peacetalk," 9 June 2014.

We would eat together on the same table, pray together and even cry together when we hear that another baby had died in the evacuation center.

The parish soon realized that helping the poor is not a matter of choice. For us Christians, it is a duty and a social responsibility. After all, when you hear the sound of mothers weeping and children crying in the night, you don't anymore ask whether they are *Lumads*, Muslims or Christians.[52]

This spirituality goes beyond the confines of the church and identifies human society as the arena for realizing God's peace and justice, recognizing the dignity of each person or group – regardless of social or religious background – and acknowledging that each person or group is seeking the good for the rest of the community. This spirituality is informed by *contextual theology* – understanding the world through the eyes of God – as well as *development theory* – understanding the world (social reality and the human condition) through the lens of attaining desirable social change.

Challenges to the Evangelical Faith Community

As discussed above, a spirituality informed by contextual theology and development strategies enabled IMC and OMF-IRD to respond effectively to a war-generated crisis by identifying and providing resources through which the community could secure and rebuild itself. But first, the IMC community had to go through intense soul searching, a process that included acknowledging the wounds that had accumulated through decades of war, which led to prejudice, mistrust, and hatred against the Muslims.

From the *GiNaPaLaDTaKa* experience and the animating role of the IMC and the OMF-IRD, we can distill several challenges for evangelical communities seeking to engage in community-based peacebuilding. First, communities will need to go through deep soul searching to discern the resources that will enable this kind of ministry. Second, they will need to identify and unlearn beliefs and practices that could hinder this ministry.

---

52. Layson, "Peacetalk," 9 June 2014.

Doing Ministry

In the evangelical tradition, ministry to those outside the Christian faith is seen as a form of evangelism – seeking to convert people to the Christian faith.

The experience of the IMC and the OMF-IRD points to the importance of being motivated by "love of neighbor" and how this principle can be applied in situations of large-scale violence, where the neighbor includes those who have hurt us. Here, love is concretized in interpersonal relations and in our response to social sufferings and systemic factors that generate conflict. Thus, confronting a war system and philosophy may be a higher expression of love of neighbor.

Participating in peacebuilding acknowledges that the church has as much at stake in peace as the rest of society. It also reflects that the church considers itself as one with humanity in seeking solutions to violence and in building a culture of peace. This expands our notion of "God-in-community." Beyond the local church and the Christian community, the larger community needs to be recognized as part of creation, where God seeks to bring about the reign of love, justice, and peace.

Interfaith Relations

The IMC community went through significant transformation in relating with people of other faith, especially those they considered as the "enemy." How should evangelical Christians relate with people of a different faith/ideology? One of the anchors of the *GiNaPaLaDTaKa* is the way that each religious belief/system is held as equal and important as the other. For evangelicals, this requires a readiness to acknowledge that other faith systems can anchor the community in times of crisis and disintegration. Such a posture assumes that God is at work in the lives and histories of communities before the arrival of the Christian influence.

As such, this posture compels us to recognize the value of dialogue. While we honestly acknowledge our differences and missional agenda, we are willing to work with each other in the spirit of respect and solidarity, sharing a common desire to draw on the life-affirming resources of each faith tradition and harness them for the benefit of the community.

In the same spirit, we need to value the social sciences and other "secular domains" of knowledge that are designed to address conflict and violence. This is especially true for faith communities, whose fundamental orientation is to defend life, human dignity, and the integrity of the created order.

Modeling Peace

In journeying with a community towards a peaceful future, we may need to pay attention to our own community so that it reflects a truly peaceful community. This peace community is, first of all, characterized by an understanding and practice of power. Community-based peacebuilding represents a radical shift in the paradigm of power. It marks a decentralization, if not the transfer or redistribution, of power from the top or center to the bottom or periphery.

The challenge for the Christian community is to purge itself of hierarchical and domineering notions of power by cultivating what Rollo May refers to as nutritive and enabling power.[53] This involves enabling all members of the community to participate in decision-making and to take responsibility in the areas that matter most. It creates opportunities for every member, especially the lowliest, to develop their capacity for collective decision-making.

Second, the peace community must address the economic inequality that defines most of the relationship in the faith community, both locally and globally. Such inequality leads to marginalization and exclusion, creating a scandalous situation where there is affluence by a few and widespread poverty and deprivation among many. Thus the church needs to live out and demonstrate a radical redistribution and sharing of resources, opportunities, rights, and privileges.

Third, the Christian community needs to interrogate its notion of violence. Where it has blindly accepted or unquestioningly assumed the legitimacy of war as a means of achieving social, political, or economic goals or resolving conflicts, the faith community needs to learn how to make peace as the default mode in times of conflict. More importantly, the faith community needs to confront the cultural and structural violence that mediates national policies and social relations, including those within churches.

Fourth, the faith community needs to recover the notion of God's redemptive act as ultimately leading to shalom, the sociological expression of which includes the reign of justice, peace, love, and ecological balance as envisioned in the new heaven and new earth (Isaiah 65). Redemption covers a person's inner life as well as the fabric and systems of society, which includes politics, economics, culture, and the natural environment.

While redemption and shalom is God's work, the process invites human participation, which includes persons and organizations outside the church or faith community. In this regard, peacebuilding contributes to the realization of

---

53. Rollo May, *Power and Innocence: A Search for the Sources of Violence* (New York: Norton & Company, 1972).

God's shalom and therefore takes on both a sacramental and practical nature as part of the missional orientation of the Christian community.

Conclusion

On the whole, participating in community-based peacebuilding offers the evangelical faith community an opportunity to actualize its calling as agents of peace and reconciliation.

But to effectively do so, the faith community must be able to live out and demonstrate the possibility of a peace community characterized by love, justice, the practice of nurturing and enabling power, sharing and solidarity, and non-violence. In this way, it will be able to generate a surplus of tangible and non-tangible resources that can be added to the task of building peace. One of these resources is a spirituality that inspires commitment to the long-term transformation of society and that envisions a sustainable peace patterned after shalom.

6

Moses, the *Datu*, and the Prince of Peace

Sources and Synergies for Filipino Leadership

Jeremy Simons

The revolution to which the biblical community is summoned is to enact in the world of social affairs a new practice of social relationships marked by justice, mercy, and peace, which touches all of life.

–Walter Brueggemann, *The Covenanted Self*[1]

This study explores how community leadership that is modeled on the life of Jesus, the Prince of Peace, can be expressed in the Filipino context. The study is twofold: first, it highlights sociocultural aspects of peacemaking leadership found in the role of a Filipino tribal *datu* (chief); second, it interposes these with narrative subtexts in the story of Israel's deliverance from Pharaoh by the prophetic action of Moses. In particular, I will trace the cultural contours of Moses's adoption into the ancient Midianite community of Jethro – a process

---

1. Walter Brueggemann, *The Covenanted Self: Explorations in Law and Covenant* (Minneapolis: Fortress Press, 1999).

that leads to the transformation of Moses's leadership and identity. As the mediator of the first covenant, Moses prefigures and elucidates aspects of the contextual leadership embodied by Jesus, the mediator of the second covenant.[2]

"Narratives do not tell us what to do but point the way toward . . . what might be true of our own experience. Their function is not to inculcate in us a certain virtue, but to involve us in exploring possibilities that would help shape our identity."[3] Thus writes Athena Gorospe in her reflection on the story of Moses's reverse migration from Midian to Egypt to free the enslaved Hebrew people. Indeed, by interacting with the narrative of Moses from the perspective of a Christian cultural worker in southern Philippines – a region profoundly affected by violence and oppression – new insights and opportunities emerge for a deeper understanding of identity and vocation in a context of conflict and within multiple sociocultural realities.

The study helps to construct a model of Filipino leadership that is biblical, culturally grounded (indigenous), and relevant within the wider church and society. It seeks to strengthen cultural correctives to Filipino leadership by affirming the value of local leadership impulses that have been dishonored and diluted because of the historical context of colonialism, spiritual oppression, and globalization. By proposing a contextualized Christian and indigenous form of leadership, Filipinos can gain a deeper understanding of what it means to live as an authentic Filipino community of reconciliation.

Mindanao's *Lumads*: Masters of Filipino Peacemaking

History of Acculturation and Accommodation in Mindanao

The question of how cultures change and yet retain continuity in response to external influences should never be asked lightly nor answered simplistically. This question is particularly challenging when interacting with minority cultures in multicultural contexts situated in a history of Western colonial penetration. The unique antecedents of the Philippines include nearly three hundred and fifty years as a Spanish colony followed by almost fifty years of American colonial subjugation.

---

2. Brueggemann states, "Moses imagined a whole new way of being in the world, a way ordered as covenant, and the commands of Sinai provide the guidance for that new way" (*The Covenanted Self*, 39).

3. Athena E. Gorospe, "Old Testament Narratives in Context: Moses' Reverse Migration and a Hermeneutics of Possibility," in *The Gospel in Culture: Contextualization Issues through Asian Eyes*, ed. Melba Padilla Maggay (Mandaluyong: OMF Literature, 2013), 216.

Out of this experience, the "modern" Philippine state was formed, which involved the Christianization of more than a hundred distinct ethno-linguistic groups scattered over three major island groups. The second largest of these, the southern island of Mindanao, is characterized by a distinctive local history that includes a resurgent story of struggle in contrast with the unifying national narrative. This local history includes the stories of over 60 percent of the remaining indigenous cultural communities in the nation, including the largest populations of Muslim communities.

The population of Mindanao is often referred to as the "tri-people" of Mindanao, demarcating the various demographics of Christian settlers, indigenous people groups, and Muslim communities. The tribal or indigenous peoples living on the island of Mindanao are referred to as the *Lumad*, and many, if not a majority, are now Christianized. Still, the identities of cultural communities in Southern Philippines retain experiences that, although altered and affected by history, reflect clearer echoes of precolonial life, along with ongoing indigenous responses to historical and current realities, relative to many other linguistic groups across the nation. As Oona Paredes remarks, "the fact of early *Lumad* conversion, does not lessen or invalidate the cultural integrity of *Lumad* peoples, nor does it make them less 'indigenous' than we have always believed them to be."[4]

Sacrificial Peacemaking

In 2009, I was facilitating a workshop for the annual retreat of *Simbahang Kristyanong Lumad*, an association of Matigsalug[5] tribal pastors from *Barangay Gumitan*[6] in the mountains of the Marilog district, Davao City. We were accompanying them as they redeveloped their capacity for ministry as authentic tribal leaders and Christlike elders who are rooted in indigenous culture. During the workshop, we asked the participants to tell stories

---

4. Oona Paredes, *A Mountain of Difference: The Lumad in Early Colonial Mindanao* (New York: Cornell University, 2013), 167. Regarding *Lumads* who stayed in their original territory and therefore faced "fission" with the encroaching mainstream in contrast to those who retreated to the highlands away from contact with outsiders, Paredes states, "the story of migration and fission is also a very modern trope, one found in all present-day *Lumad* narratives of encounters with outsiders, in which the arrival of settlers presents *Lumadnon* with a difficult choice, one with bitter consequences all around" (168). She suggests that there is an ongoing need to affirm these Lumad experiences as legitimate elements of Philippine history, to "historicize them so that they may be more easily recognized as equal stakeholders in the Filipino nation" (169).

5. The Matigsalug are a Manobo sub-tribe living in the mountains north of Davao City and adjacent areas of Bukidnon and North Cotabato Provinces.

6. The *barangay* is the smallest administrative unit in the Philippines and is the Filipino term for village or district.

of successful indigenous leadership. Their stories identified several key elements as the "positive core" of Matigsalug leadership, the highest qualities being *mahigugmaon* (lovingkindness), *manggihatagon* (generosity), and *matinabangon* (helpful cooperation).

They illustrated this tripartite cultural leadership by telling a story about a conflict or problem in the community between two families. In such cases, the *datu* (village chief or leader) is typically asked to intervene as a mediator in order to solve the problem.[7] Since indigenous communities are communal in orientation, the conflict is presumed to be a matter that concerns both the immediate and the extended families of both parties. If it is a complex or serious conflict, several *datus* will work together as a kind of conciliation team to restore the relationships between the disputing families. As part of the process, the *datus* go back and forth between the families, traversing mountain ranges if necessary, until they agree to terms that will resolve the case.

If there is a loss on one side and a need for restitution, the offender, with the help of his family, pays cash (in modern contexts), a combination of cash and/or some in-kind payment (traditionally a chicken, horse, or pig), and/or symbolic items, such as a traditional sword, tools, or instruments. The amount of restitution depends upon the gravity of the conflict, especially the amount of shame and social dishonor caused by the offense. It is assumed that the offender will appeal to his family and relatives to assist him in gathering the cash or items needed for the restitution payment. In other words, resolving the conflict is not only an individual responsibility, but also a collective obligation for the wider community.

In cases where the offender and his/her family lack the material or financial resources to make the restitution, the *datu* himself[8] helps make up the insufficient portion of the payment on behalf of the offender. However, if the *datu* is poor or unable to pay what is lacking, he has the right to go to other community members and ask them to contribute. Moreover, the *datu* is allowed to take a horse, for example, from a community member and include it as part of the restitution agreement without prior consent from the owner, a practice known to the Matigsalug as *dampas* (their close relatives, the Ata-

---

7. The *datu* functions in a quasi-judicial role, which is recognized in Philippine law by Republic Act 8371, the Indigenous Peoples Rights Act (IPRA) of 1997, http://www.lawphil.net/statutes/repacts/ra1997/ra_8371_1997.html.

8. The mediation process is usually led by a male leader called a *datu, timuay,* or *kefeduwan* (these are just three of many traditional titles used, depending upon the tribe). However, female leaders, known as *bae* or *libun*, also have significant leadership roles in community peacemaking and can also act as judges.

Manobo, call this *saplag*), thus putting himself in debt to the owner of the horse. While this may seem like a gross violation of a mediator's neutrality, complicating and adding fuel to the fire of an unjust situation (as understood in a Western context), the tribal pastors in the leadership workshop provided an alternative explanation. For them, this practice demonstrates the best values of indigenous leadership and community life – lovingkindness, generosity, and helpful cooperation. For out of deep love and concern for the peace of the community, the *datu* (along with the community) sacrifices personal resources to bring a just resolution to the conflict.

In communal society, individuals *a priori* understand that the needs of the community have a greater claim than individuals in terms of property ownership, and so it is not exceptional to make sacrifices for the good of the community. Sacrificial and personal engagement in community peacemaking is a basic element of a *datu's* leadership, since he is generally related to one, or even both, of the families involved in the conflict. In fact, his established position in the social network of village relationships, where many families are intermarried, gives him not only the credibility and the right to intervene, but also places a moral obligation on him to do so. If the *datu* does not assist, he is shirking one of the core responsibilities of indigenous leadership, which indicates how a sacrificial approach to peacemaking is at the core of Christian Filipino leadership.

Incarnational Peacemaking

"Do you know how to solve conflicts between animals, or between plants and animals?" one of the senior elders of the Talaandig tribe asked when I started researching indigenous peacemaking practices in Mindanao. The Talaandig people live in the shadow of Mt. Kitanglad in Bukidnon province, and within their oral history (*Gugud* and *batbat*), they understand their unique mandate given by Magbabaya, the creator, to be peacemakers among the tribes of Mindanao, as well as to maintain harmony with all aspects of creation. Following is an account of the Talaandig oral history that was shared during my research into Talaandig peacemaking,

> . . . in the presence of the brothers and sisters of the council, Apu Agbibilin [the ancestor of the Talaandig] entrusted to Apu Saulana the sacred jar of oil ("*puti*") and comb ("*suwat*") that would be used to comb out the tangled hair of conflicts between the clans. They were told that in times of conflict, to rely on Apu Saulana because he was given the oil and comb to make peace. The oil was kept in *Bulan-bulan* (the center of the world) and the boundary of

the territory of peace extended from there to the Kimanga River, the Manupali river and to the peak of Mt. Kitanglad . . . what remains is the abode or zone of peace because the peacekeeping tradition of the tribes is preserved here.[9]

Among the Talaandig, a *datu* is a leader who genuinely incarnates this spiritual and cultural history, channeling the moral values and cultural energy of the sacred oil and comb for the entire community. The central role of a *datu* is to maintain the peace (*kalinaw/kapayapaan*) and order (*kahapsay/pagkakaayos*) of the community by mediating conflicts, promoting and protecting indigenous culture, and ensuring harmony between the physical, environmental, and spiritual realms. In fact, in the Talaandig language, the word *datu* means both chief and mediator. Thus the *datu* is regarded as a mediator, an environmental steward, and a pastor-priest. Similar to the Matigsalug, the cultural expectation for the Talaandig is that the *datu* has the resources on-hand – both social and material – to lead, mediate, protect, educate, and strengthen the community.

However, as Oona Paredes reflects on her research with the Higaonon tribe of Northern Mindanao, a tribe closely related to the Talaandig, "'*Datu*' is, in fact, a popular adjective among lowlanders used to mark someone who has amassed considerable material wealth . . . This popular use of the word shows that the *Lumad* brand of leadership . . . remains poorly understood. We have yet to appreciate fully the most basic aspects of *datuship*."[10] Appreciating "basic aspects of *datuship*" means ascertaining the complexity and nuance of peacemaking within the tribe. The term *datu* implies an inherent authority that comes with the *datu's* recognition by the wider community of his leadership role.

There is not just one *datu* in a community; rather, most tribes have levels or role assignments for *datus,* whose titles contain implicit responsibilities. Stewart Schlegel, based on his ethnographic research among the Teduray tribe in what is now Maguindanao province,[11] states that the reference to an indigenous judge (*kefeduwan* to the Teduray) should be understood as a legal specialist or sage; it does not contain the meaning and image usually associated with judges in a

---

9. Jeremy Simons, "Guardians of the Sacred Oil and Comb: Towards an Understanding of Talaandig Spirituality, Cosmology, and Peace Practices," (unpublished manuscript, 2010), 5.

10. Paredes, *A Mountain of Difference,* 172–173.

11. The Teduray tribe is an indigenous people group living primarily in Maguindanao province of Western Mindanao, Philippines.

Western judicial system.[12] In fact, in the community where he conducted his field research on Teduray law and justice, one-third of all household heads were recognized as either major or minor *kefeduwan*.[13] Meanwhile, according to the *Batasan Adansil* (customary law) documented by one of the Higaonon tribes in Northern Mindanao, there are forty-four types of male *datu* leadership roles or specializations, six types of female *ba-e* leaders, along with *bagani* (warriors/ defenders), and *baylan* (herbalist/spiritualists) in their tribe.

Of the forty-four *datu* specialists, most are related to the practice of community peacemaking, with fifteen roles described primarily in terms of mediating, problem-solving, or judicial functions, and three of the fifteen specific to intervention roles in blood feuds. An excerpt from this list of titles and roles portrays the holistic and comprehensive coverage of the tribal conciliation structure: *Datu Lumbac – tigpatunga* (separator/go-between), *Datu Makahusay – tighusay* (reconciler of cases and blood feuds), *Datu Diamla – tigtulay sa duha ka partido or pamilya* (bridge between two parties/families), *Datu Sangcopan – tigsulbad sa bug-at nga problema* (heavy problem solver), *Datu Ayunan – tigpauyon* (agreement-maker), *Datu Kuluba – tigpanalipod sa katawhan* (people's defender), *Datu Kaubayan – maduolan sa mga problema* (ombudsman), and even one who is assigned to "cool things off," the *Datu Mayor Bayok – tigpabugnaw sa mga problema*.[14]

In other words, appreciating "*datuship*" means understanding that the leadership structure of the community is built around and incarnates intentional, dynamic, and highly nuanced community justice roles and peacemaking imperatives. For the Talaandig, this mandate begins with the creation story, where *Agtayabon Migbaya* (the highest god) brings peace in the relationship between the three supreme beings. This allows *Magbabaya* (the supreme creator being) to establish the natural order, which eventually leads

---

12. Stewart Schlegal, *Wisdom from a Rainforest: The Spiritual Journey of an Anthropologist* (Manila: Ateneo de Manila University Press, 1999). Schlegal states that the legal sages' "loyalty was not to personal interests but to the restoration of just public order. Their goal was not for either side to 'win,' but to achieve a genuine settlement in which all fault was determined and accepted and all hurt gall bladders [the psychosocial-emotional center of the person] were vindicated and restored . . . When the settlement was reached, it was invariably regarded as the joint achievement of all participating adjudicators, not a personal triumph or defeat for anyone" (167–168).

13. Stewart Schlegal, *Tiruray Justice: Traditional Tiruray Law and Morality* (London: University of California Press, 1970), 59. "Tiruray" was first used by colonial administrators, missionaries, and later researchers, but it has since been corrected to "Teduray" by the Teduray community itself.

14. Kagsabuwa Inc. and German Development Service (DED), *Batasan Adansil: Customary Laws of the Higaonon Tribe in Iligan City* (Intellectual Property of the Higa-onon Tribe of Iligan City, no date), 27–29, n. 1.

to the commissioning of *Apu Saulana*, the ancestor of the Talaandig, as the peacemaker among the tribes through the symbolic gifts of the oil and comb.

Thus indigenous stories and spiritual understanding, along with the history of intergenerational peacemaking, support a collective leadership infrastructure that engenders a culture of peace. According to Roda Cisneros, "[The] organs of IDRM [Indigenous Dispute Resolution Mechanisms] are intimately intertwined with its varied norms and procedures that generally include the jurisdictional or the justice-related functions of the indigenous communities . . . [T]he very essence of indigenous justice systems [is] playing an integral role . . . for purposes of providing justice and preserving harmony in the community."[15] In other words, the stories, leadership structure, and community roles all fit together as an organic cosmology and integrated community justice system that, at its best, enables community members to take joint responsibility to do justice and live peacefully together.

Holistic Peacemaking

A few years ago, three Ata-Manobo men living in Paquibato district – a mountainous area of Davao City, where communities are heavily influenced by the Philippines communist insurgency[16] – were gathering rattan in the forest when a Philippine army patrol chanced upon them. Assuming them to be rebel fighters, the army patrol captured and physically abused them before releasing them back to the community. The incident was reported to the local tribal chief. In order to retain the support of the community, the commanding officer of the unit agreed to follow the indigenous process of community justice. The chief, after deliberating on the situation, fined the army unit nine horses for the incident. In rural communities, horses are a valuable part of the local economy, providing crucial transportation for people and produce along the steep trails that lead to the farm-to-market roads. When asked how the chief decided on such a heavy fine, he explained that each of the three victims should receive three horses in restitution: one horse for the *sakit* (the pain and suffering), one horse for the *ulaw* (the shame), and one horse for the *kalag* (the soul and spirit of the victim).[17]

---

15. Roda Cisneros, "Recovering Olden Pathways and Vanishing Trails to Justice and Peace: Indigenous Modes of Dispute Resolution and Indigenous Justice Systems," in *A Sourcebook on Alternatives to Formal Dispute Resolution Mechanisms* (Manila: National Judicial Institute, 2008), 94.

16. The New People's Army (NPA), the armed wing of the Communist Party of the Philippines, has been waging an armed, Maoist revolutionary struggle since 1969.

17. This story was directly related to the author by indigenous leaders from the Paquibato district of Davao City in 2014.

For the Ata-Manobo, justice is not meant to be punitive, but rather holistic, healing, and restorative. The restitution marks an approximation of the harm done in multiple dimensions, addressing not only the physical effect of the violence, but also the wider social impact and the spiritual reality. In fact, the Western materialist concept of an individualistic, rights-based justice is an alien framework in a world where social interactions that leverage mutual obligations and indebtedness (*utang na loob*) are the norm. The restoration of community relationships and social harmony takes precedence over personal preference, private property, and punishment that is inflicted as pain or social exclusion (jail time).

Non-Adversarial Peacemaking

In order to accomplish restoration, the indigenous process of justice itself is restorative and conciliatory rather than adversarial. Cisneros, in her study of indigenous communities across the Philippines, notes that peaceful means characterize the actual process of indigenous dispute resolution in Mindanao.[18] Moreover, the various indigenous justice systems across Luzon and the Visayas contain similarities in that they are "generally non-adversarial, non-confrontational and participatory."[19]

Schlegal describes the Teduray process as an example of non-adversarial peacemaking, with its four-step path of "natural healing." First, the hurt is "registered"; it is neither hidden nor ridiculed, but respected. Second, anger is expected to erupt and is openly displayed within the affected community without criticism. The *kefeduwan's* (judge's) job is to help the victim figure out a response that will bring no further harm to the community and prevent a cycle of revenge. Third, the victim is given "a socially honored way to deal with the distress" via a conciliation process (*tiyawan*) involving a series of "sessions." The pain is made public and "handled with great seriousness." Lastly, the sessions result in vindication through a "public and concrete" response to "address the source of hurt and put it in its proper place," which includes a "peaceful forum for admitting fault and making restoration."[20]

This synthesis of historic and current peace and justice practices in Mindanao's *Lumad* communities portrays a Filipino cultural framework for peacemaking and justice that is characterized by sacrificial, incarnational, holistic, and non-adversarial leadership. However, given the historical

---

18. Cisneros, *Recovering Olden Pathways*, 104.

19. Cisneros, 104.

20. Schlegel, *Wisdom from a Rainforest*, 169–171.

experience of colonialism in the Philippines and the external (mostly Western) cultural infusions into the Filipino identity, an important question remains: how can Filipino leaders appropriate these concepts of *datuship* when most Filipinos neither identify as, nor have experience with, the *Lumad*?

The Leadership Journey of Moses

Dislocated Leadership

Exodus 18:13 states, "The next day Moses took his seat to serve as judge for the people, and they stood around him from morning till evening." Moses is primarily known for his part in the dramatic rescue of the Israelites from Egypt and his role as the mediator of God's law to the Israelites. But in between these two iconic events, we see the tribes of Israel waiting in line for Moses – the community peacemaker and judge – to solve their petty (and not so petty) problems. By the time Moses makes a second climb to Mt. Sinai, his community peacemaking leadership has become such an important part of the community life that he deputizes Aaron, his spokesman, and Hur, his military commander, to settle the most difficult cases in his absence (Exod 24:14).

Yet twenty-two chapters and forty years earlier, when Moses attempts to bring peace and justice to those who "groaned in their slavery" (Exod 2:23), he is cynically rebuffed by his very own people. This leads us to consider what brought about such a dramatic transformation of Moses's leadership capacity. In an extended reflection on the Christian's posture in relation to violence, injustice, and exclusion, Miraslav Volf notes that the journey to peacemaking leadership involves a process of discovering a new, "'de-centered center' of self-giving love . . . [where] judgments about exclusion must be made and the battles against exclusion fought [as] . . . the practice of embrace."[21] For Moses, this de-centering occurs through a variety of processes that raise provocative possibilities for Filipinos today.

The beginning of Exodus tells the story of the young, idealistic Moses, whose destiny is shaped while he is still in utero by the Bible's first acts of nonviolent civil disobedience: when the Hebrew midwives refuse to drown him in the Nile (Exod 1:17) and his mother hides him from Pharaoh for his first three months of life (Exod 2:2). By these acts, Moses is saved, and he is prophetically marked by his safe passage in the Nile, which is a precursor to his miraculous passage through the Red Sea many years later. He is then adopted

---

21. Miraslav Volf, *Exclusion and Embrace: A Theological Exploration of Identity, Otherness, and Reconciliation* (Nashville: Abingdon Press, 1996), 71.

by the daughter of Pharaoh and raised as an Egyptian imbued with all the privilege and power of the imperial court (Exod 2:5–10). Yet as he comes of age, Moses confronts his emergent Hebrew identity when he is provoked by an Egyptian taskmaster who is beating a recalcitrant Hebrew slave. In spite of a childhood of imperial indoctrination, Moses's conscience spurs him towards defending "his own people" (Exod 2:11). He intervenes with righteous anger, attempting to bring justice to a tribal nation, who is undergoing a slow genocide as they are murdered and starved in Egyptian labor camps. Seeking a violent and absolute justice, Moses, "[l]ooking this way and that . . . killed the Egyptian and hid him in the sand," (Exod 2:12), thus entering into the very cycle of violence that he is seeking to destroy.

The next day, having achieved "justice," Moses assumes that he has earned the right to make peace. Noticing a fight brewing between two Hebrew workers, and having somehow discerned from afar which one is at fault, Moses intervenes by asking "the one in the wrong" a question that presupposes a guilty verdict, "Why are you hitting your fellow Hebrew?" (Exod 2:13). The slave's retort is both pointed and ironic, "Who made you ruler and judge over us? Are you thinking of killing me as you killed the Egyptian?" (Exod 2:14). This response makes it clear that Moses's actions, though they reflect the best intentions of a just liberation, have somehow gone awry.

Realizing that his attempt to instigate a revolution is not provoking a widespread political uprising, Moses flees to Midian for asylum. Seething at the failure of his efforts to achieve national liberation, thirsting literally and figuratively to continue the struggle, he inserts himself into another situation of blatant oppression by driving off the shepherds who are harassing the daughters of Jethro. The daughters report back to their father, who is the priest of Midian, that, "An *Egyptian* rescued us from the shepherds . . ." (Exod 2:19; emphasis mine). In spite of the social risk, Jethro invites Moses – who appears to be a member of the cosmopolitan elite – into his simple, tribal home.

This offer of indigenous, Middle Eastern hospitality turns out to be one of the major turning points in Moses's journey towards his true leadership vocation. Gorospe suggests that by accepting the hospitality of Jethro, Moses believes that he will settle permanently in Midian.[22] In his subsequent forty years of exile with the extended family of Jethro, Moses struggles to come to terms with himself. Gorospe highlights the dynamics of this internal struggle: "In Midian, Moses described himself as a *ger* – a 'sojourner' or 'alien,' (2:22). Caught between three worlds – a Hebrew by birth, an Egyptian by upbringing,

---

22. Gorospe, "Old Testament Narratives in Context," 193, n. 136.

a Midianite by marriage – Moses lived a marginal existence in Midian, with a conflicted identity."[23]

This reality mirrors the interwoven identities that are present in Filipino society: a people of Malay cultural roots (Hebraic), who have been educated in a socioeconomic system developed primarily by Europeans and Americans (Egyptian), who are living in a social reality that is defined by regional and kinship loyalties rather than modern political allegiance (Midianite). For many Filipinos, this provokes conflicting feelings of anger, inferiority, frustration and self-disgust: anger at the history of colonialism and at the foreign "other" for dominating the local sociocultural space, inferiority at having lived with both explicit and implicit messages that de-value Filipino culture and identity, and frustration and self-disgust for allowing that domination to continue.[24]

In the desert, though Moses is geographically safe from Pharaoh and no longer under Pharaoh's jurisdiction, he has yet to reconcile his calling from birth with his Egyptian identity and his yet-to-be fulfilled vocation. When Moses moves to a new reality with greater stability by getting married and settling down as a family man, he discards the imperial veneer when he is adopted into a new (but perhaps familiar) culture in the clan of Jethro. Yet this increased stability provides the locus for a deeper transformation in the life of Moses, along with a challenge from Yahweh at the burning bush to leave this stable place.

Because the text is quiet about Moses's forty years in the desert, Gorospe argues that it must be a place of both marginalization and "liminality," a kind of transformative transition.

> Moses in Midian was a marginal person, but not a liminal one.
> It was the call of God that made Midian into a liminal period . . .
> an in-between state between the Egypt of Moses' upbringing and
> the Egypt of his prophetic calling. It was in this liminal space that
> Moses was transformed, receiving a new identity . . . [25]

While Gorospe identifies the transitory aspect of Moses's Midianite journey as one of the keys that unlocks his emerging vocation, the fact that

---

23. Gorospe, 192.

24. Gorospe states, "In Moses' story, the sense of alienation is connected not only with Moses' experience in Midian, but also with his experience in Egypt . . . Thus his experience of being marginal was not only associated with his migrant status, but springs from a certain lack of identity. By linking together migration, alienation, marginality, and loss of identity in the character of Moses, the story makes it possible for Filipino readers to explore similar themes in relation to their migrant experience" ("Old Testament Narratives in Context," 199).

25. Gorospe, "Old Testament Narratives in Context," 204.

Moses is adopted into a new family and a semi-nomadic existence is equally important. For this forty-year period[26] of rooted wandering in the desert serves as a time of cultural re-engagement, an undoing of the ways of imperial Egypt, and a re-acquisition of the ways of Moses's wandering forefathers. Moses's immersion into the cultural heritage of the Midianites, who are thought to be ancient cousins of the Hebrews, is an essential lesson in Yahweh's Abrahamic cultural reconstruction of Moses as an authentic Hebrew leader.[27] Midian, as a psychosocial space, means a simultaneous forgetting of the recent memory of life in Egypt and also a deeper grounding in the lost collective memory of Moses's Hebrew forefathers.

The indigenous Midianite knowledge, systems, and practices – which have been preserved and handed down over the generations, and to which Jethro is an heir, priest, and cultural master – are presumably re-learned by Moses. Having been rejected by his own people due to his efforts at aggressive "peacemaking" and expelled from the educational superstructure of the royal court due to his revolutionary fervor, Moses enters the school of the desert as a shepherd's apprentice. Adopted by his marriage into a semi-nomadic band of Midianites, he is radically re-oriented by forty years of life-skills education, "keeping the flock of his father-in-law Jethro" (Exod 3:1). This novitiate prepares Moses for the forty years that he will spend in this same desert as he leads the wandering, complaining, and conflicting sheep of Israel towards the promised land. Moses eventually emerges from the wilderness of Sinai, having begun to reclaim the peacemaking core of his culture and identity, after he encounters the source of this cultural well: the "I am" of his ancestors, the "God of your father, the God of Abraham, the God of Isaac and the God of Jacob" (Exod 3:6).

---

26. The number forty recurs repeatedly in the OT and NT as a Hebrew numerical symbol of completeness. It also demarcates a period of preparation, transition, judgment, cleansing, and similar forms of qualitative change or transformation.

27. Volf emphasizes the importance of situating the journey towards peace in the experience of Abraham: "The narrative of Abraham's call underlines that stepping out of enmeshment in the network of inherited cultural relations is correlate of faith in the one God" (*Exclusion and Embrace*, 39). Yet he recognizes that this does not legitimize "when an alien culture (say one of the Western cultures) is idolatrously proclaimed as the gospel in another culture (say one of the Asian cultures)"; rather, he suggests that "the solution for being a stranger in a wrong way is not full naturalization but being a stranger in the right way" (39–40). And so, "we are left with the question of how the people who trace their origin to Abraham's departure should relate to surrounding peoples and cultures" (42).

Re-centered Leadership

The Moses who is confronted by Yahweh in the burning bush on "the far side of the wilderness . . . Horeb" (Exod 3:1) while shepherding his father-in-law's sheep is not the same Moses whom Jethro invites under his tent after driving off the rebel shepherds (Exod 2:20). In Moses's dialogue with Yahweh at the burning bush, Moses both honors Yahweh and recognizes the sacred nature of their exchange. Moses employs subtle and skillful communicative expertise to determine the parameters and mandate of his and Aaron's job as Yahweh's negotiating team to Pharaoh. This is concluded by Yahweh's final delineation of Moses and Aaron's roles: Aaron will be the spokesman-prophet, and Moses will be as if he were "God to him" (Exod 4:16).

Gorospe contends that the final "rite of passage" in this transformative transition occurs *after* Moses's dialogue and commissioning with Yahweh at the burning bush, while Moses is leaving Midian to begin his prophetic negotiation with Pharaoh.[28] In an anomalous and opaque text, Exodus 4:24–26 tells the story of a "death encounter" between Yahweh and Moses almost immediately after Yahweh commissions him. Death is averted when Moses's wife, Zipporah, performs a rite of circumcision on their son. This narrative raises many questions, including, what does it mean that a Midianite woman performs the Hebrew rite of passage, which saves the life of her husband? Yet the ceremony also signifies a "loss" as her family comes to be identified with the children of Israel rather than the children of Midian. At the very least, Zipporah, a nearly invisible indigenous woman, emerges as a key figure, bridging the adopted identity of Moses as a Midianite, his birth identity as a Hebrew, and his prophetic calling as a liberator and peacemaker.

Though Gorospe argues that this marks the end of Moses's identity and vocational crisis[29] and the acceptance of his calling back to Egypt and his Hebrew identity, it may not be such a clear resolution, as it apparently involves a new separation in the family. The silent aspects of the story involve the birth of a second son, Eliezer, at an indeterminate point in time. In his naming, he

---

28. Gorospe, "Old Testament Narratives in Context," 194.

29. Gorospe, "Old Testament Narratives in Context," 196–197. Gorospe contends, "The liminal period comes to an end through an initiation rite that involves the whole family. As a rite, the act of circumcision . . . is associated with times of transition, when change of identity and status takes place. For Israel it is a mark of distinction . . . Even though what was at stake was Moses' prophetic calling, it was Zipporah – his Midianite wife – who performed the rite that would identify this half-Midianite, migrant family as belonging to the people of Yahweh . . . Yahweh's threat of death puts into relief the ambivalence of Moses toward his calling and the hybrid identity of his family . . . Through this rite the process of death and rebirth is acted out, and the ambiguity of Moses and his family is resolved."

is identified with God's divine intervention, for Eliezer means, "My father's God was my helper, he saved me from the sword of Pharaoh" (Exod 18:4). But does this son's name represent Moses's recognition that the Hebrew people will be delivered because of Yahweh's miraculous intervention? Or is this name a nod to the God of Jethro, who gives Moses refuge when he flees Pharaoh as an aspiring revolutionary? We find out later that Zipporah and their two children do not accompany Moses to Egypt, but Moses sends them back to Midian, where they are received by Jethro (Exod 18:2). Are they sent back simply because the mission is too short or dangerous to justify having the family come along? Does Zipporah have second thoughts about her decision to identify with the tribe of Moses's origin in the circumcision ritual? Though Jethro wishes Moses well, does he feel betrayed by Moses's decision to return to Egypt, thereby identifying with his own people rather than the Midianites? With many parallels to the current experience of separation and fracture in the family life of Overseas Filipino Workers, this story is full of unanswered questions, and this sub-narrative only picks back up after Moses comes out of Egypt, having freed the Hebrew people.

With his family relations under strain, Moses journeys from Midian to Egypt to serve as Yahweh's hostage negotiator by using the very skills he gained from Jethro in order to earn back the trust of Israel's elders before confronting Pharaoh. No one survives in the desert without the mandate of the community, and so Moses convinces the local Hebrew leaders through a series of patient conversations and demonstrations of God's power. His approach is engaging and compassionate, a marked contrast from when he tried to solve the Hebrews problems by killing their taskmaster and berating them as they argued.

In the ensuing contest between Moses and Pharaoh, whom the Egyptians considered divine, Moses is given equal standing with Pharaoh by the designation that he will be "god to Aaron." This comes with the understanding that Yahweh, the I-am and the highest authority, is the principal actor and the source of power, who will secure the release of the Hebrew people. The plagues, as symbolic events vis-à-vis the cosmology of Egypt, can be seen as forms of active nonviolence, providing Pharaoh with nine opportunities to negotiate a just settlement. Even the final plague of the death on the firstborn is an acknowledgement of the lives lost when the midwives were ordered to kill the male children who were born to the Hebrew slaves. It is instructive that this decision to take a life, even in the service of justice, rests with God alone through the angel of death rather than through the people's weapons. The plundering of Egypt, when the Israelites are told to ask the Egyptians for their treasures, serves as nonviolent restitution for the losses suffered during their uncompensated, forced labor. Yahweh's concern for balanced justice does not go beyond "an eye for an eye" into excess and revenge, which for the Hebrews is a concrete but mysterious demonstration of Yahweh's love and justice. As Brueggemann notes,

> When our mothers and fathers arrived at Sinai, they had just come from the land of Pharaoh . . . It had been a place of great corporate wealth in which the powerful controlled all the public processes, in which the little ones were used up and discarded, in which the weak ones were abused and oppressed, in which the marginal ones were silenced and coerced. They had groaned and cried out, until they had finally attracted the attention of Yahweh. And then they were liberated! . . . But they could never explain their departure. They regarded it as a miracle about which they could only break out in song and dance.[30]

Finally, after Moses and the people of Israel arrive on the far side of the Red Sea, Jethro reappears, accompanying Zipporah and the two children, having heard of Moses's success against the Egyptians (Exod 18:1–2). With Jethro going to Sinai to meet Moses, rather than vice versa, the scene indicates Moses's political ascent, spiritual transformation, the resolution of his sociocultural identity crisis, and an affirmation of his vocation as a leader. The encounter between Jethro and Moses follows an act of deliverance – no longer a solo performance by Moses in delivering the children of Jethro from the bullying shepherds – but rather Yahweh's decisive intervention against Egypt. Again, there is an invitation to come into the tent of the host, but here Moses receives Jethro rather than Jethro receiving "the Egyptian" who saved his daughters. The initial meeting is followed by a deep cultural and spiritual exchange. Rather than a marriage feast, where Moses is adopted as Jethro's son-in-law, Jethro brings offerings to Moses. Over a meal, Moses introduces the elders of Israel to the priest of Midian, which symbolically connects the two communities. The result is the transformation of both parties. While Jethro, a Midianite, gives praise to the God of Israel, the Israelite community accepts Moses's Midianite father-in-law and wife, and his half-Midianite children. On the following day, Jethro exercises his right as an elder and father-in-law by teaching Moses how to set up a dispute resolution system that will enable him to address the disputes that will naturally arise in everyday community life both effectively and collaboratively.

---

30. Brueggemann, *The Covenanted Self*, 76.

Resources for Peacemaking: Indigenous Filipino Leadership and the Biblical Story

Filipinos are uniquely gifted by the creator to be peacemakers through sacrificial, incarnational, holistic, and non-adversarial leadership. Understanding the indigenous roots (values and practices) of traditional leadership can help transform adversarial leadership practices. Three core aspects of Filipino leadership are illuminated by the stories above and reflect nuances of the word "*datu*" (chief): *datu* as "rich," *datu* as "mediator," and *datu* as "chief" or "leader." Thus to be a *datu* is to be "rich," yet not for personal gain, but rather to mobilize a variety of personal and collective resources for social healing and physical restoration. To be a *datu* is also to be a "mediator," yet not one who wields distant authority in order to impose punishment or settlement, but rather one who is intimately involved in holistic justice for collective dignity, honor, and spiritual transformation. Finally, to be a *datu* is to be a "leader," yet not one who seeks individual prominence, but rather one who incarnates the reconciling mandate of the creator within the spiritual history of the community and the broader "cloud of witnesses" (Heb 12:1).

In the stories and narratives of Moses's development as a leader, we see the transformation of a man who is passionate about justice, yet disconnected from his people, conflicted in his identity, and, at a deeper level, detached from his culture and the God of his ancestors. Jethro's hospitality opens up a new possibility for Moses to unlearn the ways of the dominant system of Pharaoh and re-learn what is best in his cultural traditions. This long process requires deep re-rooting in community, intra-personal displacement, family conflict, and inter-communal separation. Through the binding and loosing of ties, Moses comes to understand his leadership vocation and how to fulfill it as well as the source of its power.

From the perspectives of Jethro, Moses, and our indigenous brothers and sisters in Mindanao, a Filipino leader (*datu*) is most powerful and effective when acting in alignment with the Holy Spirit through relational peacemaking, restorative justice, and reconciliation. Filipino indigenous leadership concepts are rooted in the collective Filipino psyche, yet they need to be articulated in ways that are relevant to current realities while avoiding the tyranny of popularity and shallow conformity. The Exodus story reveals a process for exploring and articulating cultural and spiritual resources in the leadership transformation of Moses that is relevant to current realities.

As Filipinos who walk the "Midianite wilderness paths," may we discover the great I-am in a burning bush encounter beneath the shadow of Mt.

Sinai and behold God's immanent and transcendent presence in culture and community. As we read and learn from Scripture and culture, may the texts read and transform us so that we can discover the peacemaking resources that already exist without relying on fads and simplistic formulas. May we lead collaboratively, promote harmony and just relationships, and affirm the dignity and honor of all. May Filipino Christian leaders remember that the two most common meanings of *datu* ("wealthy" and "chief") have their deepest roots and most beautiful blooms in Jesus Christ, *Datu sa Kalinaw,* the prince of peace. *Datu Jesu Kristo sa Kalinaw* is the source of all spiritual and material resources, the mediator of a new covenant relationship between God and humanity, and the cosmic reconciler of all creation.

Section III

Healing and Forgiveness

7

Telling a Different Story

Rwandans Learn to Forgive After Genocide

John Steward

How do you forgive when fellow community members have decimated your family, taken your spouse, or disfigured your children, destroyed your home, stolen your animals, eaten your crops, and then mocked your poverty and taunted you for your very existence? These atrocities were committed by your friends at school, with whom you played sport and gathered sticks and fodder and collected water. Now, they treat you like poison and call your family "animals." *Why should I ever forgive them? How could I ever do that?*

I have now heard hundreds of stories from Rwanda, which provide a treasure trove of insights on the challenges and possibilities of healing, forgiveness, and reconciliation.[1]

---

1. Further detail is available in my book *From Genocide to Generosity: Hatreds Heal on Rwanda's Hills* (Carlisle: Langham Global Library, 2015).

Photo 1. Mama Deborah (Photo by Colin Smith. Used by permission.)

Mama Deborah is one of my teachers – she forgave the young soldier who came to confess, *I killed your son,* and then she requested justice: *you must replace my lost son by now becoming my son.* The strength of the radiance on her face is like an icon of hope for the reconciliation possible for Rwandans.

Rwanda's Confronting Challenge

Despite warnings early in 1994 of impending troubles, the Western world turned its back on Rwanda in its neediest hour. As a result, around eight hundred thousand Rwandan Tutsi and moderate Hutu died in one hundred days, between 6 April and 18 July, 1994 – the time it took the Rwanda Patriotic front to remove the Hutu government, which had masterminded the killings. General Romeo Dallaire, who led the moderate UN peacekeeping force in Kigali at that time, documented the buildup of the threat and pleaded for more troops. He estimated that an additional five thousand UN soldiers would have restricted the slaughter to around fifty thousand. But the stonewalling of the over-developed world gave the genocidal planners and their militia a free hand, with some support from Rwanda's colonial allies.[2]

Then about two million of the Hutu fled in fear of reprisals into camps in Zaire (now Congo), Burundi, Tanzania, and Kenya. Within three years these refugees returned to Rwanda and were shocked to find their homes and land occupied by around one million Tutsi and moderate Hutu, who had returned from long-term exile in neighboring countries.[3] Into this tense atmosphere

---

2. "I told him (the UN Secretary General) if I had four thousand effective troops I could stop the killing . . . the call ended with words of encouragement that couldn't have seemed more futile." Romeo Dallaire, *Shake Hands with the Devil: The Failure of Humanity in Rwanda* (Toronto: Random House Canada, 2003), 289. Similarly, 514.

3. Dallaire, *Shake Hands with the Devil,* 152–156.

and recipe for chaos, I walked in early 1997, a time when expatriates from the over-developed world were not greatly liked.

After my initial sense of helplessness upon arriving in Kigali, I began to listen to my new colleagues, trying to connect their faces to their names and eventually their stories. At first, I couldn't recognize some of them from the day before, and I realized I must pay attention to whatever they would share with me from their lives. I learned to observe the "language" of individual Rwandan faces – not just their individual features, but the unspoken language on their faces – some hard, others frozen, clouded with pain, troubled, distant, and pre-occupied. Few smiled. The only certainty of laughter was when the beating of the drums drew people out to dance. In those rare moments it seemed as if nobody had a care in the world. But most Rwandans were carrying heavy burdens in their hearts, which were wounded by loss, pain, and shame. As I began to know Rwandans as unique people, I could recall both their names and their faces, because their stories were so unforgettable. With time, many became good friends. And through knowing them, I came to love them.

During this time, a common Christian theme in Rwanda was, *we must forgive and forgive and then forget . . .*, adding pressure to the furrowed brows, sorrowful faces, demotivation, and confusion. A few wise souls realized the need to focus on healing, and when I attended my first "healing" workshops, I noted some clenched-fisted resistance at the very mention of forgiveness. One participant daily claimed, *I shall leave the moment I am told that I must forgive someone.*

Increasingly, I came to value the language of the body and the eloquent emotional messages on faces. I also observed a dawning gentleness, relief, and openness on the faces of those whose inner healing brought them to consider forgiving people who had done terrible things to their loved ones. I could distinguish in them a peace that was not present in those who were not yet ready to progress towards love of the *other,* their enemy.

The Longing for Forgiveness

On one occasion, I attended a celebration on the final day of a healing workshop. Each participant summarized the changes within them and their struggles and hopes for the future. They celebrated small steps forward, and we danced around the room in thanks for the small signs of progress.

Among the participants was Jacqueline, who lost all her family in the genocide. She spoke of how she came to the workshop scared and anxious. She wore dark glasses so that others could not see her tears of sadness and often left the room to weep because of her deep grief. On this final day, Jacqueline apologized for having isolated herself at times from the group; then she surprised everyone with a joyful announcement: *prior to attending this healing, a man asked for my hand in marriage seven times, and I declined each time. This week I accepted his offer. I am inviting you to come to my betrothal ceremony next month! This will be a great way to celebrate the difference this workshop has brought to my life.* The applause was vibrant and supportive.

Photo 2. Jacqueline [left] receives a hug from one of the participants after making her announcement. (Photo by John Steward)

Seven years after that event I met with Jacqueline again. Married, with three adopted children, she has found her place as an active member of the new Rwandan society. Her quiet confidence and clear thinking have made her a confidant of many women, and her peaceful smile and energy are like an inviting, open door. Jacqueline was elected by her community as a *person of integrity* to join the local tribunal, tasked with seeking to restore justice at the grassroots, through the traditional process called *gacaca.*

As a participant in the process of healing and forgiveness, she has helped lead many others towards their own forgiveness. Jacqueline shares: *In the tribunal work, as I heard the terrible acts being confessed, I felt a lot more forgiveness than anger for these people.* This change started when she began her own healing journey and chose to admit her fears and look them in the face, to grieve her losses, and to let go of her bitterness and the right to seek revenge.

Human history is a boggy swamp of the ongoing unwillingness to forgive. Powerful people, organizations, government, and special interest groups throughout the world maintain this trend. But there is hope wherever people yearn for and actively embody this graced experience called forgiveness, which is a central teaching of the Christian faith and every other major religion, despite the consistent failures of its adherents to honor the concept of forgiveness, peacemaking, and the seeking of justice with the enemy.

Photo 3. The community gathers to participate in *gacaca*, a traditional process seeking to bring those accused of involvement in the 1994 genocide to justice. (Photo by David Fullerton. Used by permission.)

The physical and emotional cues for gaining insight into the real-life struggles of Rwandans were formative in my understanding that the path to recovery from painful and traumatic events both reflects a person's spirituality and re-forms its expression. Our faces and bodies mirror what is inside us – our faith, core values, aspirations, the impact of our heroes, unresolved struggles, sub-conscious memories, and wounds of spirit.

Before living in Rwanda, I believed in forgiveness as a desirable concept, but in Rwandans I encountered the practical value and personal cost in choosing forgiveness even in seemingly impossible circumstances. Rwandan people taught me the intricacies, potential, and beauty of forgiveness after the consequences of genocide. They affirm that *forgiveness has the potential to heal the world, starting with myself.*

Forgiveness in Action

By observing how Rwandans changed as they processed their stories in small trust groups, I realized the importance of the healing journey for creating a climate of offering or accepting forgiveness.

Forgiveness is never easy. If ever a person feels pressured to forgive, they soon discover that it is a personal decision requiring an honest delving into submerged feelings and the reopening of past wounds. This is not a pleasant process and cannot be forced upon anyone. A person's resistance at this early stage is understandable, even appropriate. Their reticence to take the conversation further usually arises because the pain of the past hurt is still so real and raw. We can gently affirm the reality of the heartfelt hurt.

And that may be enough for the moment. If we seek a quick response, apart from the likelihood of a superficial process, the pressure normally increases the heartache and hurt and deepens the subconscious sense of powerlessness. Sometimes all we can do is re-affirm the difficulty and state our willingness to support the person at this time.

Whenever forgiveness is extracted or coerced, its counterpart – the required apology – will also be forced. This generates feelings similar to a dental extraction: *this hurts, it is being done to me, I would not do this if I were on my own.*

It is the good fortune of a dentist to have materials that mask the pain, and the dentist normally can ensure speedy and major relief. With the journey towards forgiveness, the opposite must occur – the pain must be faced. Most of us do not readily choose to face pain, but, as Monique Lisbon suggests, "if the truth hurts, just think what a lie can do."[4]

In Rwanda, after the genocide of 1994, the church often preached urgent forgiveness to people deeply affected by loss, grief, and anxiety. The message, "you *must* forgive," hurt many, increasing their levels of guilt, failure, shame, and resistance to let go of the bitterness. Despite good intentions, this was counterproductive.

Forgiveness Is Difficult, but Possible

Mama Deborah's ability to face the young man only three months after he killed her son and to forgive him is unique and relatively rare. Her regular prayer life, active faith in Jesus Christ, along with a confronting dream, and the appearance of a truthful, contrite offender assisted her in this process. Using the phrase, "difficult but possible," reassured Rwandans who were struggling with the challenge of forgiveness. It helped the victims of genocide when we acknowledged that forgiveness was complex and that a quick and easy solution would not be found, but that there was a place for hope on the horizon.[5]

It requires human energy to hold the pain within oneself while trying to live daily life. As a result, that energy is not available for interaction with

---

4. Monique Lisbon, *Fragments of Home* (Melbourne: Braidwood Press, 2008), 126.

5. For ten years I pondered why twice in the Gospel accounts about Jesus, there is a footnote to a passage about forgiveness, saying, "this text is not found in some early manuscripts" (see Luke 23:34 and John 8:3–11). Was this passage omitted because remembering the death of Jesus was so painful that some writers or copyists of the manuscripts found forgiveness to be a difficult, even an outrageous, idea from their leader? Might it reflect the feelings of grief and loss that predominate in a person whose wounds are still raw or unhealed?

others. When forgiveness is pushed too early, it becomes a challenging ideal whose time has not yet come. As Dennis, Sheila, and Matthew Linn say: "Do not forgive too soon."[6]

This is further complicated by common misunderstandings about forgiveness, such as a widespread belief that the prime beneficiary of forgiveness is the offender. Yet forgiveness does not exonerate the offenders, nor let them "off the hook." Nor does forgiveness erase the need for justice. We cannot simply decide to offer our forgiveness as quickly as possible, nor can we *just forgive and forget*. As Lewis Smedes writes, "We forgive . . . what we cannot forget."[7]

Forgiveness and Its Context

In this section, we will look at forgiveness within the context of other responses that we might make to painful events. The wounds in our hearts impact our responses in daily life and therefore our relationships, so it is helpful to describe the feelings that accompany our memories. The following table, which is based on insights from the Mennonite psychologist David Augsburger, outlines four responses to painful experiences.[8]

Table 1. Responses to Painful Experiences

Victim Active	FORGIVENESS	Y Y Y Y Y	RECONCILIATION
	XXXXXXX		XXXXXXX
Victim Inactive	DENIAL ZZZZZZZ	→ → →	REVENGE
	Offender inactive		*Offender active*

---

6. Dennis Linn, Sheila Fabricant Linn, and Matthew Linn, *Don't Forgive Too Soon: Extending the Two Hands That Heal* (New York: Paulist Press, 1997).

7. Lewis B. Smedes, *The Art of Forgiving: When You Need to Forgive and Don't Know How* (Milton Keynes, UK: Summit Publishing, 1996), 179.

8. Adapted by the author from David W. Augsburger, *Helping People Forgive* (Louisville, KY: Westminster John Knox Press, 1996), 93.

Denial

Of the four responses to painful events, denial is the most frequent. I estimate generally 65 percent of people are in denial. For example, in Australia, many people are unready to seek healing for personal wounds from the past, especially during times of conflict and war.[9] Denial is a specifically human response and does not favor one culture over another; it is a universal coping response. When we are in denial, we carry on with living after experiencing pain or trauma as if nothing serious has happened, or we recognize that things are not normal, but we do not know what to do about it. For offenders, denial leads them to act as if they have done no wrong. For victims, denial leads them to behave as if they have not been badly hurt or unduly disadvantaged.

Denial is like wearing blinkers over the eyes of our spirits so that we ignore or suppress our feelings. Frequently, both offenders and victims are deeply affected by the painful or traumatic experience. When we are in denial, life appears to continue as outwardly normal; however, the energy of the feelings evoked by the hurt or the hatred stays inside us and acts like a weight to slow us down, or subconsciously energizing and motivating us. Long-term denial usually has negative or undesirable consequences. Blaming another is one example of the social effect of denial.

The negative energy held within eventually drives those in denial in one of two directions, either causing inner, personal harm or outer, social harm. For example, the inner harm of denial, which is indicated in Table 1 by ZZZZ, is now apparent among Rwandans in the upsurge of suicides, broken marriages, mental illness, cancer, and depression that are emerging after years of "incubating" inner wounds. In other words, persistent problems of health, mindset, and behavior may reveal a past wounding that has been ignored, forgotten, or buried in the subconscious.

Revenge

The stored energy of denial moves outward in revenge as embittered victims seek to fulfill their wishes that offenders suffer the pain that they have endured. This hope for harm to occur in the offender is indicated by the → → in Table 1. Here, the victim becomes the victimizer, and the cycle of suffering and revenge takes a new turn.

---

9. Darryl Dymock, *A Sweet Use of Adversity* (Armidale: University of New England Press, 1995), 82.

Revenge is so deceptive. Francis Bacon says, "revenge is a kind of wild justice."[10] Shakespeare describes "a kiss . . . sweet as my revenge."[11] Yet the hope for revenge is neither just nor sweet. As the former long-term Australian prisoner and author Gregory Roberts says, "all violence begins as a wound in the heart . . . Cruelty, even my own acts of cruelty, begin as an agony in the self, before it is inflicted on others."[12]

In seeking revenge, the imagination of the victim is focused on diminishing the life of another, which perpetuates the conflict and does not lead to resolution. I have experienced situations where those who presented themselves as *victims* came to realize that their unhealed selves had unconsciously sought harm to others, thus also making them *offenders*.

How does one escape from the deceptive cycle of revenge? As with denial, we can avoid patterns of revenge by healing our inner wounds, as indicated by XXXX in Table 1.

Forgiveness

Forgiveness is the act of choosing to let go of bitterness and the desire to seek revenge. Forgiveness can occur without any pre-conditions for offenders, although it helps when victims can confront offenders about the effects of their behavior and also request justice or restitution.

We are usually hardest on ourselves and most aware of our own shortcomings and failures. In Rwanda, we surprise people when we say, *forgiveness of another is not possible until I can first forgive myself.* Forgiveness is the gift God offers us in Christ Jesus. But as the barrier XXXX indicates, something must first happen in us before we can accept our forgiveness – we need to know our pain and grieve our losses. The unhealed emotions no longer circulate within us, but are removed or redirected. This step of healing our inner wounds puts us on the path towards forgiveness.

Forgiveness *always* benefits the victim – letting go sets us free from the shackles of the one who hurt us. In contrast, forgiveness does not benefit unrepentant offenders and has no meaning for them until they apologize and

---

10. John Bartlett, *Bartlett's Familiar Quotations*, 14th ed. (London: Macmillan, 1977), 208.

11. Bartlett, *Bartlett's Familiar Quotations*, 290.

12. Gregory Roberts, "It's Our Humanity That Dies in an Execution," *Sydney Morning Herald*, August 14, 2003, 2.

ask for forgiveness. Forgiveness is a one-sided act, but this does not diminish its value or significance.[13]

We all have role models of forgiveness, both modern and ancient, secular and religious. We can learn much from sacred Scripture and our own heroes and heroines – from those who have been able to forgive their enemies. Finding the path of forgiveness takes time and is part of the journey of life.

When forgiveness in the victim coincides with the moment when the perpetrator is repentant and wishes to make an apology, then the divided parties can meet each other again; this moment brings us to the final segment of the table.

Reconciliation

Reconciliation is relatively rare because it requires deep change in both parties, leading to a willingness to face each other. In many cases, in Rwanda and in daily life, the readiness of one person may not be matched by readiness in the other. The offender must face the truth of hurting the victim (which may have been denied for months or years) and become open to repentance and apology. In Table 1, the barrier marked YYYY indicates the need for confession, apology, and restitution/justice.

Because of the chaos of the genocide in Rwanda, the other party often cannot be known. However, when we are aware of who hurt us, or whom we have wounded, a face-to-face meeting is pertinent. If the conflict is within a marriage, family, or business, then working towards this final stage is an important task.

Alice lost almost her entire family in the genocide and was left for dead in the swamps after her body was mutilated. She survived and later attended a healing workshop, where she was able to grieve her losses, symbolically nail her pains to a cross, and open her wounds to healing. When she played an active role in the local *gacaca* tribunal, Alice longed to offer forgiveness to her assailants, but no one confessed to harming her.

Emmanuel, who killed fourteen people, attended the same healing process and was in the small group with Alice. He was a subdued participant who spoke in generalities. Later, Emmanuel and Alice became volunteer members of a foundation for survivors and perpetrators who promote healing, forgiveness, and justice. One day he surprised Alice when he fell on the ground and pleaded

---

13. See "Twelve Steps of Forgiveness" in the Appendix of Steward, *From Genocide to Generosity.*

for her forgiveness. Even though she knew that this man did her harm, she said, "because of the healing workshop, I felt ready to forgive him."

Alice accepted Emmanuel's apology and embraced him. They have become friends and work together, supervising needy children and rebuilding houses for widows of the genocide. Emmanuel wanted to confess long before he actually did – he would open his mouth, but the words wouldn't come. He said that the words "I'm sorry" were so hard to say.

Without Healing There Is No Forgiveness

These words from my colleague Lincoln Ndogoni, a Kenyan psychologist, are a key to the quest for forgiveness.[14] We have seen earlier that in order to progress to more appropriate and healthy living, *both* the victim and the perpetrator need to have their inner wounds healed. Like Alice, victims often find that their healing opens them up to the possibility of forgiveness. Like Emmanuel, offenders often find that their healing opens them up to the possibility of confession, repentance, and apology.

So how does this healing take place? Slowly, with difficulty, often tearfully, and always truthfully. Healing requires us to open our hearts to at least one other person in a safe space. This is exactly what a good listener or group facilitator can offer, similar to a salve or soft cloth during the lancing of an infected sore. The holy surgery proceeds at the pace chosen by the victim, who moves forward from paralysis at the scene of the accident towards nurture, recovery, and rehabilitation.

People give their own clues that they need to open their hearts as they begin to know their deeply embedded pain. Revealing comments emerge, such as, "I'm paying the price for my foolishness," "I wish it wasn't so difficult," "I feel stuck," "the experience leaves me with a bad smell." Though the emotion may not be on the surface, and tears may not be visible, small expressions of wistfulness or distaste begin to open the heart's store, where the difficult experience has been buried.

Healing by telling our stories is not new – it is the very essence of "best practice" to bring the truth out into the open. Once we begin to speak out a painful truth, we open the wound and gain insight about the poison we have buried within. Difficult though this may be, this process brings us to a major truth: *This poison has affected my relationships with others and it will continue*

---

14. Personal communication with Lincoln Ndogoni, Kigali, April 1998.

to do so until I let it go. This insight invites us to make an active choice and opens the pathway towards confession and repentance.

Photo 4. A moment of burning papers with painful stories at a pain release ceremony at an interfaith workshop in Asia, modeled on Rwanda (Photo by Ian Stehbens. Used by permission.)

Many victims find it empowering to participate in an action to release the pain, such as a ceremony of symbolic re-enactment, a role play, journaling, an act of truth telling, or an attempt at relationship rebuilding. These empowering actions often release visible peace on the victim's face, as if the spirit can now freely express its essence publicly.

Perpetrators' wounds are double-edged; they have a prior cause (violence within), to which is added the guilt of their action to hurt others (violence without). Perpetrators also need to tell their stories, be validated in their pain, and affirmed in their desire to let go of bitterness. The sign of repentance comes in their confession and apology. I describe this as the two feet of repentance: to stop running away from the victim by turning to face them and then to step forward and say, *I'm sorry,* and offer some kind of restitution.

Whether or not reconciliation is reached, choosing to face the truth restores integrity within the person who has been damaged by the aggression of another, or within the perpetrator themselves. When we face our pain, we become like a gift to the world, a bridge for others to cross and a step towards living life with a healthy human spirit. In this, we join those who are *telling a different story.*

8

Healing the Trauma of War and Internal Displacement

Exploring the Nexus of Trauma Healing and Reconciliation

Annabel M. Manalo

This article presents trauma healing as a core component of peacebuilding. Drawing from narratives of peace and human rights advocates who have experienced war and internal displacement, it explores the processes that facilitate the healing of trauma and then reflects on the connection between trauma healing and reconciliation.

In 1992, I joined a team of medical doctors, psychologists, and social workers in a medical and relief mission in Marag Valley. Marag, which is located in Cagayan Valley, was believed to be the seat of the revolutionary government of the Communist Party of the Philippines-New People's Army (CPP-NPA) for Northern Luzon. Intense battle between the Philippine military and the CPP-NPA led to Marag being declared as a "No Man's Land" in the late 1980s through the early 1990s. One consequence of these battles was the displacement of indigenous peoples (Agays, Isnegs, and Aetas). By the time our team arrived, the war had already ended. My role was to assess the psychosocial impact of the war and provide psychosocial support to those who had been internally displaced by the armed conflict.

During my week in the Marag Valley, I was exposed to platoons of military men in operations, the deplorable conditions of the internally displaced persons (IDPs),[1] and the graves of children who had died in crossfires or evacuation centers. These images of war and the stories of trauma and survival of the people I encountered remained lodged in my memory. Because of the impact of this experience, I changed the course of my counseling practice and ministry involvements, first volunteering with and later joining Balay (an NGO that provides psychosocial services to survivors of organized political violence). As a resident psychologist with Balay, I did therapy with survivors of torture and enforced disappearances and also trained grassroots leaders in communities displaced by armed conflicts.

In the course of my work over a six-year period, I saw two trajectories among survivors of violence and internal displacements in conflict settings. Some survivors remained stuck in their experience of victimization, acted out of their unhealed trauma, and resorted to counter-violence. Yet more common were those who, despite their suffering, not only demonstrated resilience but also developed the courage to transform their trauma into actions for social change. This stirred up my curiosity and led me to explore the processes and conditions that could bring about such positive outcomes.

In the following sections, I will present the preliminary findings of a qualitative study that sought to explore these processes. The context of the study was the long-drawn war between the Philippine government and secessionist Muslim rebel movements in Mindanao, Philippines, which spanned more than forty years and displaced millions. In the next section, I offer a brief introduction to this conflict, describe its devastating impact, and explore how unhealed trauma fuels the cycle of violence.

The Socio-Political Context of the Mindanao Conflict

Internal displacement due to armed conflict in the southern regions of Mindanao is a humanitarian and peace issue of serious concern, for it continues to be one of the most life-threatening and destructive problems affecting the Muslims, Christians, and *Lumads* (indigenous people). The Muslim people's struggle for freedom and self-determination and the establishment of the

---

1. Internally displaced persons (IDPs) are persons or groups of persons who have been forced to flee or leave their homes as a result of armed conflict, situations of generalized violence, violations of human rights, and natural or human-made disasters. See UNHCR Guiding Principles on Internal Displacement, http://www.unhcr.org/protection/idps/43ce1cff2/guiding-principles-internal-displacement.html.

Bangsamoro are at the heart of this war.[2] This internal conflict has displaced over four million since 2000[3] and caused massive destruction of livelihoods, properties, infrastructures, and other unquantifiable social costs, such as breaking down social ties that bind individuals, families, and communities, especially between Muslims and Christian settlers.

Among the most notable displacements was the "all-out war" by President Estrada in 2000, which displaced 140,000 families or 755,761 individuals.[4] More recently, the Zamboanga siege[5] by the Moro National Liberation Front (MNLF) in 2013 displaced 118,819 people, killed 208 rebels and nineteen government forces, wounded 236, and destroyed more than 10,160 homes.[6]

---

2. *Bangsamoro* means Muslim (*Moro*) nation (*bangsa*) and expresses the Muslim people's struggle for self-determination after centuries of colonization and marginalization. The creation of the Bangsamoro homeland will enable the Bangsamoro people to exercise control over their ancestral domain and manage the natural resources found within these domains. In Judith M. De Guzman and Charlie Inzon, "Shared and Contested Meaning in the Mindanao Conflict: Exploring People's Understanding of Bangsamoro," *Philippine Journal of Psychology* 44, no. 1 (2011).

3. Gari Acolola, "Forced to Flee: How Many Have Been Displaced Due to Conflict?," *Rappler.com*, July 11, 2017, https://www.rappler.com/newsbreak/iq/175236-fast-facts-world-population-internally-displaced-persons-conflict.

4. The "all-out war" was a military offensive launched in March 2000 to "weaken primarily the MILF capability to undermine the territorial integrity of the Philippines and inflict harm on both government personnel and civilians." It ended in July with the Armed Forces of the Philippines (AFP) capturing the MILF Camp Abubakar headquarters in Maguindanao and some towns in Lanao Del Sur. It is estimated that the war affected communities in 14 provinces, 4 cities, 89 municipalities and 489 barangays of Central Mindanao. In Cesar Pobre and Raymund Quilop, eds., *In Assertion of Sovereignty, vol. 1: The 2000 Campaign Against the MILF* (Quezon City: Office of Strategic and Special Studies, Armed Forces of the Philippines, 2008). Retrieved from https://www.academia.edu/184241/In_Assertion_of_Sovereignty_The_2000_Campaign_Against_the_MILF.

5. The Zamboanga siege involved disgruntled factions of the MNLF, who felt eased out in the peace negotiation between the Government of the Philippines and Moro Islamic Liberation Front (GPH-MILF). It started on September 9, 2013, when about 200 members of a Misuari-led faction of the MNLF attacked and occupied several villages of Zamboanga City in Mindanao. It caused a clash and standoff between MNLF and the AFP. The siege was reportedly aimed at thwarting the government's peace negotiation with MILF, a secessionist group that broke away from the MNLF. The siege ended by the end of October, with the AFP rescuing all hostages and driving back the rebels. In "What Went Before: The MNLF Siege of Zamboanga City," *Philippine Daily Inquirer*, Sept 8, 2014, http://newsinfo.inquirer.net/635995/what-went-before-the-mnlf-siege-of-zamboanga-city.

6. National Disaster Risk Reduction and Management Council (NDRRMC), "Situational Report re Emergency Management for the Displaced Persons Resulting from Armed Conflict in Zamboanga City and Basilan Province," Sept 25, 2013, 2–3, http://www.ndrrmc.gov.ph/attachments/article/2655/Emergency_Management_for_the_Displaced_Person_Resulting_from_Armed_Conflict_in_Zamboanga_City_and_Basilan_Province_as_of_25SEP2013_0800H.pdf.

Even more recently, the Marawi siege[7] between May 23 and October 16, 2017, which was led by a group that declared allegiance to ISIS, displaced 359,680 people and killed 847 Maute fighters, 163 government troops, and forty seven civilians.[8] Thousands of IDPs still remain packed in crammed spaces that serve as evacuation facilities.

In 2014, after decades of conflict and seventeen years of negotiation, a peace settlement was finally reached between the Government of the Philippines (GPH) under former President Aquino and the Moro Islamic Liberation Front (MILF) through the Comprehensive Agreement on the Bangsamoro (CAB). The CAB called for the creation of a new Autonomous Region of the Bangsamoro,[9] which was hailed not only as a milestone for resolving the armed conflict but more importantly for offering opportunities for meaningful development in the Muslim Mindanao regions. However, the failure of the 16th Philippine Congress in 2014 to pass the first Bangsamoro Basic Law (BBL),[10] an organic law that aimed to provide for the creation of the autonomous region, resulted in demoralization and a loss of trust in the sincerity of the GPH. This failure undermined grassroots peace initiatives, such as interfaith dialogues and collaborative efforts by Christian and Muslim development institutions. Peacebuilders believe that the formation and aggressiveness of groups such as Maute could have been prevented if the BBL had been signed in 2014.

Despite these setbacks, many continue to hope for the prospect of lasting peace, which the enactment of a new BBL under current President Duterte

---

7. The Marawi siege involved an armed conflict between the government and Maute (a Muslim clan that swore allegiance to ISIS) in Marawi Islamic City of Lanao del Sur Province. The conflict was an attempt by Maute and Abu Sayyaf (a group that started as radical Islamic group and turned into a kidnap for ransom group) to make the Islamic City of Marawi the center of Islamic State movement in Southeast Asia. Under attack by Philippine state forces, the group fortified and engaged the government forces in urban guerrilla warfare, which started on May 23, 2017 and ended with the death of the group's leaders (Isnilon Hapilon of Abu Sayyaf and Omar Maute of the Maute clan) on October 16, 2017. The AFP regained control of the city a few days after. During the siege, several hostages were held, but all were eventually rescued. In CNN Philippines, "Timeline: The Marawi Crisis," last updated Oct 28, 2017, http://cnnphilippines.com/news/2017/05/24/marawi-crisis-timeline.html.

8. CNN Philippines, "Timeline: The Marawi Crisis."

9. Conciliation Resources, "History: Mindanao Conflict and the Moro Islamic Liberation Front," http://www.c-r.org/where-we-work/southeast-asia/history-mindanao-conflict-and-moro-islamic-liberation-front.

10. The Bangsamoro Basic Law (BBL) is supposed to be the organic law, which will create the new autonomous Bangsamoro political entity and provide the basic structure of government for the Bangsamoro Autonomous Region. The creation of the BBL is the fundamental provision of the Comprehensive Agreement of the Bangsamoro and upon which all other provisions hinge. In GMA News, "FAQs About the Bangsamoro Basic Law," Sept 10, 2014, http://www.gmanetwork.com/news/news/nation/378530/faqs-about-the-bangsamoro-basic-law/story/.

could bring. Ghazali Jaafar, Vice Chairman of the MILF and Chairman of the Bangsamoro Transition Commission, claims that the new BBL proposal is their new formula for the elusive peace in Mindanao. In his message to President Duterte during the submission of the draft BBL, he said:

> "We believe that this new proposed Bangsamoro Basic Law (BBL) reflects the diversity of interests of the Bangsamoro people, non-Bangsamoro indigenous people and settler communities; yet, these interests are all united under one goal of establishing a just dignified and lasting peace in the Bangsamoro, in Mindanao and the country in general. We humbly submit this new proposed Bangsamoro Basic Law (BBL) is the best antidote to violent extremism that has wrought havoc in many parts of the Bangsamoro. Once legislated, this new BBL would erase the doubt on the peace process, that mistaken notion, which is fueling violent extremism among some Moros."[11]

Many peace advocates and workers, however, argue that peace agreements alone will not guarantee peace, a sentiment that is reflected in the Catholic Bishops' Conference of the Philippines' (CBCP) earlier statement regarding the first BBL and the peace process:

> The present social context is one of mutual biases and prejudices, of mutual charges of injustice. Such social climate demands moral consideration . . . Bias and prejudice are part and parcel of the deep mistrust between Christians and Muslims, two peoples coming from the same Abrahamic faith.[12]

The statement emphasizes the need for a comprehensive peacebuilding process at the core of which is rebuilding and promoting harmonious relationships between Muslims, Christians, and *Lumads*. It also highlights the importance of transcending biases and prejudices and of forging trust by way of dialogue.

Archbishop Antonio Ledesma, a highly respected peace advocate, asserts that if peacebuilding is to succeed, it must begin at the grassroots level because

---

11. Ghazali B. Jaafar, "Peacetalk: This Bangsamoro Basic Law Is Our New Formula for the Very Elusive Peace in Mindanao," *MindaNews*, July 22, 2017, http://www.mindanews.com/mindaviews/2017/07/peacetalk-this-bangsamoro-basic-law-is-our-new-formula-for-the-very-elusive-peace-in-mindanao/.

12. "Striving for a Just Peace, the Moral Road," *CBCP News*, July 11, 2015, http://www.cbcpnews.com/cbcpnews/?p=59874.

the impact of armed conflict is most keenly felt at this level.[13] He emphasizes that if the peace agreement is not acceptable to the local communities, it will remain a peace process on paper alone. These comments highlight the need to work at the grassroots for peacebuilding and reconciliation. Furthermore, they indicate that the hatred that fuels the war mentality must be healed in order for a consolidated peace and reconciliation to work.

In the next section, I will explore how trauma healing and reconciliation are integral components of any peacebuilding effort. Failure to heal trauma and address psychosocial problems resulting from armed conflicts and internal displacements can prevent peace from taking root in the lives of people and their communities.

Psychosocial Impact of War Trauma

Trauma is derived from the Greek word meaning a wound or injury that is produced violently. Violent exposure in armed conflict settings creates both visible and invisible wounds, such as a response of intense fear, helplessness, or horror. Some people may develop post-traumatic stress disorder (PTSD), which involves the following diagnostic criteria: exposure to actual or threatened death or serious injury; presence of disturbing thoughts, feelings, or dreams related to the event, along with mental or physical distress with reminders of the trauma; attempts to avoid trauma-related cues; changes in how a person thinks and feels; an increased arousal or reactivity associated with traumatic events.[14] Other manifestations of trauma among survivors of armed conflict include anger, depression, anxiety, substance abuse, difficulties with affect regulation, and interpersonal difficulties that cause one's overall well-being or quality of life to suffer.

Carolyn Yoder, a peace advocate, identified the limitations of defining trauma through a strictly clinical frame and questioned the usefulness of PTSD diagnosis, especially in large-scale events, ongoing traumas, and with non-Western societies.[15] The full impact of trauma is seen not only in impaired individual and family functioning but also in the way it affects the quality of relationships among community members.

---

13. "Archbishop Urges Peace Building at Grassroots Level," *CBCP News*, Oct 10, 2012, http://www.cbcpnews.com/cbcpnews/?p=5342.

14. American Psychiatric Association, *Diagnostic and Statistical Manual of Mental Disorders*, 5th ed. (Arlington, VA: American Psychiatric Publishing, 2013), 271–274.

15. Carolyn Yoder, *The Little Book of Trauma Healing* (Intercourse, PA: Good Books, 2005), 31.

IDPs in Mindanao experience trauma in individual as well as collective/communal dimensions – physical, psychological, spiritual, social/relational, and societal. The impact of this trauma may be manifested in deeper relational issues, such as mistrust, bias, prejudice, and hostile attitudes between Christians and Muslims.

Melinda,[16] an internally displaced person who has lived through three wars, suffers profoundly from the cumulative distress of daily survival and ongoing conflict. She laments the many losses, disruptions, and dislocations of her family:

> *"Dahil sa giyera, maraming nawala na mahalaga sa buhay ko at ng aking pamilya. Marami akong hinanakit at matindi pa rin ang galit ko sa mga Muslim. Sa ngayon mahirap pa rin sa aking magtiwala sa kanila. Alam kong mali pero naiisip ko pa rin kung paano ako makakaganti. Noong 2000 all-out war, nasunog ang bahay ko, pati generator na ginagamit ko panghanapbuhay ay ninakaw. Sa giyera noong 2008, hindi ko na napalitan ang ibang mga nawalang gamit sa bahay. Itong kasalukuyang gulo na naman, nahinto sa pag-aaral ang mga anak ko. Pati ako nawalan na ng ganang magtrabaho. Gulo na rin isipan ko, pati na rin ng pamilya ko . . . Ilang buwan pagkatapos ng giyera palagi pa ring may kaba at takot. Ngayon medyo wala na pero nag-iba na ang ugali ng aking asawa, naging maiinitin ang ulo niya at palagi kaming nag-aaway kahit sa maliliit na bagay. Masakit sa dibdib ang mga pangyayari."*

(Because of the war, I have lost many things that are important to me and my family. I am still filled with resentments towards Muslims and it is very difficult to trust them. I know it is wrong, but I still have fantasies of revenge. During the 2000 "all-out war," my house was burnt down, even the generator set that I used for my livelihood was stolen. After the 2008 war, I was not able to replace some of the household appliances that were lost. Now, as a result of the recent hostilities, my children's schooling stopped. My mind is very troubled, and I lost interest in work. My family is also affected. My youngest cannot sleep and is so scared. It has been months after the war, but there is still anxiety and fear. These have subsided now, but my husband's behaviors have changed. He

---

16. Not her real name.

has become irritable and we always fight even over simple stuff.
It's really painful.)

This story exemplifies the profound impact of armed conflict and
displacement. The visible effects, such as the social, economic, and cultural
impact, can be identified readily in the dislocations and loss of home and
livelihood; the violation of the right to safety, security, and peace; and the denial
of justice and human dignity.[17] The invisible wounds of war – pain, suffering,
grief, helplessness, powerlessness, and other psychosocial effects – are more
difficult to recognize, as are the relational impacts, such as disruptions in family
life and intensification of animosities, mistrust, prejudice, and polarization
between Muslims and Christians. Feelings of victimization, anger, and hatred
fuel the desire for revenge and counter-violence.

Unhealed Trauma and the Cycle of Violence

In situations of protracted conflict and massive displacements, trauma is
cumulative and therefore difficult to heal. People are unable to grieve their
losses out of fear of being overwhelmed by intense painful feelings. Others
are able to grieve only in part; they never get to complete the grieving process
because they have to focus on day-to-day survival.

Violent exposure leads to trauma, and unhealed trauma can lead to
violence. The trauma creates intense negative energy that is trapped inside the
body and is often acted out by hurting or harming others.[18] Thus the danger of
unhealed trauma is that it can get reenacted or transferred. As Richard Rohr
puts it, "If we do not transform our pain, we will most assuredly transmit it."[19]

Yoder elucidates the psychological processes involved in the cycle of
violence resulting from unhealed trauma.[20] The model, which Yoder adapted
from Botcharova,[21] explains how people move from being victims to becoming
aggressors. It starts when a person or group develops a victim identity as a

17. Cf. Ernesto Anasarias, *Rebuilding Communities* (Quezon City, Phils.: Balay
Rehabilitation Center, 2005).

18. Yoder, *Little Book of Trauma Healing,* 20, 32.

19. Richard Rohr, "Transforming Our Pain," Center for Action and Contemplation, Feb
26, 2016, https://cac.org/transforming-our-pain-2016-02-26/.

20. Yoder, *The Little Book of Trauma Healing,* 37–44.

21. Olga Botcharova, "Implementation of Track Two Diplomacy: Developing a Model
of Forgiveness," in *Forgiveness and Reconciliation: Religion, Public Policy, and Conflict
Transformation,* ed. Raymond G. Helmick and Rodney L. Petersen (West Conshohocken, PA:
Templeton Foundation Press, 2002), 279–304.

result of the experience of aggression or violence. The danger in identifying the self/group as a victim is that it can be a powerful driving force. The strong feelings of hurt, grief, rage, powerlessness, shame, humiliation, and being unjustly treated may drive the person/group towards acts of counter-violence, justifying their violent actions in the name of self-defense or seeking justice. It becomes easier for the person/group to resort to acts of aggression after creating enemy images and demonizing their enemies. The victim is neither responsible nor accountable for acts of counter-violence, because the enemies are less human and are a threat to the person's/group's safety and security. This "us versus them" mentality justifies the use of violence. The victims now become the victimizers, setting in motion a cycle of violence and counter-violence. Violence cycles across generations, a phenomenon referred to as inter-generational transmission of violence.

The trauma of human-induced violence need not always lead to the path of counter-violence. The cycle of victimhood and violence can be mitigated by understanding and recognizing the impact of trauma and by experiencing healing from trauma.

The trauma of war and internal displacement may not easily heal, but it can be transformed. This is the experience of the many survivors who chose a different path than victimization and counter-violence and are now at the forefront of peace, relief, rehabilitation, and human rights work in war-torn communities in Mindanao. In the rest of this article, I explore the trauma healing processes that best facilitate reconciliation.

Trauma Healing to Facilitate Reconciliation

The data presented here are culled from the narratives of thirty-seven peace and human rights advocates – community leaders, social workers, and NGO workers who participated in a three-day trauma healing and reconciliation workshop that I facilitated. This group was mixed (Muslims and Christians), and all experienced being internally displaced as a result of armed conflict. The workshop provided space for participants to tell their stories and facilitated healing encounters within the group. It made use of psycho-spiritual group processes and expressive/creative approaches, such as art, metaphor, psychodrama, meditation, visualization, music, rituals, and prayer dance. The research component of the workshop involved abstracting trauma healing themes and identifying processes that facilitate reconciliation between participants from conflicting groups.

Themes and Processes

Eight themes emerged from the narratives of participants, which point to several processes that can be implemented to facilitate trauma healing.

Using Metaphors and Symbols to Tell Stories

The trauma experience is highly emotionally charged, overwhelming, or simply indescribable. Some survivors are unable to speak about trauma, because talking about distressing memories can trigger the same emotional response as the original trauma. Thus finding a metaphor or symbol to help describe the experience can be therapeutic.

Using metaphors and symbols to tell stories provides a safe context for participants, allowing them to talk about their trauma indirectly and giving them a choice about how much or little to share. Participants can access the depths of their pain without having to talk about the details of their experience.

Storytelling also provides space to acknowledge the impact of the trauma on participants' lives and facilitates the exploration of grief issues resulting from their losses and dislocations. As one participant shares:

> *"Ang buhay ko ay gaya ng palayan na dati ay malusog ang bunga. Ngunit dahil sa dalawang giyera na aking pinagdaanan, di na malusog, di na tulad ng dati, wala ng kabuhaybuhay . . . nawala ang aking mga pangarap at nawalan ako ng ganang mabuhay . . . Sa unang giyera (1972) kami ay lumikas at nahiwalay ako sa aking mga magulang. Hindi na kami nagkasama-samang muli . . . Natanggap ko na ang naging buhay ko, bagama't nalulungkot pa rin ako kapag naaalala ko ang pinagdaanan ng pamilya."*

> (My life is like a rice field. It used to be robust and fruitful. But as a result of the two wars that I went through, it is no longer healthy and is lifeless. Gone are my dreams and I lost the zest for life. During the first war (1972), we evacuated, and I got separated from my parents. I have never been reunited with them . . . I have come to terms with how life has turned out, although I still feel sad whenever I remember what my family had been through.)

By telling their stories, participants can try to explain and make sense of what happened. Some survivors need to tell their stories many times, and through the retelling gradually come to terms with their losses and pain. The storytelling provides space to integrate their trauma into their life stories and, consequently, to find a meaningful place within their hearts and minds.

Acknowledging Pain and Grieving Loss

War and displacements involve grave losses. Avoidance is a normal response to memories of those losses. Pain makes some people avoid talking about what happened so they can get on with their lives. Thus the healing process begins by helping survivors open up to painful feelings and embracing their pain. According to one participant, "*Damhin* (Feel) . . . I realized that I need to feel and accept the pain so that I can heal."

Acknowledging the pain and naming the losses can facilitate the acceptance of those losses. Grieving losses is essential to the healing process. As one participant shares: "I was able to cry over everything I have lost, the loss of our properties, sources of livelihood and hopes for my family . . . It is now easier to accept what happened . . . and accept our present crises and difficulties."

Reflecting on the Experience

Trauma can shatter the sense of order, predictability, and meaningfulness of life. In armed conflict settings, being confronted with the brutalities of war and what we are capable of as humans can be deeply jarring, creating a need to understand and make sense of the trauma. This reflective process involves the challenge of reconstructing a life when that life has been lost or shattered.

Reflection can facilitate meaning making. Providing a safe and accepting space to reflect on the trauma opens up a new way of looking at life. A reflective visioning exercise enables survivors to develop a vision of what's possible and to look into the future with hope. As one participant shares, "Reflecting on what has happened helped me understand why I behave this way towards my family . . . and the meditation exercises helped me to reflect on my dreams for myself and my family."

Discovering Inner Resources for Healing

In the midst of their suffering, survivors tend to disconnect from their inner selves. Providing space to reflect on their experiences can help participants touch base with inner strengths and resources, which can be very empowering. Most participants are surprised to see how much strength they have inside:

> "*Ang aking karanasan ay gaya ng isang halaman na namumulaklak, nakabaon sa lupa na ugat ng buhay . . . dahil sa pangyayari kami ay lumikas, nawala ako, nahulog ang bulaklak . . . Ngunit di nagtagal unti-unting gumaling, tumubo uli . . . Ngayon mas malakas at matibay . . . Di ko rin akalain na kinaya kong lahat ang pinagdaanan ko.*"

(I liken my experience to a plant that blooms with flowers, anchored to the soil which is the root of life . . . because of the events, we evacuated. I was lost, the flower fell . . . But it did not take long for it to get healed and bloom again. Now I am stronger and sturdier . . . I could not imagine how I was able to cope with everything I went through.)

Another participant describes how staying connected with inner resources and with God enables her not only to resist the "typhoons" of life but also to thrive:

"I can relate my life experiences to the plants. There are different kinds of plants . . . there are plants that cannot resist typhoons but there are also those which can sway with strong winds, like the bamboos . . . I am more like a bamboo. I continue to live despite the many trials in my life for as long as I continue to trust myself and God."

Drawing Strength from Family and Community

Trauma disconnects survivors not only from themselves but also from others. In the context of relationships and in the process of re-connection, healing starts to occur as survivors draw strength from loved ones and receive emotional connection, intimacy, and care from family members. As one participant relates, *"Ang aking dalawang anak ang pinagkukunan ko ng lakas at sigla. Dahil sa kanila pinipilit kong magsimula ulit."* (I draw my strength and zest from my two children. It is because of them that I struggle to start life all over.)

In the same way, the community spirit of *damayan*, that is, looking after and caring for one another, enables survivors to withstand tragedies: "In life, we experience the cycle of happiness and tragedies. We can relate this to our experiences of war and the support we get in the community. There are many experiences of calamities and trials in life but we continue to stand."

Being Sustained by Faith and Hope

Many survivors draw strength from their faith in the midst of war and displacements. For these survivors, maintaining faith and hope is central to healing. One participant shares how an attitude of letting go and surrendering to God helped her family to survive all the wars: "I offer myself and totally surrender to God . . . I know that my family survived all these wars because I always pray for God's protection . . . Prayer is what strengthened us in times of war."

Maintaining a hopeful attitude and a sense of connection to a higher being enables participants to persevere in the midst of suffering: "*Sa kabila ng lahat ng hirap na pinagdaanan namin di ako nawalan ng pag-asa. Alam kong kasama ko ang Diyos at di ako nag-iisa . . . Life must go on.*" (In spite of all the hardships that we went through, I did not lose hope. I know that God is with me and I am not alone . . . Life must go on.)

Discovering the Humanity of the "Enemy"

The "social wounds" of war are manifested in damaged relationships, an "us-versus-them" mentality, and division according to enemy lines. Creating opportunities for "healing encounters" that cultivate the ability to empathize with members of other groups can facilitate reconciliation.

Many participants respond to the in-depth sharing of stories with acceptance and understanding, counteracting the silence or isolation that characterized their previous way of relating and connecting them to one another through their common experiences of suffering. Learning about shared suffering helps participants see the humanity of the "enemy" or the "other," opening possibilities for them to unite and work together as peacebuilders. According to one participant, "I realized that Muslims and Christians are not enemies . . . we all have suffered the effects of war and have experienced many losses. To have peace we must learn to unite."

Seeing the humanity of the "enemy" breaks down prejudices and stereotypes and makes it easier to forgive past transgressions. As one participant relates, "*Ngayon nakita kong pare-pareho pala tayo ng pinagdadaanan at hindi tayo dapat nag-aaway-away . . . kailangang matuto tayong patawarin ang mga may atraso sa atin.*" (Now I realize that we are all going through the same path and we should not be fighting each other . . . we need to learn to forgive those who have wronged us.)

Community Rituals: Collectively Acknowledging Losses and Grief

Communities suffer losses on many levels – the loss of loved ones, support networks, homes, and livelihood. Shared acknowledgement of losses and collective mourning can facilitate healing. Community rituals and meditative prayer dances, where participants collectively bring their pain and grief before God, are powerful healing moments.

One participant shares that "*sisidlang basag*" (broken vessel) evoked in him an image of a broken urn, signifying the many losses suffered by his townmates as a result of war: "In my hometown, many people place their money only in chests or vessels. When war strikes, people evacuate and lose all their savings and other valuables through looting by soldiers. It is like a broken urn."

Nevertheless, most survivors have never collectively acknowledged these losses, even though as one participant observes, "all people are grieving because of the war." Being able to grieve losses collectively as a community can reconnect survivors and restore social ties that bind individuals, families, and communities together. As one participant observes, *"Kailangang pagsaluhan natin ang luksa . . ."* (We all need to share one another's grief).

These collective rituals strengthen participants' resolve to pursue their work for justice and peace. As the following participants share:

> "As community workers, we carry together the pains and wounds of our country and put the grains of pain on God's table so we can carry on with our work for justice and peace."

> *"Ipina-nalangin namin kay Allah na sana mabigyang lunas ang problema na nagdudulot ng kaguluhan at ng di na madagdagan pa ang mga naibuwis na buhay . . . Sana'y bigyan kami ng lakas ng loob na makabangon muli at maipagpatuloy ang gawaing pangkapayapaan."*

> (We are praying to Allah for the resolution of the problems that cause the conflicts and that there will be no more lives lost . . . that we be granted inner strength to be able to rise again and continue on with our work for peace.)

Insights for Peace Workers

Is it possible for trauma healing and reconciliation to take place in situations of on-going conflict? The trauma healing processes gleaned from the narratives of the participants provide important insights for those working for peace on the ground. While healing is a process that may take a long time, fostering certain conditions can start the healing process.

Creating Safe Spaces and Acknowledging Trauma

Creating safe and supportive spaces for people to tell their story, speak about their pain and seek acknowledgment for their suffering, provides a context conducive to healing and reconciliation. When pain, grief, anger, vengefulness, and other unexpressed emotions are contained and acknowledged, trauma is tended and the healing process can start. When the emotions are not recognized they come out as violence against self or others.

The re-storying of trauma can facilitate finding meaning in the experience, a new self-understanding, and a new vision for the future.

Adopting Culturally-Sensitive Psychospiritual Processes

Psychospiritual processes that utilize expressive, creative, and meditative approaches, can facilitate re-storying and shifts to more healing narratives. This requires cultural sensitivity – using processes and symbols that reflect the needs and wishes of the parties in conflict.

The use of metaphors and rituals can facilitate healthy mourning/grieving that is key to trauma healing. Grief is a normal, healthy response to trauma and losses; it is a wound that needs be observed, named, and recognized in order to heal. One must look carefully into its source, acknowledge it, and care for it, with compassion.[22] Giving oneself permission to grieve heals the pain. Grieving "allows us to break through the immobility, numbness or suppression that at first defended us from unbearable pain."[23] Grief that is unexpressed is grief that lasts indefinitely and can create problems in personal life and relationships.

Utilizing group processes that bring together people from conflicting groups and foster reconnection is equally important. Group processes that are experiential and provide space to listen to others' story and bear witness to their suffering can reduce prejudice and break down stereotypes. Processes that facilitate encounter between conflicting groups result in group cohesiveness and deeper connection. This is referred to as a "corrective emotional experience" that allows perspective taking and empathy towards those previously considered as enemies.

Transforming Perceptions and Restoring Relationships

Carolyn Yoder describes the potential of traumatic events to change and transform relationships, but this requires the work of reconciliation:

> But there is another side to trauma . . . traumatic events and times have the potential to awaken the best of the human spirit and, indeed, the global family. This is not an automatic process,

---

22. Thich Nhat Hahn, *True Love: A Practice for Awakening the Heart* (Boston: Shambhala Publications, 1997).

23. Yoder, *Little Book of Trauma Healing*, 35.

however. It requires that we acknowledge our own history *and our enemy's,* search honestly for root causes, and shift our emphasis from national security to human security. At the core, it is a spiritual work of the deepest sort, calling forth nothing less than the noblest ideals and the faith, hope, and resilience of the human spirit.[24]

Restoring the humanity of the "enemy" plays a key role in reconciliation. Those who have developed a victim identity as a result of trauma tend to "demonize" and "dehumanize" the enemies or aggressors. These enemies are labeled as evil, inhuman, non-human, beasts, criminals, rebels, and other negative identifiers. Depersonalization underlies atrocities and violence in times of war.

For healing and reconciliation to take place there must be a shift in perception of the "enemy." This involves seeing the humanity of the other. Restoring the humanity of the enemy involves seeing them as persons created in the image of God – with dignity, worth, and rights that need to be respected and protected.

Redeeming Trauma Through Forgiveness and Survival Mission

Humanizing the enemy makes it easier to forgive, which is an important component in completing the trauma healing journey. John Steward, a peace advocate, shares many stories of survivors of the genocide in Rwanda, who discovered the healing power of forgiveness and its role in post-conflict reconciliation.[25]

In another trauma healing workshop which I facilitated among survivors of ethnic/tribal conflict in Northern Philippines, forgiveness was a key theme that surfaced. One participant, a peacebuilder, reported that during the meditation exercise that we did, he saw an image of faceless people who represent those who killed his brother. He said he never thought he would have the courage to face the offenders without exploding in anger. Surprisingly, he was able to meet and converse with them calmly: "I spoke to them and said I am ready to forgive but all I want is for you to come out publicly and tell the truth about what really transpired and why you killed him."

---

24. Yoder, *Little Book of Trauma Healing*, 6.

25. See John Steward, *From Genocide to Generosity: Hatreds Heal on Rwanda's Hills* (Carlisle: Langham Global Library, 2015).

Judith Herman states, "While there is no way to compensate for an atrocity, there is a way to transcend it, by making it a gift to others. The trauma is redeemed only when it becomes the source of a survivor mission."[26] A survivor mission involves engaging in the wider world through some form of social action – reaching out to others who have been victimized, providing practical support, and engaging in advocacies to improve their plight.

Developing a survivor mission requires nurturing a kind of spirituality that integrates contemplation and action.[27] Contemplative practices create healing spaces that allow God to form our inner being and empower us to work for the renewal and transformation of life both at a personal and societal levels.

Nurturing Faith and Spirituality

Faith and spirituality are important resources for trauma healing. From the perspective of faith, the survivor recognizes that pain and struggle are an important part of character development. The survivor is able to accept, embrace, and value the difficulties, in the hope that something beautiful can emerge out of the struggle, because God is right there in the midst of it.

Thus, faith can counteract helplessness and powerlessness which are at the heart of trauma. It can sustain and restore inner strength and a sense of power. It can provide a sense of meaning and purpose that can enable survivors not only to heal but also to transform trauma into something meaningful.

Working for Shalom in All Areas of Life

Trauma healing and reconciliation find their basis in God, who seeks to bring shalom to all areas of brokenness. The Lausanne Movement articulates this vision of God's shalom as follows:

> Shalom is a state of wholeness, well-being, peacefulness and flourishing of all that God has created in all of its dimensions and all of its relationships. Shalom includes right relationships of human beings with God, within themselves, with one another and with the created world. Shalom as God's peace encompasses

---

26. Judith L. Herman, *"Trauma and Recovery: The Aftermath of Violence – From Domestic Abuse to Political Terror"* (Philadelphia: Basic Books, 2015).

27. See Charles Ringma, "Contemplation in a World of Action," available at https://www.northumbriacommunity.org/wp-content/uploads/2015/06/Contemplation-in-a-World-of-Action.pdf.

all dimensions of human life, including the spiritual, physical, cognitive, emotional, social, societal and economic.[28]

We need to reconceptualize our understanding of trauma healing to include work on multiple dimensions (body, mind, spirit, and relationships) and on multiple levels (personal and communal). For trauma healing to be effective, it must be situated in a broader peacebuilding program that addresses the psychological, relational, and structural dimensions of violence in an integrated manner. It must be seen as equally valuable as governance and policy making, restorative and transitional justice, humanitarian assistance, advocacy, community development, and other components of peacebuilding.[29]

Conclusion

The process of trauma healing and reconciliation is very challenging and involves the creation of conditions for mutual support, empathy, and compassion where the wounds of war and displacements can be held and transformed. To be truly meaningful, this process must be consciously directed at contributing to the transformation of all areas of life – from one marred by violence, woundedness, and dehumanization to one characterized by peace, justice, truth, and wholeness.

On a personal note, my years of engagement in trauma healing among survivors of organized political violence, such as war and internal displacements, has developed my sensitivity to people's suffering and their struggle to transform it into something meaningful. It has also sensitized me to the challenges of bringing God's shalom into the context of deeply traumatized communities. It has changed my understanding of what the gospel means in this context, how my faith/spirituality should be expressed, and how to do ministry in the context of violence. In the course of my involvements, I was transformed into a counselor-advocate, ready to speak about human rights, social justice, and peace issues whenever I am given the opportunity. This work also opened up questions that touch on the basics of my faith. I feel that the best response to these questions involves a theology that engages people where they hurt and suffer, based on a discernment of God's mysterious action in a world of conflict and violence.

---

28. David Claydon, ed., *A New Vision, A Renewed Heart, A Renewed Call (Vol. 2): Lausanne Occasional Papers* (Pasadena, CA: William Carey Library Books, 2005), 513.

29. Cf. Fermin Manalo Jr., "Community Development Animating Peacebuilding from Below: The Case of GiNaPaLadTaKa Space for Peace in Pikit, North Cotobato," *Philippine Journal of Social Development* 15 (2013): 112–142.

9

Family Reconciliation among Survivors of Incest and Abandonment

A Case Study in Accompaniment

Tricia Mazo

This case study traces the difficult journey of five girl survivors of incest and abandonment in their attempts to forgive and reconcile with their families. The study describes the survivors' relationships with God during this part of their journey and explores the roles and responsibilities of the social work minister who accompanied the survivors.

The ministry of accompaniment is beyond counseling or companioning, as the social work minister actively participates in specific activities, such as searching for missing family members, engaging with family members who caused hurt, assessing the possibility of reconciliation with the survivors, and preparing for and being present at the meeting, which may include confrontation and reconciliation.

In counseling or companioning, the desire for reconciliation needs to be expressed by the survivor and not suggested by the counselor, who must remain sensitive to the thoughts and feelings of the counselee about reconciliation. Forgiveness is an integral part of holistic healing, but it is an intensive and arduous process that is best explored when counselees perceive it as integral to their healing journeys.

The road to reconciliation is long and rocky for survivors of incest and abandonment, but it is a path worth taking because of the promise of peace. The journey becomes more bearable with the accompanying care and presence of a minister.

Family Abuse as the Context

This study traces the stories of five girls: four incest survivors and one who was abandoned by her parents. These girls were part of a group of twenty-four young people who came from various local non-government organizations and the Department of Social Welfare and Development (DSWD) shelters, where psychosocial, educational, home life, and other services were provided.

The social worker met and engaged with these girls in a Christian NGO, where she was the program manager and resident counselor. This Christian NGO operated in partnership with the DSWD through a Character Leadership Training Program with the aim to prepare disadvantaged youth for independent living, which might include family and/or community reintegration. The social worker journeyed with these girls for two years and continued on in a personal capacity after the Christian NGO phased out in 2013.

The girls were provided with psychosocial, spiritual, home life, recreational, educational, health, and practical vocational services using a multidisciplinary approach, where they were engaged in a vibrant and fruitful youth ministry that taught character leadership and shared the love of Jesus.

This case study will focus on the story of Grace and then also offer vignettes of the stories of Annie, Lisa, Suzzie, and Jenny.[1]

Grace

Sexual Abuse

Grace was the youngest of three children, with an older sister and brother. Her childhood memories included Sunday School, and so at a young age she had already heard the gospel and knew many Bible stories. As far as she could recall, her father was often away at work, and her mother was often ill, and so a pastor would visit to pray for her mother.

---

1. To protect the identities of the girls, their real names are withheld.

When Grace was nine years old, her mother died. Shortly after this, her father started to sexually abuse her. She became pregnant at the age of twelve. When her aunt heard that she had missed her menstruation, she made her abort the child by giving her abortive medicines. After hearing what had happened, some relatives tried to hide her, but other relatives took her to DSWD and reported the abuses.

Grace stayed at a DSWD facility for girls for four years and did not disclose the abortion. A child abuse case was filed against her father, who went into hiding. She started to have nightmares, such as her father running after her or hearing a crying baby. She also had many physical symptoms, with frequent leg and knee cramps and stomach aches.

Processing the Pain

In the center for girls, Grace tried to cope with these traumatic symptoms by actively involving herself in school and church youth activities. The staff saw her leadership potential, and so they nominated her to participate in the character leadership training for youth in Manila, where she joined other young people at the Christian NGO.

At her first interview with the social worker at the Christian NGO, she disclosed the abortion. During the first few weeks, her nightmares became more frequent, and she was afraid that her father might come to harm her. The counseling session with the social worker focused on processing the fear towards her father, anger towards her mother, and guilt feelings over the abortion. She vented out her anger against her mother, whom she thought was the root cause of her suffering, crying out: "Had she not died, had she not left me, I would have not suffered this much!"

Grace understood that her father had made wrong choices in violating her. He broke the law and would need to face charges in court. She also came to realize that her father was afraid, because he was the one hiding, and this realization eased her fears. She also came to understand that consenting to the abortion was not her full responsibility, because she had only been twelve years old and lacked discernment.[2] Moreover, she had been under threat, afraid, and confused.

Grace blamed God for what happened to her, saying: *Tita, hindi naman ako bad girl* (Tita, I am not a bad girl). This statement suggested that bad things

---

2. Philippine law (Republic Act 9344) exempts a child from criminal liability at age fifteen and below, http://www.officialgazette.gov.ph/2006/04/28/republic-act-no-9344-s-2006/.

happened to bad people, a perspective that needed reframing, and so lessons about "Why bad things happen to good people?" were discussed in discipleship sessions. Grace resented God for not intervening and for allowing the horrible abuse to happen to her, but during this phase in her journey, she surrendered her life to Jesus. Although she knew about Jesus from Sunday School, she did not make a conscious decision to accept Jesus as Lord and Savior until she began to search for answers during the time of intense psychological and spiritual processing. Lisa Rudolfsson and Inga Tidefors explain: "Although sexual abuse might lead to distrust and disappointment in God, however, many victims still express a longing for a trusting relationship with God."[3] During this time, her nightmares and dreams dramatically decreased, along with the physical symptoms of knee and leg cramps and stomach aches. She also became more engaged in school and ministries.

Forgiveness and Attempts at Reconciliation

Grace shared that she was able to forgive her father because Jesus had forgiven her. The desire to forgive her father happened after Grace surrendered her life to Jesus. It came on her own initiative because of what she had learned from her discipleship lessons and personal quiet times. She was never asked by any of the discipleship leaders or staff to forgive, and she did not wait for her father's repentance before she made the decision to forgive. Grace's forgiveness is an "embodiment of its continuation to the extent that she is transformed by it."[4]

With a desire to restore the broken relationships in her family, Grace began to communicate with her sister and brother. When she was ready to visit them, her social worker and team leaders accompanied her to her home province, where they were warmly welcomed by her siblings. They decided to stay a couple of nights so that Grace could have some bonding time with her sister.

Grace finished high school while she was with the Christian NGO. She trained in Teaching English as a Second Language (TESOL) to be able to teach English to children. She then briefly worked in a beverage manufacturing company and then ministered overseas, teaching English to children in Taiwan. When she came back from Taiwan, she got engaged with her boyfriend.

---

3. Lisa Rudolfsson and Inga Tidefors, "I Have Cried to Him a Thousand Times, But It Makes No Difference: Sexual Abuse, Faith, and Images of God," *Mental Health, Religion & Culture* 17, no. 9 (2014): 911, http://dx.doi.org/10.1080/13674676.2014.950953.

4. James Voiss, *Rethinking Christian Forgiveness: Theological, Philosophical, and Psychological Explorations* (Collegeville, MN: Liturgical Press, 2015), 389.

On her own initiative, Grace sought contact with her father through their relatives. With mixed emotions, she talked to him over the phone. She was angry with her father's sarcastic reply, *Heto, payat na ako, walang makain* (Here, I am thin, there's no food to eat). She felt that her father was blaming her for his situation, since he was hiding from police authorities due to the pending arrest warrant and was doing odd jobs in order to survive. She decided to meet him and confront him about how she had suffered because of his actions. Even though she had forgiven her father, she still needed to hear him acknowledge the wrong he had done to her, and she wanted him to hear the suffering she had endured as a result of his wrong decisions.

Grace called up the social worker to help her clarify her motives in deciding to meet with her father. She asked the social worker to accompany her during the meeting. The court case against her father was taking too long, and so she wanted to drop it and start anew. She also wanted to give her father a chance to live freely without hiding and for her siblings to be able to visit him freely so that they could be a family again.

Grace wanted to hear her father ask for her forgiveness and to surrender to the police as a form of justice. She wanted him to have some time in prison, but she was planning to stop the court case later so that her father could gain his freedom.

This put the social worker in a dilemma. Should the social worker report to the DSWD that Grace knew the location of her father, so that the DSWD could issue a warrant of arrest and pursue the case? Or should she let Grace exercise her agency and give her the space needed to make her own decisions about her father, an action that was empowering for her? It was a choice between a high-risk activity versus a healing opportunity. The social worker opted for the latter, but with a mitigation plan to lower any ethical or safety risk.

Preparing for the Reconciliation Meeting

The following steps outline the mitigation plan that the social worker made before Grace met with her father. First, Grace informed her previous social worker in the DSWD shelter for girls about her decision to meet with her father and not to pursue the case once her father is jailed. Second, as a security check, Grace's boyfriend visited the location the day before the meeting in order to survey the nearest police and barangay stations and to check entry and exit points in case of any dangerous or inappropriate incidents. Third, to establish trust with the father, Grace's brother was asked to act as a go-between, communicating with the father about the plan for a meeting so that he would not think that he was being setup to be arrested by the authorities.

Before the meeting, the social worker and Grace prayed and talked about the plan, particularly how she wanted the meeting to go and what she would tell her father. Then they rehearsed the plan.

The Reconciliation Meeting

The meeting happened outside her father's residence, which was a tiny shack that he shared with other tenants. Grace sat on a bench beside the social worker, waiting for her father to come out of the shack. Her father came and sat on a stool next to her. The atmosphere was tense, and only a few words were uttered. From a distance, the boyfriend and the brother could see what was happening, but they could not hear the conversation.

Grace trembled and cried as she poured out her heart to her father – especially what she had been through because of his actions, including her stay at the shelter and how she felt betrayed by the fact that her siblings had withheld the location of his hideout from her.

Her father listened but said very little. He looked down most of the time and whispered, "sorry." Grace asked what he said to make sure she heard him right and he repeated the word, "sorry."

During this conversation, the social worker held Grace physically while Grace shook and wept to keep her from falling off the bench. At the same time, the social worker held Grace figuratively, silently praying for the release of Grace's anger, bitterness, and fear, and for healing and restoration of the relationship. The social worker did not speak a word. Her role was to be present and accompany Grace, who executed the plan and did all the talking herself.

After Grace's father said, "sorry," she regained composure, and they began to talk about her siblings and other relatives. The atmosphere became lighter. As a result, everybody – Grace, her boyfriend, her brother, and her social worker – left the meeting with bright faces and smiles, released from tension and anxiety.

Attaining Peace and Justice

After the meeting, Grace continued to communicate with her father over the phone. When she decided to marry her boyfriend, she thought of inviting her father to the wedding, but felt it was too risky, since he had not surrendered to the police and the warrant of arrest was still valid. Grace and her boyfriend asked the social worker to walk her down the aisle on their wedding day. This posed another dilemma for the social worker. Professionally, being part of a client's wedding might be construed as unethical, but the social worker felt she was being called to go beyond professional boundaries by accompanying Grace spiritually on her wedding day. By walking Grace down the aisle, the social worker felt she would be ushering Grace to the next level on her journey, having moved from her dark past into a new life and a new relationship. Social workers and those in the other helping professions are expected to accompany people in times of pain and risk, but their accompanying presence is also necessary in times of joy and celebration, thereby affirming the wholeness of a person's life.

Through this long process of forgiveness and reconciliation, Grace affirms that she has almost achieved peace. She still feels that justice is lacking, which she feels will only happen if her father surrenders to the police, and she goes to court to desist the case and set him free. This is how Grace imagines attaining justice and restoration. She is still waiting for her father to accept responsibility for his decisions under the law. If this happens, she will attain full peace.

Annie, Lisa, Suzie, and Jenny

Annie: Abandonment

Annie was only three years old when she and her brother were abandoned by their parents due to the parents' involvement with prohibited drugs. Even though she had other half-siblings through her parents' previous relationships, her brother decided to leave her at an orphanage, opting to stay on the streets and look for odd jobs. Occasionally, her father would visit her at the DWSD shelter, where she moved after the orphanage closed. She has fond memories of her father, even though he was not able to take her with him since he was sick. Her mother, who was involved in another relationship and was still peddling drugs, never came to visit her. While living at the DSWD shelter, she learned that her father had died of an illness, and so she was unable to pay him respect for the last time. She mourned the loss of her father, and she longed one day to see her mother.

Annie tried to trace the whereabouts of her mother, together with her social worker from the Christian NGO. They were informed that her mother was in the women's correctional center, serving a sentence for peddling prohibited substances.

To prepare for the meeting with her mother at the women's jail, Annie met and prayed with her social worker. The social worker accompanied Annie to facilitate the visit and help Annie process her feelings afterwards.

Upon seeing one another for the first time in fifteen years, Annie and her mother were very emotional and began weeping. At first her mother was in shock, unable to believe that her daughter would visit her, and then she embraced Annie and did not want to let go. Annie was too overwhelmed with mixed emotions to speak many words. She had wanted to ask her mother a lot of questions, but her mother's answers were not coherent, because her mind had been affected by drug abuse.

After the meeting, Annie continued to communicate with her mother, siblings, and other relatives. Even though Annie had forgiven her mother, she opted not to stay with her mother after she was released from jail, because she knew that it would be a long process before her mother would be rehabilitated from drug use and peddling. After her training with the Christian NGO, Annie worked as an office assistant in a Christian company and supported herself through school. Once Annie has completed her bachelor's degree, she plans to help her mother and siblings live comfortable and sober lives.

Lisa: Abuse and Betrayal

After Lisa was sexually abused by her father, she told her mother, but her mother did not believe her. So Lisa decided to leave home and stay with friends. Later, people helped her report the abuse to the DSWD, and a case was filed against her father, who went into hiding.

With her social worker at the Christian NGO, Lisa met with her mother and other relatives. Her mother urged her to withdraw the case against her father, but Lisa was determined to pursue the case. Nevertheless, the meeting with her mother and relatives eased the animosity between them, paving the way for regular communication.

Lisa enrolled at the university and worked, living independently from her family, but maintaining communication with them and her other relatives. Later on, her father was captured by the police and imprisoned. The family begged Lisa to withdraw the case, and so Lisa went to visit her father in jail. Her father was repentant and asked for her forgiveness in front of the family, and so Lisa decided to withdraw the case.

Lisa now has her own small perfume business and regularly visits her family.

Suzie: Abandonment and Molestation

When Suzie was an infant, she and her mother and two brothers were abandoned by her father. Growing up, her mother told her that her father had died, but then the family received a letter from her father in prison. When they visited him in prison, Suzie was hesitant to meet him at first, since she had thought her father was dead for as long as she could remember.

When her father was paroled, Suzie stayed with him for a couple of months so that they could form a father-daughter relationship, but then he started to molest her. Suzie kept this a secret from everyone, including her mother, since she did not know how to handle the situation.

Suzie first disclosed the incident to the Christian NGO director and the social worker, but she was resolved not to report the abuse to the police or to file a case against her father, since doing so would cause conflict among her family and relatives. She later on disclosed the molestation to her mother but maintained her decision not to report her father to the police.

Her father later asked for her forgiveness over the phone, and she found herself able to forgive him and to allow him and her mother to come visit her at the Christian NGO.

Suzie just graduated with a Bachelor's Degree in Fine Arts and is looking for a job. She now stays with her mother, while her father, who is working elsewhere, visits them occasionally. However, when her father is around, both she and her mother are careful to ensure that Suzie has her own space and that her father no longer molests her.

Jenny: Sexual Abuse and Denial

Jenny was repeatedly sexually abused by her father when she was in high school, but when she told her mother, her mother beat her up. Eventually, Jenny related everything to a high school friend, who sought help from the school's guidance counselor, who referred Jenny to the DSWD. As a result, her father was arrested by the police, and a court case ensued. After Jenny testified about the sexual abuse in court – which was a harrowing experience – her father was convicted of eleven counts of rape. Her mother, however, denied the rape and abandoned Jenny.

At the Christian NGO, Jenny expressed a desire to release all her negative emotions against her father and mother. Afterwards, she made several steps to reach out to her family. First, she wrote a letter to her father in prison to pour out all her pain and suffering. Second, accompanied by the Christian NGO social worker, she visited her brother and grandmother in the province while her mother was working in another city. This visit restored communication with her grandmother, brother, and other relatives.

Through this visit, she got her mother's contact number. Since Jenny was ready to talk with her mother, the social worker contacted the mother to assess the possibility of a meeting. But before the meeting, Jenny received a phone call from her mother. Her father, who was still in prison, came on the phone line and surprised Jenny by asking for her forgiveness, as did her mother.

The social worker scheduled a meeting between Jenny and her mother, who was emotional and full of tears. The social worker gave Jenny and her mother time to talk alone together while praying from a short distance away.

Jenny is now finishing college while working in a call center and volunteering as a Sunday school assistant. She is now able to visit her mother and relatives in the province without accompaniment from her social worker.

Insights from the Case Studies: The Role of an Accompanying Minister

For survivors of incest and abandonment, the road to reconciliation is long and rocky. Because this road is also risky, there needs to be corresponding mitigation. Even though this road is painful, it paves the way for further healing and invites the promise of peace.

As we have seen in these case studies, when a minister is present to offer counseling, care, and accompaniment through the most salient moments in the process, victims of abuse and abandonment can make the arduous journey towards reconciliation and healing. This is especially important for children and youth, who need the guidance and protection of an adult. Accompaniment involves being present both in moments of pain and risk, joy and celebration.

In cases of sexual abuse and abandonment, the accompanying minister focuses on the survivor's healing and empowerment, nurturing a space where the survivor can exercise his or her agency while also ensuring ethical decision-making and taking practical precautionary measures for the survivor's safety and security.

In the ministry of accompaniment, the minister does not do all the talking, planning, and execution, but rather helps to facilitate space where the survivor can feel free to initiate, act, and talk at a pace that feels safe and comfortable. The minister's primary role is often to remain silent and prayerful, inviting God to be present and remaining dependent on God through the entire process.

It is important for a different minister to be designated to accompany the perpetrator, keeping in mind that many perpetrators were also victims of sexual abuse in their childhoods.[5] This precaution ensures that there will be no conflict of interest in accompanying the survivor. In cases where reconciliation is possible and where restoration and justice are realizable, family counseling may be beneficial if all members of the family agree to counseling.

Forgiveness and reconciliation are integral aspects to holistic healing, but forgiveness is an extensive and arduous process that is best explored only after a survivor is ready, as depicted by the Apostle Paul in his exhortation to the Ephesians: "Get rid of all bitterness, rage and anger, brawling and slander, along with every form of malice. Be kind and compassionate to one another, forgiving each other, just as in Christ God forgave you" (Eph 4:31–32). This passage sheds light on the process that the five girls in the case studies went through in coming to the decision to forgive and reconcile with their families. All of the girls went through counseling sessions to process their bitterness, anger, pain, shame, guilt, and other negative emotions because of their abuse and abandonment. Once these negative emotions and actions were exposed and released at the counseling sessions, they no longer had as much power over the survivors. After these sessions, other emotions surfaced, such as kindness and compassion towards the perpetrators. This compassion paved the pathway towards forgiveness as the girls began to express a desire to forgive those who had hurt them because they had experienced forgiveness through Christ.

---

5. John B. Murray, "Psychological Profile of Pedophiles and Child Molesters," *The Journal of Psychology* 132, no. 2 (2000): 219.

Section IV

Liturgical and Cultural Resources

10

Franciscan Peacemaking

Making Connections with the Wider Christian Tradition

Charles Ringma

We are living in anxious and fearful times, with the specter of violence all around us and domestic violence within our own homes. The hope that World War II would be the last war to end all wars lies tattered and bloodied behind us. M. Ignatieff calls the twentieth century "a century of total war."[1] In this part of the twenty-first century, we are traumatized by images of terrorism and war destroying whole cities and displacing millions. And Syria is only one place of conflict!

As contemporary Christians, we are pulled in three directions at the same time. On the one hand, we resonate with D. J. Hall's assertion that "God is at work healing the creation, [and] making the tragic kingdoms of the earth a kingdom of peace."[2] He continues, this vision of God's shalom is "not just the absence of hostilities, but a condition of well-being, justice, mutuality of concern, harmony between all creatures, [and] gratitude for being."[3] The second impulse, in contrast to this theological "idealism," is to regretfully accept the

---

1. Michael Ignatieff, *The Needs of Strangers* (New York: Picador, 2001), 139. It is estimated that one hundred million people have been killed in the wars of the twentieth century.

2. Douglas John Hall, *The Stewardship of Life in the Kingdom of Death* (Grand Rapids: Eerdmans, 1992), 13.

3. Hall, *Stewardship of Life*, 15.

violence that continues in our world. In light of this, mainstream Christianity has maintained the just war theory as the "dominant theological position."[4] The core idea is to kill in order to create peace,[5] or in the words of M. E. Jegen, "the world still depends on war to put an end to war."[6]

The third impulse is in following Christ, one embraces the suffering that it will bring. Not only do many who work for a just peace "experience emotional and mental fatigue,"[7] but both Gandhi and Martin Luther King Jr. lost their lives in the cause of peacemaking. With the renunciation of violence, a new relationship between adversaries becomes possible, with the aim of the "reconciliation of the oppressor and not only the liberation of the oppressed."[8]

In further exploring this third option, I will engage the Franciscan tradition.[9] But I do so from a particular perspective. My concern is that St Francis and his tradition can be seen as being so different, and therefore so undoable, that we dismiss it even before we start the process of careful listening. And so, we leave St Francis with birds on his shoulders, stroking a wolf, and singing about brother sun and sister moon![10]

In order to overcome this possible dismissal, I wish to make four moves, through which I seek to show that the Franciscan vision of peacemaking is closer to mainstream Christianity than first expected. This involves: (1) analyzing some fifteen hundred hymns, (2) looking at a number of Christian lectionaries, (3) examining the missional documents of the Lausanne movement, and (4) listening to the Anabaptists. I could, of course, have turned to various denominational theological positions to engage a similar dialogue. But I am taking this approach because hymns and lectionaries are closer "to home" for

---

4. John Howard Yoder, *The War of the Lamb: The Ethics of Nonviolence and Peacemaking*, ed. Glen H. Stassen, Mark Thiessen Nation, and Matt Hamsher (Grand Rapids: Brazos Press, 2009), 95.

5. Yoder, *War of the Lamb*, 102.

6. Mary Evelyn Jegen, *Just Peacemakers: An Introduction to Peace and Justice* (New York: Paulist Press, 2006), 9.

7. Jegen, *Just Peacemakers*, 10.

8. John Howard Yoder, *Nonviolence: A Brief History, The Warsaw Lectures*, ed. Paul Martens, Matthew Porter, and Myles Werntz (Waco: Baylor University Press, 2010), 44.

9. There is, of course, a wider tradition within the Christian church on peacemaking. See Michael Braswell, John Fuller, and Bo Lozoff, *Corrections, Peacemaking, and Restorative Justice: Transforming Individuals and Institutions* (New York: Routledge, 2015); Daniel P. Horan, *The Franciscan Heart of Thomas Merton* (Notre Dame: Ava Maria Press, 2014); and Irfan A. Omar and Michael K. Duffy, *Peacemaking and the Challenge of Violence in World Religions* (Oxford: Wiley Blackwell, 2015).

10. St Francis, for many, is the icon of ecology, but they may not see peacemaking as key to his ministry.

most laity, while theological statements tend to be the domain of scholars.[11] I will then set out some of the salient concepts of Franciscan peacemaking and conclude that these resonate with important, if not dominant, aspects of the Christian tradition.

Voices in Hymnody

In exploring the church's understanding of the nature and scope of peace and the task of being peacemakers,[12] I have examined more than a thousand hymns in various church hymnals.[13] The following broad themes occur in the hymns.

First, the nature of God the Father as "Father of Peace, and God of Love" (*TinS*, no. 482). Second, Christ as the Prince of Peace: "Hail, Saviour, Prince of Peace" (*TinS*, no. 225). Third, Christ as the giver of peace: "in peace that only thou canst give . . . let me live" (*TinS*, no. 601). Fourth, Christ as the agent who brings us peace with God: through his blood "sealing our peace with God" (*TinS*, no. 221); "while he offers peace and pardon let us hear his voice today" (*BofW*, no. 95). Fifth, the Holy Spirit as peacemaker: through the Spirit's "fertile ground from which your peace and justice spring like rain" (*TinS*, no. 416).[14] Sixth, peace in the faith community:[15] "joining together in peace those once divided by sin" (*TinS*, no. 423); "take from our souls the strain and stress and let our ordered lives confess the beauty of thy peace" (*AHB*, no. 519). Seventh, God's eschatological peace:[16] "with all your church above . . . in one unbroken peace" (*TinS*, no. 521).

It is important to note that these do not exhaust all the themes, but they are important ones. Another theme that could readily be added is peace as an

---

11. With the Anabaptists, I have taken a slightly different route by looking at their spirituality. But this, too, is the domain of the laity and not simply that of the theologians.

12. The core theological concept I am working with is that peace is a gift from God through Christ and as such becomes a task, in that we are called to be peacemakers, drawing on the gift given to us.

13. *The Australian Hymn Book:With Catholic Supplement* (Sydney: Collins, 1977), henceforth cited as *AHB*; *Book of Worship* (Geelong: Reformed Churches Publishing, 1990), henceforth cited as *BofW*; *Together in Song: Australian Hymn Book II* (East Melbourne: Harper Collins Religious, 1999), henceforth cited as *TinS*.

14. The first and fifth themes are seldom used, while the second, third, and fourth themes are used repeatedly, with the second one used in *TinS* some thirteen times.

15. A frequent theme, particularly around the theme of forgiveness: "Where pity dwells, the peace of God is there" (*AHB*, no. 503) and that of Christian unity: "Peace with the Father, peace with Christ his Son, peace with the Spirit, keep us ever one" (*AHB*, no. 402).

16. Used often. Further examples include: "and take us home to you in peace" (*TinS*, no. 550); "our wanderings cease . . . our souls arrive in peace" (*TinS*, no. 564).

inner disposition: "take my heart . . . guide it to be at peace" (*TinS*, no. 593); "God blesses you with peace" (*BofW*, no. 147).

But of interest for our purposes is the theme of God's peace for our world, with the cessation of war, the flourishing of goodness and justice, and the role of the people of God as instruments of that peace. This brings us back to the theme of peace as gift and task. Following are four important emphases within this theme. First, God desires a world of peace: "Bring to our world of strife your sovereign word of peace, that war may haunt the earth no more and desolation cease" (*TinS*, no. 616).[17] Second, Christ is the way to peace: Hail to the Lord's anointed "and over every nation His peaceful rule shall be" (*BofW*, no. 72). Third, this is the Spirit's work: "till compassion builds the peace the nations seek," through the Spirit (*TinS*, no. 420). Fourth, this is the task of the church: "Cleanse the depths within our souls and bid resentment cease" and "our lives will spread your peace" (*TinS*, no. 635). A well-known hymn emphasizes this: "Make me a channel of your peace" in the places of hatred, sadness, injury, doubt, despair and darkness (*BofW*, no. 451).

In light of the above, the following conclusions may be drawn. First, most of the hymns focus on Christ the Prince of Peace, who brings us peace with God through his redemptive work, calls us to an inner peace, calls us to be a church community marked by love, forgiveness, and peace, and promises us a peace in the age to come. At the same time, there is a Trinitarian emphasis that the Father, Son, and Holy Spirit are involved in this peace-giving activity.

Second, the peace of God is a gift for the whole world, and the church is to be an agent of God's peace to penetrate our wounded, troubled, and war-like world. This peace is not simply the cessation of conflict, but a quality of life marked by God's shalom.

Voices in Liturgies

In exploring the church's understanding of the nature and scope of peace and the task of being peacemakers, I have also examined various liturgical resources.[18]

---

17. See also *TinS*, no. 616. And also: "He [God] causes war to cease; the weapons of the strong destroyed. He makes abiding peace" (*BofW*, no. 46).

18. *The Book of Alternative Services of the Anglican Church of Canada* (Toronto: Anglican Book Centre, 1985), henceforth cited as *BAS*; *Catechism of the Catholic Church* (Manila: ECCCE, Word of Life Publications, 1994), henceforth cited as *CCC*; *Celtic Daily Prayer: From the Northumbria Community* (New York: HarperOne, 2002), henceforth cited as *CDP Book 1*; *Celtic Daily Prayer, Book Two: Farther Up and Farther In* (London: William Collins, 2015), henceforth cited as *CDP Book 2*.

Anglican Liturgy

In the modern version of the traditional Anglican *The Book of Common Prayer*,[19] there are numerous references to peace in the prayers, the canticles, the litanies, the baptismal liturgies, the Eucharistic liturgies, services for Sunday and other Holy Days, marriage ceremonies, and services for the sick.

The themes identified in the church's hymns are also present here. First, God is the source of peace: "O God, the author of peace and lover of concord" (*BAS*, 130).[20] Second, Christ is the "Prince of Peace" (64). Third, peace has come through Christ's sacrifice: we are "all gathered into peace by his death on the cross" (95); "by his death he opened to us the way of freedom and peace" (201). Fourth, the church is to be a community at peace: "may we who share this sacrament live together in unity and peace" (291). Fifth, there is a promise of final peace: "receive . . . [name] into the blessed rest of everlasting peace" (586); "that we may at length fall peacefully asleep in you" (602).

What is noteworthy, however, is the emphasis on the call to pray and work for peace in our world: "for the whole human family, that we may live together in justice and peace" (116); "from civil strife and violence, from war and murder . . . good Lord, deliver us" (139); "that justice and peace may increase" (311); and, by way of full integration: "give peace to your church, peace among nations, peace in our homes, and peace in our hearts" (677).

The call to be peacemakers is rooted in God's call to us: "that we may hear and respond to your call to peace and justice" (118). It is the call of the Beatitudes: "Blessed are the peacemakers" (85; Cf. Matt 5:3–12). This call finds its beginning in our baptismal vow, where we respond to the question, "Will you strive for justice and peace among all people," with, "I will, with God's help" (159, 332, 627). At the end of worship, we are reminded of this in the challenge: "Go in peace to love and serve the Lord" (215).

Clearly, this lectionary sees peace as both a gift through Christ's salvation, an inner disposition, a relational reality in the church, and a missional task in the world.[21]

---

19. *The Book of Common Prayer* (New York: Oxford University Press, 1990).

20. All the page numbers in this section are from the *The Book of Alternative Services of the Anglican Church of Canada* (*BAS*).

21. David J. Bosch summarizes that "mission is a multifaceted ministry, in respect of witness, service, justice, healing, liberation, peace, evangelism, fellowship, church planting, contextualization, and much more" (512), but gives peace no treatment in his extensive discussion of "Elements of an Emerging Ecumenical Missionary Paradigm" (368–510), even though he acknowledges that peacemaking is "integral to the church's missionary existence" (119) in *Transforming Mission: Paradigm Shifts in Theology of Mission* (Maryknoll, NY: Orbis, 1991).

Roman Catholic Catechism

The Roman Catholic faithful, in the reflection on the fifth commandment, "You shall not kill," are challenged to safeguard peace (*CCC*, 511).[22] We could also say that they are to shepherd peace since peace is not an automatic reality in our beautiful yet broken world. Peace is something that needs to be birthed and maintained.

The catechism reminds the faithful that peace is an inner quality and thus speaks of a "peace of heart" (519). This inner peace rejects "murderous anger" (519) and recognizes that "hatred is contrary to charity" (520). It embraces the call to "love your enemies" (520) and realizes that "peace is the work of justice and the effect of charity" (520). As such, "peace is tranquility of order" (520).

This peace is not simply the absence of conflict and war, but is a quality of life. It is the calling of the Christian community, as well as the government, to work for goodness and justice and "the avoidance of war" (520–521).

The catechism then notes that a government "cannot be denied the right to a lawful self-defense" (521) and can legitimately use military force. It supports the idea that the government can impose on its citizens the call to "national defense" (521) and points out that soldiers in fulfilling their duties contribute to "the common good of the nation" (521). The catechism then makes three key moves. First, it allows for citizens, on the basis of conscience, to refuse to bear arms (521). Second, it rejects disproportionality in conflict, stating that "extermination of a people" and "destruction of whole cities" is a "crime against God and man[kind]" (522). Third, it is deeply concerned about the arms race and notes that this "does not ensure peace" (522).

This catechism, however, instructs the faithful to forgive enemies, on the one hand, and to participate in legitimate warfare, on the other. This may leave the laity to place forgiving enemies only in the intra-personal sphere and the latter in the public sphere. Such an interpretation implies that peacemaking is always a possibility in the Christian-Christian and Christian-neighbor sphere, but it is less likely at the national level.

This is hardly surprising, since the catechism provides this sober assessment of the human condition: "injustice, excessive economic or social inequalities, envy, distrust, and pride among men [women] and nations constantly threaten

---

22. All the page numbers in this section are from the *Catechism of the Catholic Church* (*CCC*).

peace and cause wars" (522).[23] This catechetical instruction forms a contrast to the Anglican liturgies we have examined above. While hymns and liturgies can celebrate the peace that Christ brings, instruction includes some form of just war theory. This approach of the catechism is likely to maintain a dualism that continues to see peacemaking in the personal spheres of life, but not in the socio-political arenas.

Celtic Liturgies

In the Northumbria Community's liturgical resources, the daily Morning Prayer ends with the blessing: "May the peace of the Lord Christ go with you, wherever He may send you" (*CDP Book 1*, 19).[24] The daily readings refer to finding again the sacred paths "well-walked with the Gospel of Peace" (*Book 1*, 55). It stresses speaking a "word of peace" (*Book 1*, 63) and notes St Aidan's peace prayer for the Holy Island of Lindisfarne: "Here be the peace of those who do thy will. Here be the peace of brother serving man [woman]. Here be the peace of holy monks obeying. Here be the peace of praise by dark and day" (*Book 1*, 61–62).

The complines are riddled with the theme of peace. The Ita Compline includes: "Be the peace of the Spirit mine this night. Be the peace of the Son mine this night. Be the peace of the Father mine this night. The peace of all peace be mine this night" (*Book 1*, 29).[25] The Aidan Compline refers to a peaceful sleep (*Book 1*, 31) and includes the prayer, "Circle me, Lord, keep peace within, keep evil out" (*Book 1*, 33). The Felgild Compline opens with, "Let all the tumult within me cease. Enfold me, Lord, in your peace" (*Book 1*, 38). The Boisil Compline has the prayer, "that awake we may watch with Christ, and asleep may rest in his peace" (*Book 1*, 43).

These themes on peace clearly focus on one's inner disposition, which is gifted by Christ, the peace giver. But in the Celtic liturgies, there is also an emphasis on the calling and task of peacemaking. While inner peace is the source for removing "resentment and argument" (*Book 2*, 1099) so that "all the strife that my life once was made of, turn to peace" (*Book 2*, 1135), the calling is to "go peaceful in gentleness through the violence of these days" (*Book 2*, 898).

---

23. For a much fuller Roman Catholic discussion see "The Challenge of Peace: God's Promise and Our Response" (US Catholic Bishops, 1983) in *Catholic Social Thought: The Documentary History*, eds. D. J. O'Brien and T. A. Shannon (Maryknoll, NY: Orbis, 1992), 492–571.

24. All the page numbers in this section are from the *Celtic Daily Prayer* (*CDP*), *Book 1* or *Book 2*.

25. This line is repeated in the other complines of the week.

The lectionary cites three historical examples on the topic of peacemaking. Telemachus (d. 391), a Christian, tried to stop a gladiator in the arena and lost his life as a result. The lectionary uses this example to call us all to a life of prayer and "active peace-making" (*Book 2*, 1098). It makes the point that in "facing the powers," we are to extend "the peace of Christ" and "amidst conflict and violence," we are to live and proclaim, "the peace of Christ" (*Book 2*, 1100).

The second example is St Pedrog (n.d.), a former soldier, who becomes a "soldier" of Christ. Two symbols are associated with this saint: a "broken spear" and a "tame wolf" (*Book 2*, 1198). The former symbol illustrates the cessation of violence. The taming of the wolf symbolizes the transformational theme of a whole new way of being. Peace is not simply the absence of war. It is the "fullness of life" (*Book 2*, 1222). It is a state of being that reflects God's shalom.

The third example is Reinfrid (d.c. 1084), a former mercenary, who became a monk at Evesham in the UK. The reflections in relation to Reinfrid are noteworthy. Peace does not fall out of the sky. Peace is costly and must be won by suffering – not by vengeance. The lectionary reflects that "Peace must often be made before it can be enjoyed" (*Book 2*, 1134).

A peacemaker does not withdraw from conflict but enters conflict in a different way. The lectionary articulates this different way as follows: to be a peacemaker is to be a "remedy finder; bridge-builder; breach-repairer; a new-way maker; a relationship broker" (*Book 2*, 1135). Thus peacemaking is a constructionist project. It is about rebuilding on a new foundation. At its most basic level, it is about love and forgiveness and "going the extra mile" and "not returning evil for evil" (*Book 2*, 1496).

Some Observations on the Liturgies

The Roman Catholic Catechism strikes a note of hope and bitter realism. While suspicions and hatreds continue in our world, conflict and war are the likely result. However, the task of governments is always to seek for peaceful solutions, even though war may be the final result. Christians need to work out whether they will support the government at this point or not. Yet peacemaking is the major theme of the Christian life.

In the different liturgies, we are struck by the familiar theme that peace is God's gift in Christ, which calls us to peace with God and with each other in the faith community. This peace, however, is not only a gift for ourselves, but for the whole world. Christians, therefore, are not only called to live in internal peace, but are also called to be peacemakers in our world. This is a sacrificial and costly ministry. Through the power of forgiving love, we are called to disarm the power of "the powers"[26] by embracing a whole new way of being and acting in the way of Christ.

Voices in Evangelical Missional Documents

To what extent do the missional documents of the Lausanne movement "representing" global Evangelicalism incorporate the notion of peace as gift and task in the mission of the church in their reflections?[27]

The Lausanne Covenant (1974)

"The Lausanne Covenant" highlights the urgent need for world evangelization and emphasizes that "evangelism is primary"[28] over social concern and societal and cultural change, even though it acknowledges that the Christian community is to "transform and enrich culture" (39). This document does not significantly engage the topic of peace and does not call the Christian Church to the task of peacemaking in our world.

The main reference to peace is in relation to the responsibilities of governments. The document states, "It is the God-appointed duty of every government to secure conditions of peace" (44). The main orientation of this call is so that the church can play its missional role in conditions of societal peace (44). This language reflects the older Christendom model of thinking, where society has one task – governance – and the church has another task – evangelization. The former creates the conditions for the latter to do its work, and the latter leaves the societal domain of life to governments. It is difficult to see how this kind of dualistic thinking allows the call to "transform and enrich culture" (39) to be outworked in significant ways. Surely the faith community is also to play a role in creating societal peace.

---

26. Charles Ringma, *Resist the Powers with Jacques Ellul* (Vancouver: Regent College Publishing, 2009).

27. See John R. W. Stott, ed., *Making Christ Known: Historic Mission Documents from the Lausanne Movement, 1974–1989* (Grand Rapids: Eerdmans, 1996).

28. Stott, *Making Christ Known*, 28. Except as otherwise stated, all page numbers in the following sections are from this book.

The Glen Eyrie Report (1978)

"The Glen Eyrie Report on Muslim Evangelization," while not addressing the peacemaking role of Christians in the world, does touch on some themes that have implications for peacemaking.

First of all, the report acknowledges that historically, both Christians and Muslims have used "various forms of coercion" (134). Thus violence is not simply a societal problem, but also a religious problem.

But the report probes a little deeper. If peacemaking does indeed involve reconciliation and includes an appreciation of "the other," then Christians have not always reflected these values. The report acknowledges that "Christians . . . have all too readily cherished and cultivated an antipathy towards Muslims" (122) and have often been "critical of Islamic culture" (123). It goes on to point out that our own culture is also flawed (122). While the document does not further develop this point, there is a startling implication here. To the extent that contemporary Christianity is significantly influenced by Western culture,[29] Christianity is therefore also flawed to some extent.

All of this opens up some key insights, which the report does not explicitly make, about the dynamics of peacemaking. Most simply put, peacemaking involves a sympathetic understanding of "the other" and a critical view of oneself.[30]

An Evangelical Commitment to Simple Lifestyle (1980)

While "An Evangelical Commitment to Simple Lifestyle" makes no direct reference to the Christian task of peacemaking, there are some important themes that play into this task, since this document seeks to challenge the personal values of contemporary Western Christians (146). The focus here is our self-focused lifestyle, our commitment to "much-having," and our lack of concern about poverty and injustice (145).

This document also calls us to pray and act, recognizing that "saving-faith" is exhibited in "serving love" (149). It highlights that serving love calls "all Christians . . . [to] participate in the active struggle to create a just and responsible society" (148). This struggle is based on the recognition that "poverty and excessive wealth, militarism and the arms industry, and the

---

29. See Lesslie Newbigin, *The Gospel in a Pluralist Society* (Grand Rapids: Eerdmans, 1989) regarding his concern about the cultural captivity of the Western church.

30. See Dave Andrews' acknowledgement of these dynamics in *The Jihad of Jesus* (Eugene, OR: Wipf & Stock, 2015).

unjust distribution of capital, land, and resources are issues of power and powerlessness" (148). And as we have seen in the Roman Catholic Catechism, these conditions are often also the conditions for oppression, violence, and war.

There are several important implications here for the Christian task of peacemaking. The first, is that we need to undergo a conversion in relation to our "much-having." Second, there is a direct link between the work of justice and that of peacemaking. The rectification of injustices makes a way for peace to flourish. Third, this document calls all Christians to be involved in the task of working for a more just society and in this way contributing to conditions that make for peace. These implications should have been drawn out in the document but are not.

The Grand Rapids Report (1982)

"The Grand Rapids Report on Evangelism and Social Responsibility: An Evangelical Commitment" deals more directly with the matters under discussion,[31] and notes that in evangelization: "the people of God should become deeply involved in relief and development and the quest for justice and peace" (177).

This statement is framed within the broader discussion of the relationship between evangelization and social concern, with the point that: "evangelism and social concern, while distinct from one another, are integrally related in our proclamation of and obedience to the gospel" (182).

The document calls Christians to penetrate the world and every dimension of life, including the realm of politics (189, 199).

In looking at Scripture, it concludes that: "The Bible lays great emphasis on both justice (or righteousness) and peace" (198). It makes the claim that "churches which visibly demonstrate the righteousness and the peace of the Kingdom . . . will make the greatest evangelistic and social impact on the world" (198).

In a world of "terrorism and war" (202), Christians are to work and pray for the "evangelization of the world" and "the quest for peace and justice" (200).

This document places peacemaking as part of the church's mission in the world. It also recognizes the link between peacemaking and the work of justice and points out that "the emergence of justice and peace in the wider society" cannot be called "salvation" in the full sense of the word (185–186). It also

---

31. This was written only two years after the Thailand Statement (1980), which retains the emphasis on the priority of evangelization while calling for a commitment "to seek . . . relief and justice" for the poor. See Stott, *Making Christ Known*, 159, 162.

notes that "war may be in some circumstances the lesser of two evils" (194). But concludes that "we should all . . . seek to be peacemakers" (194).

This document reflects the stance of the Roman Catholic Catechism, which emphasizes the importance of peacemaking as part of the calling of the people of God in the world, while at the same time recognizing the role that governments may need to play in executing war as a last resort.[32]

Cape Town Commitment (2010)

Regarding the gift and task of Christian peacemaking, the Cape Town Commitment[33] is much more explicit than any of the previous Lausanne documents. It recognizes the challenges of our time as: "global poverty, war, ethnic conflict, disease, the ecological crises, and climate change" (3).

It clearly calls Christians to love their neighbors, including foreigners and enemies (4), and calls Christians to embrace a way of life that includes, among many other themes, the call to compassion, hospitality, the work of justice, and "peace-making [and] non-retaliation" (8). It rejects the posture of retaliation and revenge (10) and calls Christians "to denounce evil and injustice wherever they may exist" (9).

This document is framed within the over-arching theme of the love of the Father, the Son, and the Holy Spirit for each other, the church, all humanity, and the creation, with a view to the full restoration of all things. From this foundation, it sets out a major discussion on building the peace of Christ in our divided and broken world (16–19). Discussions include Christ's peace in ethnic conflict, for the poor and oppressed, those with disabilities, people with HIV, as well as a major section on expressing the love of Christ to people of other faiths (19–22). The document also makes the following commitment: "in the name of the God of peace, we reject the path of violence and revenge in all our dealings with people of other faiths, even when violently attacked" (20).

The document identifies that the peace of Christ is also "for his suffering creation" and suggests that this is part of the church's "missional calling" (19).

---

32. "The Manila Manifesto" (1989) does not significantly move the discussion further. In discerning present-day evils, including violence, corruption, and exploitation, it makes no mention of war. However, it helpfully states, but does not develop, the following: "the proclamation of God's Kingdom of justice and peace demands the denunciation of all injustice and oppression both personal and structural" (Stott, *Making Christ Known*, 231).

33. The Lausanne Movement, "The Cape Town Commitment: A Confession of Faith and a Call to Action," 2011, https://www.lausanne.org/content/ctc/ctcommitment. The page numbers in this section are from the PDF file available on the website, https://www.lausanne.org/docs/CapeTownCommitment.pdf.

It challenges our consumptive lifestyles and urges us into the work of "the protection and restoration of the earth's habitats" (19).

In conclusion, the Cape Town Commitment calls us not only to witness and service in the cause of Christ, but also to pray. These prayers include: "the establishment of justice, the stewardship and care of creation, and the blessing of God's peace in communities" (25).

While this document does not elaborate on the Christian stance towards war, it makes it clear that the peace of Christ is not simply an internal disposition, nor a relational dynamic within the faith community, nor a blessing of God in an eschatological future, but rather part of the church's missional ministry to the world, particularly in places of poverty, marginalization, and violence. Thus the Cape Town Commitment engages the peacemaking theme far more than earlier Lausanne documents.

Voices of the Radical "Other": The Anabaptist Tradition

If you are surprised that these voices are being included in this attempt to understand peace as gift and task, it can be pointed out that Anabaptism is also part of the larger Christian tradition – just as much as Evangelicalism or the Roman Catholic tradition. Moreover, there are always blessings and challenges in listening to the voice of the "radical other,"[34] for we learn not through a tired monologue, but through dynamic dialogue.[35]

Several of the early Anabaptist leaders can get us started in this challenging journey. Hans Denck, in referring to Moses killing the Egyptian (Exod 2:12), comments: "if Moses had . . . perfect love, he would have given himself to be killed in the place of his brother."[36] He goes on to say that we are called "to forsake all violence for the Lord's sake" (120).

Menno Simons suggests that the matter of peacemaking is not simply an event in the face of violence, but a lifestyle. He hopes that "we may walk our whole life long . . . in peace" before the Lord (272).

The most penetrating insight, however, comes from Peter Walpot in the Hutterite Anabaptist tradition, who suggests that "greed is a serious and evil

---

34. See Emmanuel Levinas, *Humanism of the Other*, trans. Nidra Poller (Chicago: University of Illinois Press, 2006).

35. See Hans-Georg Gadamer, *Truth and Method*, 2nd ed., trans. J. Weinsheimer and D. G. Marshall (London: Sheed & Ward, 1993); Charles Ringma, *Gadamer's Dialogical Hermeneutics* (Heidelberg: Universitätsverlag C. Winter, 1999).

36. Daniel Liechty, ed., *Early Anabaptist Spirituality: Selected Writings*, The Classics of Western Spirituality (New York: Paulist Press, 1994), 114. The page numbers in the following paragraphs are from this book.

sickness" (192), which is the cause of "many wars" and that these wars arise "from private possessions and greed" (139–140).

Hans Hut theologizes this by recognizing that "peace in our world will be born from . . . [the] assault on the flesh" (78), which is the perishing of the old man "in baptism" (77), and bearing "suffering after the example of the head [Christ]" (79).

Moving forward to contemporary Anabaptist voices, D. Augsburger's central thesis is that peacemaking involves "habitual nonviolence" as a way of life.[37] In discussing a variety of possible responses to one's enemy, Augsburger calls us to "uncalculating enemy love."[38] He says that this reflects the way of Jesus and cuts across the "domination system" of our present culture.[39] He concludes that no one is an enemy, no one is disposable, and through repentance, good can triumph if we seek reconciliation and commit to peacemaking.[40]

Stuart Murray gives a very sober assessment of the peacemaking position of the Anabaptist and modern Mennonite tradition. Though he makes it clear that "peace is fundamental to the gospel,"[41] he observes that "through the centuries [Anabaptists] have been guilty of passivity in the face of injustice" (130).

While supporting the Anabaptist pacifist position, Murray raises the following concerns: it may allow injustice to flourish; it may be effective only at the micro level; and it can be easily confused with passivism (128). But he strongly rejects what he sees as the position held by mainline churches: they "have endorsed lethal violence, blessed the weapons of war, prayed for military success, celebrated victories [of war] in acts of worship, and deployed missionaries under the protection of conquering armies" (126). This approach, Murray notes, is based on what he calls "the myth of redemptive violence" (131), which is the opposite of the biblical vision of redemptive suffering.

Noting with approval the many contemporary Anabaptist/Mennonite initiatives, such as Christian Peacemaker Teams, conflict transformation initiatives, and victim-offender reconciliation programs (130–131), Murray concludes that many Christians are now convinced that peace is at the heart of the gospel and that this calls the church to love of enemies (129).

---

37. David W. Augsburger, *Dissident Discipleship: A Spirituality of Self-Surrender, Love of God, and Love of Neighbor* (Grand Rapids: Brazos Press, 2006), 134.

38. Augsburger, *Dissident Discipleship*, 140–142.

39. Augsburger, 138.

40. Augsburger, 142–144.

41. Stuart Murray, *The Naked Anabaptist: The Bare Essentials of a Radical Faith* (Scottdale, PA: Herald Press, 2010), 124. The page numbers in the following section are from the *Naked Anabaptist*.

The most important contemporary voice in this tradition is J. H. Yoder. Following is a salient but very basic summary of his extensive writings on Christian nonviolence and peacemaking.[42]

First, the Old Testament wars did not have the theme "fight boldly," but trust in Yahweh. And stress, do not make military alliances with other nations whom you will then trust instead of Yahweh (75).

Second, we cannot reduce Jesus's preaching to a gospel of the inner life and the future life of God's final kingdom (77). Jesus's way was "neither quietism nor zealotry," (91) but a whole new way of life based on reconciliation, healing, and peace in the form of a community that was a witness to the false powers of the time.

Third, Yoder rejects the logic of the just war tradition. He notes that Christians rejected military service in the first three centuries of the Christian era and that all the church fathers condemned participation in war (50–51).[43] Changes to this position occurred with Constantine. He goes on to note that the limits set by Augustine and Aquinas in their articulation of a just war no longer apply, as wars today are no longer subject to proportionality (57), and the "entire economy is mobilized for military production" (56). Importantly, Yoder notes that the just war position in the Roman Catholic tradition is "not *the* official" position of the church (125). Here, Yoder makes reference to The Challenge of Peace (1983) of the USA Catholic Bishops,[44] which holds that pacifism is close to the New Testament, that the just war theory and pacifism "are complimentary,"[45] that strategies such as those used by Martin Luther King Jr. are positive, and that the use of some weapons, nuclear or biological, are morally wrong.

Finally, Yoder sets out all sorts of strategies for peacemaking. He notes that peacemaking is activist. It empowers people, builds coalitions, demonstrates, and is willing to suffer for an alternative vision of what it means to build a just and humane society.[46]

---

42. All the page numbers in the following are from Yoder, *Nonviolence*.

43. In a major review of the scholarly debate about the early Christian involvement in war, George Kalantzis confirms much of Yoder's thesis. He summarizes: "the literary evidence confirms the very strong internal coherence of the Church's non-violent stance for the first three centuries," in *Caesar and the Lamb: Early Christian Attitudes on War and Military Service* (Eugene, OR: Cascade Books, 2012), 7. He concludes that the early Christians saw themselves as peacemakers as an expression "of the Kingdom on earth" (202).

44. For the entire text, see David J. O'Brien and Thomas A. Shannon, eds. *Catholic Social Thought: The Documentary Heritage* (Maryknoll, NY: Orbis, 1992), 492–571.

45. Yoder, *War of the Lamb*, 97.

46. Yoder, 156–157.

What we learn from the Anabaptist or Mennonite tradition and the other historic "peace churches," including the Friends and Brethren, is that Christ as the normative human being, the New Adam, and Christ's way in the world, is how we are to live. The way of Jesus is not simply the way of our personal lives, but our social life as well. Thus peacemaking in the way of Christ is how we live, not simply what we believe. And within this tradition, this means that we refuse to participate in all forms of violence, including war.

Peacemaking in the Franciscan Tradition

In this section, we will summarize this theme from the primary writings of St Francis before engaging the wider Franciscan tradition.

The Writings of St Francis

One may be surprised that in these writings of St Francis,[47] the peace theme does not seem to be that prominent. In "The Testament," Francis states: "The Lord revealed to me a greeting, as we used to say: 'May the Lord give you peace'" (155). In "The Admonitions," he makes a more significant statement: "The true peacemakers are those who preserve peace of mind and body for the love of our Lord Jesus Christ despite what they suffer in the world" (132). And goes on: "where there is inner peace and meditation there is neither anxiousness nor dissipation" (35). Here Francis notes that peace is a profoundly Christological matter[48] and that peace is to be maintained in the face of difficulty.

This theme of maintaining peace occurs elsewhere. In "The Canticle of Brother Sun," Francis states: "Blessed are those who endure in peace" (39). In "The Canticle of Exhortation to Saint Clare and Her Sisters," he states: "Those who are weighed down by sickness and the others who are wearied because of them, all of you: bear it in peace" (41).

Apart from these statements, Francis gives a number of peace benedictions. In the first, "The Second Version of the Letter to the Faithful," he states: "To all Christian religious: clergy and laity, men and women, and to all who live in the whole world, Brother Francis, their servant and subject, [offers] homage and reverence, true peace from heaven and sincere love in the Lord" (67). In

---

47. Francis, of Assisi, *Francis and Clare: The Complete Works*, in The Classics of Western Spirituality, trans. Regis J. Armstrong and Ignatius C. Brady (New York: Paulist Press, 1982). The page numbers cited in this section are from this book.

48. In "The Parchment Given to Brother Leo," Francis speaks about God, stating: "You are inner peace" (100).

the second, "A Letter to the Rulers of the Peoples," he exclaims: "To all mayors and consuls, magistrates and rulers throughout the world . . . peace to all of you" (77).

Though none of this seems very significant, Francis's statements in "The Earlier Rule" and "The Later Rule" show otherwise (107–135; 136–145). Here he speaks about *a way of life* in Christ shaped by the gospel that creates the basis for being peacemakers in our world. These two rules should be read by all, but in the following I make a point-by-point summary.

First, the Franciscan brothers were not to own property so that they could live a "disarmed" lifestyle, with nothing to protect or defend. Since much violence is about possessions, the cause of violence is removed.

Second, the brothers were not to exercise leadership and dominance over each other or others. Thus there was no one to "put down" and no one to dominate. Power *over* others can so easily lead to various forms of oppression and this can result in violence.

Third, the brothers were to see themselves as nothing much except for the grace of God. Thus they had no sense of being powerful or privileged. They saw themselves as God's "little ones" in God's grand scheme of things. This posture of humility eschewed all sense of power.

Fourth, the Franciscan brothers were called to the love of neighbor and love of enemy.

Fifth, the brothers were called to see others – including Muslims – as part of God's world. Thus they were to respect those who were different.

Finally, they were invited to see the whole created world – both the social world and the natural world – as reflecting the image of the incarnate Son of God. This called them to care for all, rather than destroy some.

This meant that Francis did not see peacemaking as a strategy, but rather as a way of life in Christ. Peacemaking is not something one does in certain circumstances, but rather what one becomes through rebirth in the life of Christ. Thus being a person of peace is ontological rather than pragmatic. If peace is ontological – a primal state of being – then it is fundamental to who we are to become in Christ. It is not an optional extra. It is not something we only do from time to time. The reason for this is that Christ has become our peace by embracing the unjustified violence against himself. Thus Christ has put aside every attempt to bring peace and well-being into the world through violence or the misuse of power.

The Broader Franciscan Tradition

In this section, we seek to remain as close as possible to the heartbeat of St Francis by taking note of what Francis *did* (not only what he wrote) and by engaging a number of older and contemporary Franciscan scholars. Since this is a huge field, I will begin with an eight-point summary.

First, as the Franciscan scholar Ilia Delio points out, Francis saw peace as a gift from God as he "encountered the God of peace in the crucified Christ."[49] Thus to be a "peacemaker is to accept the gift of peace given to us by Christ."[50] This means that the *gift* of peace precedes the task of peacemaking.

Second, to grow in the love of God is to become more fully a person of peace. And "peace . . . is the path of active love."[51] Thus, sanctified service includes peacemaking.

Third, a person of peace is "willing to suffer . . . out of love for another."[52] Peace comes at a price. Rather than retaliation, it involves redemptive suffering.

Fourth, Bonaventure (1221–1274), the Franciscan theologian and Minister General of the Franciscan Order, points out that Francis "in all his preaching . . . proclaimed peace" and that he received this "in a revelation from the Lord."[53] Peace was thus central to Francis's gospel.

Fifth, Francis sent out his brothers as emissaries of peace: "Go, my dear brothers two by two . . . *announcing peace* to the people and *penance for the remission of sins.*"[54] And this was possible because the brothers were to be "children of peace."[55] Francis makes the point: "Let everyone be drawn to peace and kindness through your peace and gentleness."[56] Peace is thus a way of life, a gift of grace that had become deeply embedded in the brothers.

Sixth, in case one might think that Francis was only concerned with helping people find peace with God, or finding an inner or relational peace,

---

49. Ilia Delio, *Franciscan Prayer* (Cincinnati, OH: St Anthony Messenger Press, 2004), 165.

50. Delio, *Franciscan Prayer*, 155.

51. Delio, 165.

52. Delio, 168.

53. Bonaventure, *The Life of St. Francis*, trans. E. Cousins (New York: HarperOne, 2005), 24.

54. Quoted in Delio, *Franciscan Prayer*, 167. Italics in original.

55. Quoted from "The Assisi Compilation," in Michael H. Crosby, *Finding Francis, Following Christ* (Maryknoll, NY: Orbis, 2007), 186.

56. Quoted from "The Anonymous Perugia," in Crosby, *Finding Francis, Following Christ*, 188.

in an age "rent by civil wars,"[57] Francis helped to settle political disputes – not only in Assisi, but also in Arezzo, Perugia, Siena, and Bologna.[58]

Seventh, Francis's era was not only a time of civil wars – he was involved in one before his conversion – but it was also the time of the Crusades. While there is no evidence that Francis publicly condemned the Crusades, he nevertheless subverted them by his very actions. The Franciscan brothers made many attempts to engage Muslim leaders. To give only one example, five brothers went on a mission to Seville, which was under Mohammedan control. They were expelled from the city, but they returned, and were beheaded.[59] In 1221, Francis and some brothers joined a crusade as peacemakers in order to get to the Sultan, Malik al-Kamil. While first mistreated, Francis was able to earn the Sultan's respect, and they were able to talk about matters of faith.[60] M. H. Crosby observes that Francis moved "from a violence-based approach to Islam, to a respectful way of dialoguing with it."[61]

Finally, in terms of some of the key dimensions of St Francis's comprehensive understanding of peacemaking, we note his approach to creation and the environment. As W. J. Short points out, Francis was never simply a lover of nature. For him, all creatures reflected "the face of the beloved Son."[62] And all things "bear the traces of him [Christ]."[63] As Bonaventure observes, Francis saw a "universal reconciliation with each and everything" and "perceived a heavenly harmony in all things."[64] Thus peacemaking is not only God-oriented, relationally relevant, and reflective of an inner Christlikeness, but it is also related to the stranger, enemy, and our care for nature.

Now, in order to obtain a more comprehensive understanding of Franciscan peacemaking, I will expand on these eight key points.

---

57. Jorgen Jorgenson, *Saint Francis of Assisi: A Biography*, trans. T. O. Sloane (New York: Longmans, Green & Co., 1913), 99.

58. Jorgenson, *Saint Francis of Assisi*, 99; Crosby, *Finding Francis, Following Christ*, 186. Francis also settled a powerful family feud in Bologna and brought reconciliation between a mayor and a bishop (Crosby, *Finding Francis, Following Christ*, 190–191, 193–194). Bonaventure notes that Francis did not see these peacemaking initiatives in programmatic terms. In Arezzo, "shaken by civil war," Francis was able to "command the devils to leave the city" (Bonaventure, *Life of Francis*, 64).

59. Jorgenson, *Saint Francis of Assisi*, 163, 192, 199–200.

60. Crosby, *Finding Francis, Following Christ*, 194–197.

61. Crosby, 194.

62. William J. Short, *Poverty and Joy: The Franciscan Tradition* (Maryknoll, NY: Orbis, 1999), 111.

63. Short, *Poverty and Joy*, 113.

64. Bonaventure, *The Life of St. Francis*, 9, 94.

Franciscan peacemaking is not simply a strategy for creating harmony that reduces everything to some common – and often anemic – denominator. Peacemaking is at the heart of the gospel, for through the cross of Christ, peace with God, each other, the enemy, and the whole created order becomes a possibility. Furthermore, peacemaking is a whole way of life in obedience to the gospel. St Francis is clear: "that I should live according to the pattern of the Holy Gospel."[65]

Peacemaking has everything to do with our Christology. Constantine conquered in the name of Christ with a sword in his hand. Colonialism acted in the name of a conquering Christ. Peacemaking, however, becomes a possibility when we follow the incarnate and suffering Christ into the world. St Francis cries out: "Look, brothers, at the humility of God"[66] in the incarnation.

Delio points out that peacemaking involves the rejection of all forms of "dominion theology."[67] The way of God in the world is not one of conquest, but redemptive suffering. Yet throughout history, the church has often assumed that the more power it has, the better its mission will be. But Celano, the earliest Franciscan biographer, rightly notes: "only a wounded body can bring about peace."[68] Leonardo Boff, the Latin American Franciscan, reminds us that the urge to dominate and to have power *over* others is present in all of us.[69] He points to the subtlety of this when the church relates to the poor "through power" by its ministries of "assistance" marked by "paternalism."[70]

Another key concept is that Franciscan peacemaking should arise from a maternal spirituality. Bonaventure notes that Francis "seemed like a mother who was daily in labor pains bringing . . . [others] to birth in Christ."[71] Delio reiterates this, observing that Francis displayed a "mysticism of maternity," that is, giving birth to Christ in our lives and in the life of the world.[72] As the people of God, we are to be a "second incarnation" through the birthing of the Holy Spirit.[73] Boff helpfully points out that in a world of paternalism,

---

65. Quoted in Crosby, *Finding Francis, Following Christ*, 125.

66. Quoted in Short, *Poverty and Joy*, 43.

67. Delio, *Franciscan Prayer*, 170.

68. Quoted in Delio, *Franciscan Prayer*, 174.

69. Leonardo Boff, *Saint Francis: A Model of Human Liberation* (Quezon City: Claretian, 1984), 39.

70. Boff, *Saint Francis*, 78.

71. Bonaventure, *The Life of St. Francis*, 80.

72. Delio, *Franciscan Prayer*, 13.

73. Delio, 69.

Francis was able to integrate "the feminine."[74] Without buying into the over-generalization that men make wars and women make homes, we do need to recognize both the historical reality of male dominance and the current reality of male domestic violence. Boff reminds us that "the heart and spirit of kindness constitute the central reality of the human being and of humanizing culture."[75] He further notes that "true gentleness is born of strength" and not of passivity or cowardice.[76]

So far, we have noted that St Francis and his brothers, St Clare and her sisters, as well as the early formation of lay tertiaries, lived in a world of regional wars, crusades, and paternalism. But they also lived in a feudal world of hierarchy, with its inherent propensity for oppression and other abuses of power. In contrast to this, and in contrast to the powerful landowning monasteries of that time,[77] Francis created a "fraternal" order.[78] Thus, as Crosby notes, Francis created a new familial order of the kingdom of God.[79] As Boff observes, this way of being "breaks the rigidity of the feudal hierarchy."[80] A fraternal order based on relationships of mutuality undermines potential misuses of power, which are inherent in all forms of hierarchy. This was revolutionary for its time.[81]

In "The Anonymous Perugia," Francis exclaims: "Lord, if we had any possessions, we would need arms to protect them because they cause many disputes and lawsuits. And possessions usually impede the love of God and neighbor. Therefore, we do not want to possess anything in this world."[82] Bonaventure notes that because "they possessed nothing," as a consequence, "they had nothing to defend and feared to lose nothing."[83] Thus Franciscan asceticism is related to peacemaking. Franciscan identification with the poor is about empowering the weak rather than pulling down the strong. Moreover, in this identification, St Francis discovered the surprise of God: "what seemed

---

74. Boff, *Saint Francis*, 28.

75. Boff, 15.

76. Boff, 22.

77. Some monastic orders, particularly the Templars, the Knights of Malta, and the Teutonic Knights, participated in the Crusades. See Desmond Steward, *The Monks of War: The Military Orders* (London: The Folio Society, 2000. First published in 1972).

78. Crosby, *Finding Francis, Following Christ*, 62.

79. Crosby, 135.

80. Boff, *Saint Francis*, 22.

81. Mario von Galli, in *Living Our Future: Francis Assisi and the Church Tomorrow* (Chicago: Franciscan Herald Press, 1972), is right to call Francis a revolutionary figure.

82. Quoted in Crosby, *Finding Francis, Following Christ*, 162.

83. Bonaventure, *Life of St. Francis*, 37.

bitter to me [in kissing the leper], became sweetness of body and soul."[84] This caused Francis to embrace a spirituality of descent, which contrasts with our present-day orientation towards a spirituality of ascent. We assume that the more socially powerful we become as a Christian community, the greater our influence will be, which follows the old Christendom model, with its propensity towards the misuse of power. Boff makes the point that Francis led a life of "de-class-ification"[85] as a countermove to the inherent oppression of the class system of his day. Thus Francis's orientation to life was one of "disappropriation,"[86] which is the opposite to a life of much-having and its temptation to exclusion.

Francis's core passion expressed in "The Testament" is clear: "that I should live according to the pattern of the Holy Gospel."[87] Crosby notes that Francis believed "that the pattern of Jesus's life might be replicated in our own."[88] This Christification made Francis a builder, which relates to his call: "Francis, don't you see that my house is destroyed? Go, then, and rebuild it for me."[89] This rebuilding was multi-directional: Francis's relationship with God, himself, the church, the stranger, the human community, and all of the created reality. Crosby notes that this call involved "everyone and everything in it [as] part of God's domain or household."[90] This commitment to building up in following Christ demonstrates relational peacebuilding, which poses a challenge to us. We tend to be self-serving rather than regarding others. We are denominationally and missionally territorial and tribalistic, dividing rather than building the whole. Just think of our fragmented and competitive evangelicalism!

Francis did not see "the other" as one to be feared, but as one to be loved. He did not denigrate the other, particularly not the radical stranger. As Bonaventure notes, Francis rejected "the vice of detraction,"[91] which allows one to pull the other down and even justifies some sort of violence towards the other. So instead of hatred towards Muslims, Francis saw them first and foremost as fellow creatures wrapped in the love of the crucified God. Sadly, we are all too quick to demonize others – and the more we do this, the more we justify the legitimacy of our violence towards them. Delio agrees: "we

---

84. Quoted in Boff, *Saint Francis*, 68.
85. Boff, 67.
86. Boff, 69.
87. Quoted in Crosby, *Finding Francis, Following Christ*, 125.
88. Crosby, 105.
89. "The Legend of Three Companions" in Crosby, *Finding Francis, Following Christ*, 52.
90. Crosby, 57.
91. Bonaventure, *Life of St. Francis*, 82.

are fragmented, divisive, dominating and oppressive."[92] As she continues, "Christians play a part in the constant violence in our world."[93]

Much more could be explored,[94] but it should be clear that Franciscan peacemaking is not simply about certain strategies – though strategies are involved[95] – but rather with a whole way of life in following Christ. Delio helpfully points out that the Franciscan way is a "disarmament of the heart,"[96] embracing, imbibing, and living a "crucified love," which is a "love for the sake of the other."[97] For peacemaking, this means that the Franciscan way explores and practices the "connection between peace in your heart and peace in the world."[98]

To conclude, Jorgenson notes that "by paying evil with evil," we simply participate in and accentuate the sins of others, and so our task as peacemakers is to lead others to "love God in peace and joy."[99] This peace is not simply an internal disposition, but peace for all. M. von Galli is right: "a non-violent revolution is the only possible revolution for Christians."[100]

Integration and Conclusion

We have engaged the hymns, liturgies, catechism, spirituality, and missional praxis of the Anglicans, Reformed, Evangelicals, Roman Catholics, and Anabaptists regarding their perspectives on the topics of peace and peacemaking.

From these Christian resources, it is clear that peacemaking is an important part of the Christian tradition. Key themes are peace with God through Christ, the inner peace of faith, and relational peace within the Christian community. The theme of the church as a peaceful presence in the world is also readily acknowledged, but it is much weaker, except in the Franciscan and Anabaptist traditions. Following are some summary statements about these themes.

---

92. Delio, *Franciscan Prayer*, 178.

93. Delio, 175.

94. For example, Francis's theme of peacemaking with the environment. See Jorgenson, *Saint Francis of Assisi*, 34–35, and Crosby, *Finding Francis, Following Christ*, 198.

95. See Ken Butigan, Mary Litell, and Louis Vitale, *Franciscan Nonviolence: Stories, Reflections, Principles, Practices, and Resources* (Las Vegas, NV: Pace e Bene, 2003).

96. Delio, *Franciscan Prayer*, 178.

97. Delio, 177.

98. Delio, 178.

99. Jorgenson, *Saint Francis of Assisi*, 216.

100. Von Galli, *Living Our Future*, 169.

In the hymns, we sing, "bring to our world of strife your sovereign word of peace, that war may haunt the earth no more, and desolation cease" (*TinS*, no. 616) and "our lives will spread your peace" (*TinS*, no. 635).

In the liturgies, we pray, "give peace to your church, peace among nations, peace in our homes, and peace in our hearts" (*BAS*, 677). *Celtic Daily Prayer* calls us to prayer and "active peace-making" (*CDP*, Book 2, 1098).

In the Lausanne documents, the call is to compassion, hospitality, the work of justice, and "peace-making [and] non-retaliation."[101]

Augsburger, reflecting a contemporary Anabaptist perspective, notes that in this tradition, the emphasis is on "habitual nonviolence" as a way of life.[102]

And the Franciscan perspective is well summarized by Bonaventure: because "they possessed nothing," as a consequence, "they had nothing to defend and feared to lose nothing."[103] This freedom, which was centered in Christ, gave them the freedom to work for peace in their world.

There is a clear division between Anabaptists, who hold a pacifist position, and those who maintain that Christians, along with others, need to play their part in supporting the war effort of their respective countries as their civic duty. However, there are always legitimate questions that need to be raised regarding the political justification for a particular war. While Christians may not be pacifist, they may object to supporting a particular war, as with the Western invasion of Iraq.

It is clear that even though all the Christian traditions we have considered affirm that the Christian church should be an instrument of peace in the world, both the Franciscans and the Anabaptists give this task a much greater priority.

The Franciscan tradition poses a particular challenge, in that peacemaking in the world is not simply a task, but is intrinsic to what it means to be a follower of Christ. Because salvation and peacemaking are linked, peacemaking is ontological and not simply pragmatic. When this is backed by a lifestyle of radical relinquishment, the fruit of the peace of Christ can all the more readily blossom in our world.

---

101. *Cape Town Commitment*, 8.
102. Augsburger, *Dissident Discipleship*, 134.
103. Bonaventure, *Life of St. Francis*, 37.

11

Kapayapaan at Pagbasa ng "Pasyong Mahal"

Pagtuklas sa Ugnayan[1]

Ronaldo H. Magpayo

H oly Week centers on the death of Jesus as a demonstration of God's sincere offer of peace and reconciliation. In the Philippines, *Semana Santa* (Holy Week) is the most significant religious celebration, and perhaps the communal reading of the *Pasyon Mahal* or most commonly known as *Pasyon* – an indigenous and vernacular rendering of the passion narrative – is the most powerful expression of Filipino folk religion.[2] *Pasyon* is a poetic composition that recounts the life and works of Jesus Christ. Used during the Lenten season as a commemoration of the Lord's passion, death, and resurrection, this practice has been kept alive for centuries in the Philippines.[3]

---

1. Peace and the Reading of "*Pasyong Mahal*": Exploring the Relationship.

2. The most influential of all the Tagalog *Pasyon* texts is the *Casaysayan nang Pasiong Mahal* (narrative of the passion; the genitive is spelled alternatively as *Pasiong* or *Pasyong*) printed in 1814. Traditionally known as the work of Padre Pilapil, the *Casaysayan* remains the most popular text chanted in the *Pabasa* (a Lenten ritual involving the uninterrupted chanting of the *Pasyong Mahal*) every Holy Week.

3. Rodel E. Aligan, *The Biblical and Folkloric Elements of the First Tagalog Pasyon* (Manila: UST Publishing House, 2001), 3.

This paper focuses on the faithful readers of the *Pasyon*,[4] exploring the devotees' appropriation of the cross in the context of the *Pasyon*, which centers on the message of God's offer of peace and reconciliation through the sacrifice of Jesus. Does this message affect the lives of the devotees of the *Pasyon*? Do they experience a deeper sense of forgiveness and peace before God? Does their devotion influence their understanding of forgiveness and reconciliation in their relationships with others?

This paper adopts an *interpretive content analysis*[5] of the narrative of the devotees rather than a literary analysis of *Pasyon* as a text. This method requires greater interpretative judgment in coding and analysis. Unlike *basic content analysis,* interpretative content analysis does not assume that meaning is simply contained in the text, but instead allows the researcher to interpret the whole, or the gestalt of the communication.[6] Researchers may use this method to describe the content and meaning of a text and even summarize and make inferences about thoughts, feelings, and intentions based on various forms of communication.[7]

In this research, personal in-depth interviews, semi-structured interviews, and observations of the participants were the primary means of gathering data. This process is based on the belief that the knowledge of a social world is constructed through informal conversation and personal interviews, since these forms of communication set the participant's perspectives within the context of personal history and experience. Interviews were given during Holy Week as the respondents actively took part in reading the *Pasyon* during the *Pabasa* (uninterrupted chanting of the *Pasyon* during Lent). The religious environment during Holy Week heightens the imagination of the devotees as they appropriate the suffering of Christ in their lives.

---

4. The respondents are devotees from the towns of Bulakan, Plaridel, and Santisima Trinida. Others are from the small barrios (a town district) of Sumapa and Dakila. Their ages range between late-sixties and early eighties. They have been actively participating in the *Pabasa* for more than two decades.

5. James W. Drisko and Tina Maschi, *Content Analysis: Pocket Guide to Social Work Research Methods* (New York: Oxford University Press, 2016). Generally, *content analysis* is defined as a "structured research approach using specified research design and methods to make replicable and valid inferences from texts and similar materials" (6). There are two types of content analysis. *Basic content analysis* assumes that meaningful content is fully contained in the text under study. It is objective, descriptive, and quantitative in its method and analysis. *Interpretative content analysis* is based on a constructivist epistemological foundation, which operates on the position that the researcher's purpose and frame of reference may make an important difference in the understanding of words in context (67).

6. Drisko and Maschi, *Content Analysis*, 4.

7. Drisko and Maschi, 65.

Pasyon as *Pagninilay* (Reflection) and *Pakikibahagi* (Identification)

The reading of the *Pasyon* is meaningful for the devotees because it leads them to reflect on the suffering of Jesus in a way that is not purely rational. Since the reflection includes emotions and feelings, the devotees "connect" or "identify" with the suffering of Christ. Thus the theme of *awa* (mercy, empathy) is very prominent in their narratives.

For the devotees, *Pasyon* serves as *pakikibahagi sa paghihirap ni Kristo* (sharing in the suffering of Christ). Since *Pasyon* centers on the suffering of Christ, it is done with respect and meditation. Devotees use various words to express the manner of reflection one should have in order to appreciate the powerful impact of *Pasyon*: *pagninilay* (reflection), *pagsasaloob* (internalization), *pagdibdib upang matimo sa isipan* (serious and deep reflection), *pagsasapuso* (take into heart), and *pagdama* (empathy). *Pasyon* should be performed with sobriety in order to internalize the message behind the song.

For Ka Dely and Ka Saring, reading the *Pasyon* is like reading the Bible. For more than fifty years, they have meditated on the sufferings of Jesus every Holy Week. The sufferings of Christ strike a sensitive emotional cord to Ka Dely, who is a mother, as she recites a verse in the *Pasyon* that depicts the scene where the lifeless body of Jesus is placed on Mary's lap:

> *Ito baga ang buhok mo*
> *tuwi na'y sinusuklay ko*
> *hinuhusay kong totoo?*
> *bakit ngayo'y gulong-gulo*
> *natitigmak ng dugo mo?*

> (Is this the hair you once owned?
> one I used to touch
> and care for so much?
> Why now disheveled
> and seemed filled with your own blood?)

Pasyon is a form of deep reflection on the sufferings of Christ (*pagninilay sa paghihirap ng Panginoong Jesus*) and also their means of sharing the suffering of Christ (*pakikidamay sa paghihirap ni Kristo*). Again, Ka Dely recites a verse from the text:

> *Nasaan baga bunso ko*
> *ang taong pinakain mo*
> *mahigit na limang libo,*
> *bakit ngayo'y wala rito*
> *at di dumamay sa iyo?*

(Where now, my young child
are the people you fed?
there were more than five thousand
but now not even one is here,
to weep with you, not even one is left)

This line invites all to share in Christ's suffering, since he died for our sins to redeem us. After reciting this line, Ka Dely reflects, "*Sinakop tayo ni Kristo, dapat pasakop din tayo, tularan natin sya . . .*" (Since Christ has subjected us, we ought also to be subjected to him; let us imitate him.) Ka Dely believes that we do not need to inflict pain in our body like flagellants: "*yong iba nga nagpipinitensya, nagpapadugo pa ng likod, kami ay hindi na ganoon . . . iniisip ko makasunod lang ako sa kalooban nya, higit pa sa pagpapadugo ng katawan ang nagawa ko.*" (Others inflict pain on themselves, even to the point where their backs bleed; we are like that. I think that if I can follow his will, it will be regarded as superior to inflicting my body with pain.)

According to Rodel E. Ilagan, the *Pasyon* at first was read for the purpose of consoling the sick and the dying and was originally known as *Magpa-Hesus*.[8] But Aquino De Belen's *Pasyon* shifted the emphasis from the dying to those who are present on the deathbed, who are chided for being materialistic and worldly. Rene B. Javellana notes that although the *Pasyon* genre is unquestionably Spanish in origin, the originality of Aquino de Belen's *Pasyon* lies in the lessons or *aral*.[9]

These lessons (*aral*) or moral sermonettes draw implications out of the different scenes in the passion of Christ, inviting readers to join in the spirit of penitence. Ka Marciana reflects that "*Parang may pangangaral siya (pasyon) . . . makikita mo ang buhay mo*" (*Pasyon* is like an invitation for introspection). After enumerating the many penetrating lessons about life from the *Pasyon*, many respondents say, "*nandoon po lahat sa Pasyon yon, mababasa nyo*" (You can read it all there in the *Pasyon*).

The lessons help devotees see their lives before God and how they relate with other people. For Ka Tessie, the *Pabasa* is an opportunity to come to God and ask for forgiveness and renewal. Meditation on the *Pasyon* gives her

---

8. According to Rodel Aligan during the early years of evangelization, *Magpa-Hesus* was part of a pastoral solution to the problem of taking care of the sick and the dying. The prefix *Magpa* means someone who causes other persons to do something. Customarily, the *Magpa-Hesus* was used to pray the rosary over the sick and the dying. Also, the reading of the Gospel brought great consolation to those who were sick and dying. *Biblical and Folkloric Elements*, 10.

9. Rene B. Javellana, "The Sources of Gaspar Aquino de Belen's Pasyon," *Philippine Studies* 32 (1984): 321.

an opportunity to renew her heart before God (*pagbabalik-loob*). Ka Tessie admits that she seldom attends church and still struggles with sins in her life. She sheepishly reflects that in reading the *Pasyon*, "*nababawas-bawasan yong nagsisikip kong kalooban dahil sa kasalanan*" (It lessens my guilt and provides a sense of relief).

Pasyon and Themes Related to Peace and Reconciliation

In describing the experience of reading the *Pasyon*, devotees often identify two prominent themes: *Ginhawa* (comfort, relief) and *pakikipag-kapwa* (in solidarity with others). *Ginhawa* refers to the experience of forgiveness and *pakikipag-kapwa* flows out of this experience, which is the result of *pagninilay* (deep reflection).

Ginhawa

Ginhawa has the same wide range of meaning as *shalom* in the Hebrew Scriptures. Shalom is generally translated as "peace" (*kapayapaan*). All of the respondents share the same experience of "*ginhawa sa kalooban*" (inner relief) in their narratives. The devotees' experience of *ginhawa* comes from their reflection on Jesus as a friend and co-journeyer (*katoto, kaibigan*), as he is depicted in the *Pasyon* without denying his divinity. Thus devotees find strength and inspiration in the suffering of Jesus.

    Ginhawa is expressed in various ways. Respondents describe it as "*masarap po ang pakiramdam*" (I feel good), "*napakalakas po ng aking pakiramdam*" (I feel so strong), "*maligaya po ang pakiramdam*" (there is a feeling of joy), and "*nakakagaan po ng loob*" (it lightens my burdens). They speak of satisfaction and contentment, of having a sense of joy and fulfillment in doing their devotion: "*parang kulang po ang araw mo pag hindi ka nakabasa ng pasyon*" or "*parang hindi kumpleto ang Mahal na Araw mo pag hindi ako nakabasa*" (it seems that your day or your Holy Week is incomplete without participating in the reading of *Pasyon*). Their feeling of *awa* (sympathy/empathy) towards the sacrifices of Jesus in turn becomes their *pagpapasalamat* (thanksgiving, gratitude).

    Moreover, the experience of healing contributes to some respondents' concept of *ginhawa*. In addition to realizing the kind of love they receive from God through the suffering and death of Jesus, some narratives describe how their families experience God's healing and protection. as a result of their devotion. They say, "*Hangga't kami ay binigyan ng lakas ng Panginoon, patuloy kaming babasa*" (As long as the Lord gives us strength, we will continue to read).

The only male among my respondents is Ka Vic Esteban. Diagnosed with an "unknown" health problem he had found healing from God when he became a devotee and gave his vow (*panata*) to the *Pasyon*. He saw this healing power in the life of his father, who had a similar experience. Ka Vic reflects, "*Talagang sa Dios ay walang imposible*" (Truly, with God nothing is impossible).

Ginhawa sa kalooban (inner relief) includes God's provision for the family of devotees. Given an offer to work as *kasambahay* (housemaid) and an opportunity to have a small business, Ka Virgie keeps going back to her *panata* (vow). She says, "*Sa paglilingkod ko, hindi naman ako pinababayaan ng nasa itaas . . . pasalamat ako sa loob ng isang taon di ka man lang nagkakasakit*" (Never has God abandoned me as I serve him. I am thankful that I never got sick for a whole year).

A widow for more than twenty years, Ka Milagros's son was able to graduate from college when she made the reading of *Pasyon* her *panata*. With tears in her eyes, she recalls the words of her son, "*Gusto ko po mag-college*" (I want to go to college). Even though she had no one to turn to for provision, God provided for her son's educational needs.

For the devotees, *Ginhawa* does not mean having material possessions, financial security, or absence of pain and suffering. In fact, all of the respondents have their own stories of tragedies. But according to Ka Fely, *Pasyon* is the story of Jesus and human experience in this world. "*Ganito pala ang buhay ng tao na naghihirap, parang si Cristo . . . kung nanamnamin mo*" (So this is how it feels when humans suffer – it is being like Christ . . . if you really try to feel and experience it). A person who experiences *ginhawa* has *kapayapaan* (peace). Ka Trining speaks about her experience of life as taught to her by the *Pasyon*, "*masarap mabuhay kung kasama mo ang Dios . . . ang kasayahan ng buhay ay hindi yong tawa ka ng tawa . . . yong may kapayapaan ka . . .*" (Life is meaningful if you are with God . . . having joy in life does not mean you laugh and laugh . . . but it is when you have peace).

The theme of *ginhawa* is dominant among the narratives of the respondents. *Ginhawa* is experienced first and foremost in their *kalooban* (inner being). The respondents receive *kapatawaran* (forgiveness), *kagalingan* (healing), and *pangangailangan* (provision) as part of their devotion. Thus the experience of *kapayapaan* (peace) is about having peace with God and experiencing inner peace.

Pakikipag-kapwa

The respondents' devotion to the *Pasyon* helps them meditate on the suffering of Jesus and then appropriate its message in their lives. *Pagninilay* (meditation, reflection) is an invitation to imbibe the lessons and truth of the *Pasyon*, which is a spiritual exercise that carries significant moral and ethical implications.

The ethical implication of the *Pasyon* can be attributed to how Christ is represented in the text. Unlike the presentation of Christ in the Gospels, which is unadorned and spare, in the *Pasyon*, Christ is more rounded and multi-dimensional. Christ is shown to be interacting with others in situations that are not found in the Bible, portrayed as a man rather than a god.[10] For this reason, devotees naturally see the relevance of the passion story to real life situations.

An important analysis of the first Tagalog *Pasyon* identifies two important contributions of the *Pasyon* text to the inculturation of Christianity in the Philippines. First, it had a catechetical function. Literature played an important role in the Christianization of the Philippines, and the folk idiom in the *Pasyon* ingrained the Christian faith into people's consciousness. Second, *Pasyon* served as a promoter of Christian and Filipino values. The Tagalog *Pasyon* helped to shape moral, religious, and social values that are integral to the Christian faith.[11] The moral values find relevance in this research on *pakikipag-kapwa tao* (respect for the other person).

Another important theme that surfaced in the interviews reflects a slight different understanding of *pakikipag-kapwa* as being a good neighbor. The *Pasyon* is not just about an individual's relationship with God, but has social and ethical dimensions as well. According to the narratives of those interviewed, *pakikipag-kapwa* is expressed in various ways – through *pakikisama* (conformity, fellow feeling), *paggalang sa karapatan ng tao* (respecting the rights of others), and *pagmamahal at pagtulong sa kapwa* (helping other people).

The message of the *Pasyon* leads a person to engage with people. Aling Gay Villegas (age 72) says, "*Kung inuunawa mo ang mga binabasa mo magiging malapit ka sa mga tao . . . kasi nalalaman mo ang kanilang kalooban*" (If you would truly understand what you are reading, you would get more familiar and intimate with other people . . . because you discover who they really are). Ka Rosario and Ka Lourdes say that their devotion to the *Pasyon* has gained them many friends, which is not surprising given their joyful and resilient spirit during the interviews. Like other devotees, they have their own stories

---

10. Elena Zarco Rivera, "Christ in the Tagalog Pasyon" (master's thesis, University of the Philippines, 1976), abstract.

11. Aligan, *Biblical and Folkloric Elements*, 61.

of pain and sufferings, but their reflections on the suffering of Jesus inspire them to be a *catoto* (friend) to others.

Pagpapatawad (to forgive) is part of *pakikipag-kapwa*. Since Jesus's death on the cross opens the way for God's forgiveness and reconciliation, we are also expected to forgive those who sin against us. Ka Aunor (age 63) says, "*Kasi ginawa sa atin ng panginoon pinatawad tayo, e di hindi tayo makapagpapatawad kung sakali man, kaya kailangan kung may kaaway ka, e patawarin mo na.*" (It is because God has forgiven us; if not, we won't be able to forgive others. Thus, it is a must that, if you have an enemy, you must forgive.) When asked how the *Pasyon* influences her relationship with other people, Aling Lydia De Chavez answers "*pagtulong sa kapwa . . . yong bukal sa puso . . . at yong wag gagawa ng kasalanan sa iba*" (Helping others . . . help that is sincere . . . and not doing bad things to other people). *Pakikipag-kapwa* is priceless and has eternal value. One should not get tired of doing good to others. Ka Leonora (age 78), in referring to the truth that we will reap what we sow, states, "*para na ring nag-aalkansya ka, ipon ka ng ipon . . . pag dumating ang wakas ng buhay meron kang nagawa.*" (It is like having your own piggy bank. You keep saving . . . When the end comes, you will discover that you have done something good.)

Some respondents mention lessons on family relationships. Couples who don't get along with each other cannot receive the blessings of God, so they need to learn to love and forgive each other. Referring to children who defy the authority of their parents, Mang Vic says, "*Nakaka-isang salita ka pa lang, nakaka-isang libo na sila . . . nasa Pasyon po yon!*" (While a child has only spoken one word, parents have already uttered thousands. That is mentioned in the *Pasyon*!) On making friends, the *Pasyon* teaches Vic, "*pag may kwarta may kaibigan, pag wala, wala na . . . malalaman mo sino ang iyong kapanalig . . . sabi nga nila e 'kabigan' hindi 'kaibigan'.*" (If you have money you have friends. But if you don't have money, no one stays . . . you will really find out who your true friends are . . . and as they say, it is like being "user friendly," but not a friend.)

Conclusion

The reading of the *Pasyon* is a liturgical exercise where devotees contemplate the suffering, death, and resurrection of our Lord Jesus Christ which serves as their *pakikibahagi sa paghihirap ni Kristo* (share in the suffering of Christ). In this sacred duty, those who offer a *panata* (vow of devotion) are affirmed of God's costly love. As they offer their service to God, their vow becomes a *panalangin* (prayer) for healing, protection, and provision, sufficient to survive a day or a week.

The *Pasyon* is not only a time for meditation, prayer, and worship but also a celebration of God's love, a time for fun and food. *Ginhawa* is not only about having peace with God and with oneself (*ginhawa sa kalooban*) but also about being reconciled with others (*pakikipag-kapwa*) in order for peace (*kapayapaan*) to reign over families as well as the whole community. For devotees, their devotion to the annual reading of the *Pasyon* invites them to experience a glimpse of *shalom*.

12

The Aestheticization of Violence and the Poetics of Peace

John Robert Rances

In 2015, the photo of Aylan Kurdi, a three-year-old Syrian boy lying face down on a Turkish beach, brought home to the world the plight of Syrian refugees, who had to leave their homeland to escape the fierce fighting between Islamic State insurgents and Kurdish forces. While trying to get to Kos in Greece across the Aegean Sea, the refugees' unseaworthy boat capsized. The little boy, along with eleven others, drowned and then the waves washed their bodies to the beach.

The horror and pathos of Aylan's death inspired artists all over the world to depict his death as a way of voicing their protest – *Humanity Washed Ashore!* Through visual arts, these artists denounced the inhumanity and violence that had led to the young boy's demise. The various artistic renditions of Aylan, lying face down on the beach, evoked painful emotions from viewers. As the audience was informed of the circumstances that had led to the boy's death, they also became aware of the impact of the military conflict in Syria, which was causing its inhabitants to flee their homeland.

The practice of incorporating violence into the arts is referred to as the *aestheticization of violence*. In this essay, the aestheticization of violence is defined as the general use of violence – its intensity, nature, frequency, and volume – in terms of depiction, allusion, and integration in any form of creative human activity regardless of the intent for its inclusion. It is the integration of violence in any form of aesthetic craft.

Such aesthetic convention brings terrible violence into the comfort of our homes. However, while one may be entertained by violence in the form of art, witnessing real-life savageries brings discomfort, even if the victims are portrayed aesthetically. These literary depictions and graphic portrayals of brutality may produce a distinctive aesthetic experience – where the mind and the heart refuse to approve of the violence that is being aestheticized.

This essay attempts to show the value of the aestheticization of violence in the arts to communicate peaceful poetries. Violence in various forms may function as an aesthetic import that can evoke the horrors and unpromising repercussions of armed conflicts and other violent encounters. With strong semiotic framing and the purposeful play of signs and symbols, amicable resolution can be embraced by the audience as a better alternative.

My main thesis is that aestheticizing actual violence through the arts changes the viewing experience from entertainment to alarm. In this process, the audience is dissuaded from embarking in the same acts of violence or develops a disdain for the type of violence being portrayed.

This paper explores the peculiar phenomenon of aestheticizing violence in popular culture, where real-life acts of violence are taken as the focal elements of an aesthetic work and, whether deliberate or not, transmute the viewing experience from being entertaining or cathartic into something repulsive. Such a phenomenon reinforces a non-violent agenda and facilitates peacemaking and peacekeeping efforts.

Art as Medium of Influence

Intellectuals in early antiquity recognized the power of the arts as a medium of influence.[1] Plato, in a vision of an idyllic polis, supposed that a sensible restraint of the arts would positively influence the psychic formation of an ideal leader – a philosopher-king.[2] Aristotle proposed that the selection of melodies should be beneficial for education, *catharsis*, and enjoyment.[3] He

---

1. Art eludes an airtight definition. This essay prefers a definition that respects the concept's openness in terms of content and purpose. As such, art is taken to mean the product of any creative human activity serving a particular aesthetic interest. For definition of arts in the same vein, see George Dickie, *Art and the Aesthetic: An Institutional Analysis* (Ithaca, NY: Cornell University, 1974); George Dickie, *The Art Circle* (New York: Haven, 1984); Monroe Beardsley, *Aesthetics* (New York: Harcourt Brace, 1958).

2. See Plato, "The Republic," in *The Portable Plato*, ed. Scott Buchanan (New York: Penguin, 1976), 353–363.

3. See Aristotle, *Politics*, trans. Benjamin Jowett (Kitchener: Batoche, 1999), 182, 187, 190–191.

also thought that a space for tragic and sacred melodies was allowable, owing to their quality to have a healing or cathartic effect.[4]

Art can be a powerful medium that can capture and shape both the imagination and reality. Patricia Johnston argues for the pivotal role that visual art plays not only in portraying social conditions but also in influencing the way they are perceived.[5] She highlights how visual culture contributes to the shaping of social values. Other impact studies explore the socio-cultural value and economic importance of the arts[6] and how they act as catalysts in preserving cultural identity and improving communal well-being. Many studies claim causal connection between the use of the arts and the betterment of specific populations. Studies cited by Joshua Guetzkow measure the effects of the arts in terms of educational, social, economic, and personal advantages,[7] although he raises some research concerns about how to measure art's impact on societies.

As a medium of influence, the arts can influence the opinion and thinking of its audience, shape its social values, and provoke a variety of responses within viewers. In this respect, the arts can help to foster a peace agenda.

A Culture of Images and Signs

Over time, humanity's perception and engagement of the world has shifted from *oral,* to *scribal,* to *typographical,* to *visual.* The influx of the new media has further widened the disjuncture between a previous text-based culture to a culture of images and signs. With such a paradigm shift, Neil Postman comments that public discourse "must change and be recast in terms that are most suitable to television."[8] This shift restructures public discourse to accommodate a new medium (i.e. television), thereby "creating new forms of truth-telling."[9]

French postmodernist theorist Jean Baudrillard supposes that the changes in the rupture of modernity and postmodernity have something to do with *simulation* and *play of images and signs.* The capitalist agenda of the previous consumer society centers on production and consumption,

---

4. Aristotle, *Politics,* 190–191.

5. See Patricia Johnston, ed., *Seeing High and Low: Presenting Social Conflict in American Visual Culture* (Berkeley: University of California, 2006).

6. See Keith Evans, et al., *Cultural and Creative Industries in Pakistan* (London: British Council, 2004).

7. See Joshua Guetzkow, *How the Arts Impact Communities: An Introduction to the Literature on Arts Impact Studies* (Princeton: Princeton University, 2002), 2–11.

8. Neil Postman, *Amusing Ourselves to Death: Public Discourse in the Age of Show Business* (London: Penguin, 1986), 8.

9. Postman, *Amusing Ourselves to Death,* 16–29.

whereas postmodernity's consumerism is centered on commodity's cultural significations – the "sign-value."[10] Aided by mass media and advertising, this form of consumerism regards commodities not in relation to their *use* but rather to the *image* they project. These images are disengaged from their social or linguistic contexts and disengaged from reality. Postmodernity's consumer culture assigns significant value to a commodity's cultural representation – perhaps as a status symbol – rather than its actual use. Fredric Jameson aptly dubs these images as "free-floating signifiers."[11]

This play of images and signs are devoid of reality, mere *simulations* that appeal to human senses and thereby create an unreal world in the process. Baudrillard calls this unreal world a *simulacrum*, and he refers to the mass of disconnected culture as *hyperreality*.[12] In the aftermath of the disintegration of modernist capitalism, images and signs now characterize postmodernity. Baudrillard incisively comments, "[O]ne day the image of a person sitting watching a television screen voided by a technicians' strike will be seen as the perfect epitome of the anthropological reality of the twentieth century."[13]

In the wake of postmodernity, art – together with other spheres of life – has been liberated.[14] Thus Baudrillard says, "Everything is sexual. Everything is political. Everything is aesthetic. All at once."[15] As categories of distinction have become confused, aesthetics penetrates all other facets of human existence,[16] creating what he calls *trans-aesthetics*.[17] Pushed to its greatest extent possible, art is dissolved into a "general aestheticization of everyday life . . . *a transaesthetics of banality*,"[18] thus resulting in *indiscriminate aestheticization*.

---

10. See Jean Baudrillard, *The Transparency of Evil: Essay on Extreme Phenomena*, trans. James Benedict (London: New Left, 1993), 16.

11. Fredric Jameson *"Free-floating signifiers,"* quoted in Kenneth Allan, "The End of Everything: Jean Baudrillard," in *Contemporary Social and Sociological Theory: Visualizing Social Worlds: Visualizing Social Worlds,* 2nd ed. (Los Angeles: Sage, 2011), 310.

12. An image of an image of reality that never existed and never appears. See Allan, "The End of Everything," 310.

13. Baudrillard, *Transparency of Evil,* 13.

14. Baudrillard, 3.

15. Baudrillard, 9.

16. This collapse of categories is characterized by what Baudrillard calls *transpolitics, transsexual,* and *transaesthetic.* Collectively, they form what we conventionally label as culture, which Baudrillard qualifies as "a sort of all-pervasive media and advertising-led semiologization: 'culture degree Xerox.'" See Baudrillard, *Transparency of Evil,* 9.

17. Baudrillard, *Transparency of Evil,* 10.

18. Baudrillard, 11. Emphasis mine. Baudrillard further writes, "It is often said that the West's great undertaking is the commercialization of the whole world, the hitching of the fate of everything to the fate of the commodity. That great undertaking will turn out rather to have been

Indeed, if everything *is*, nothing *is*.[19] However, the profusion of art in the mundane has stripped art of its *soul* – its very reason for being.[20] Its value and criteria are fading into the abyss as well.

Contemporary society is not only an advanced consumer society but also an aestheticized culture. Thus we can say that our society is an "aestheticized consumer society." In this movement towards signs, images, and symbols, art, although different from its classical and modernist precursor, is given a new thrust. Because art pervades all of life, it has the potential to become a powerful medium of instruction once again. Postman himself argues negatively against a television-based epistemology. However, he also admits the unexplored potential of television to become a "theater for the masses." Although the medium undermines rational discourse, it can nevertheless "arouse great emotional power" from its audience towards a cause (e.g. racial discrimination).[21] Postman recognizes that "these and other possibilities are not to be taken lightly."[22]

Violence in Aesthetics

Some suggest that the motif of violence in aesthetics has Hellenistic and post-Enlightenment precursors.[23] Artists of the fifteenth and sixteenth centuries portrayed disturbing emotions and gruesome depictions of human pains and fears of the netherworld and other similar motifs.[24] The inroad of horror movies, such as *Dracula*, *The Wolf Man*, and *Frankenstein*, in mainstream cinema in the 1930s reinforced these motifs. In the 1950s to 1960s, cinematic violence was revolutionized by the introduction of color. Aestheticizing violence became more explicit and dramatic, and cinematic effects further highlighted this phenomenon.

Margaret Ervin Bruder, a film studies professor at Indiana University, identifies the aestheticization of violence in films when the use of violence is

---

the aestheticization of the whole world – its cosmopolitan spectacularization, its transformation into images, its semiological organization." See, *Transparency of Evil*, 16.

19. Allan, *End of Everything*, 311.

20. Allan, 14. Baudrillard suggests that art is an adventure and has the power to create illusion, to negate and evoke realities.

21. Postman, *Amusing Ourselves to Death*, 28–29.

22. Postman, 29.

23. See Luc Boltanski, *Distant Suffering: Politics, Morality and the Media* (Cambridge: Cambridge University, 1999).

24. See the works of Heironymous Bosch, Peter Brueghel, and Mathis Gothart-Neithart.

"stylistically excessive in a significant and sustained way."[25] Hence, some violent films, such as *Die Harder*, are not to be included in this category, because even though it has a disproportionate number of brutalities in relation to the total screen time, the violence is not presented in an aesthetically significant way.[26] Yet the use of violence in the arts is not exclusive to visual arts, such as film and paintings. Literature also utilizes violence in its creative agenda. Voltaire's magnum opus, *Candide*, reports massacre, rape, and other hideous encounters casually, adding to the picaresque quality of the novel as it wrestles with the important question of evil.[27]

People's fascination with aestheticized violence is difficult to justify. However, if recent movie attendance reflects our parameters, according to Bruder, "it seems that we do manage in one way or another to get around our moral qualms."[28] As film producer Lawrence Gordon comments, one of the chief reasons for the industry's attraction to the "action genre" is that violence "travels well."[29]

With violence becoming a cinematic norm, or a norm in the media in general and accepted by mainstream audiences, efforts are being made to analyze its effects on the audience. Some critics suggest that violence is desensitizing, whereas others think that violence is cathartic.[30] For the former, violence as an added stylistic feature or a superficial appendage and foil for a film causes its audience members to be desensitized to brutality, which has the potential to increase aggression. For the latter, aestheticized violence serves a "cathartic or dissipating effect . . . providing acceptable outlets for anti-social impulses."[31]

There is no clear benchmark to determine which of these two dominant interpretations is applicable. Audiences' exposure to aestheticized violence can go either way based on a host of other factors (e.g. gender, psychological

---

25. Margaret Ervin Bruder, "Aestheticizing Violence, or How to Do Things with Style," *Postmodern Discourses* (1998), accessed on November 20, 2015, http://www.gradnet.de/papers/pomo98.papers/mtbruder98.hhtm.

26. Bruder, "Aestheticizing Violence."

27. See Voltaire, *Candide and Other Stories,* trans. Roger Pearson (Oxford: Oxford University, 2006).

28. Bruder, "Aestheticizing Violence."

29. Ken Auletta, "What Won't They Do?" *The New Yorker* (May 17, 1993), quoted in Bruder, "Aestheticization of Violence."

30. Bruder, "Aestheticizing Violence."

31. Thomas R. Atkins, "Images of Violence," in *Graphic Violence on Screen,* ed. Thomas R. Atkins (New York: Simon & Schuster, 1976), 4.

health, length of exposure, age, etc.).[32] It seems that the bifurcated line of interpretation regarding the effects of aestheticized violence on its audience is not an either–or option.[33] Certain nuances in the spectrum should be observed, for either interpretation can be true under certain conditions. This tension invites us to question the circumstances under which one in interpretation is truer – or more operational – than the other.

Paradox of the Aestheticization of Violence

Among other possibilities, aestheticized violence can evoke a quasi-religious awe from its audience. Observing violence in different art forms may be entertaining, but this may not be the case in watching violence in real life – except for those who have psychological leanings towards the enjoyment of violence. It is one thing to relish the sight of aestheticized violence, gore, or hideous altercations portrayed realistically through film, sports, or other mass media; it is another thing to enjoy the sight of violence in real life.

The American philosopher of art Noël Carroll observes this paradox, particularly in people's fascination with horror as a movie genre. He comments:

> We do not, for example, attempt to add some pleasure to a boring afternoon by opening the lid of a steamy trash can in order to savor its unwholesome stew of broken bits of meat, moldering fruits and vegetables, and noxious, unrecognizable clumps, riven thoroughly by all manner of crawling things. And, ordinarily, checking out hospital waste bags is not our idea of a good time. But, on the other hand, many people . . . do seek out horror fictions for the purpose of deriving pleasure from sights and descriptions that customarily repulse them.[34]

Carroll wonders why people enjoy the gore in horror films, but turn away from, or even cringe, at the sight of such things in ordinary life circumstances.

---

32. See Bruce D. Bartholow and Craig A. Anderson, "Effects of Violent Video Games on Aggressive Behavior: Potential Sex Differences," *Journal of Experimental Social Psychology* 38, no. 3 (May 2002): 283–290; Christopher R. Engelhardt, et al., "Effects of Violent Video Game Exposure on Aggressive Behavior, Aggressive-Thought Accessibility, and Aggressive Affect Among Adults With and Without Autism Spectrum Disorder," *Psychological Science* 26, no. 8 (August 2015): 1187–1200.

33. See Sissela Bok, *Mayhem: Violence as Public Entertainment* (Boston: Addison-Wesley, 1998).

34. Noël Carroll, *Philosophy of Horror or Paradoxes of the Heart* (New York: Routledge, 1990), 158.

He says, "[I]n the ordinary course of affairs, people shun what disgusts them. Being repulsed by something that one finds to be loathsome and impure is an unpleasant experience."[35] The paradox he observes, however, is that people find pleasure or are attracted to something that is "explicitly repulsive,"[36] which, in the usual state of affairs, would be avoided.

This paradox could lead us to believe that there is an observable rupture between the perception of violence that performs an aesthetic function, such as in film and literature, and the perception of actual violence and gore before one's eyes. Perhaps people approach and construe violence differently under different sets of circumstances, thereby altering their perception of the violence they are witnessing. This change of perception – from an aesthetic scene to a real experience – transmutes violence into something vile rather than pleasing, alarming rather than amusing.

Re-Considering the Phenomenon

Lilie Chouliaraki proposes a theory that could serve us well in understanding this paradoxical phenomenon, supposing that mediation is critical to this change of interpretive reception. Appropriate mediation involves audience members connecting "emotionally and culturally with the distant (suffering) 'others,'"[37] creating *immediacy* with the "distant other" and its target audiences. Although spatio-temporal distance can be bridged through a medium, the manner of mediation significantly shapes the message being conveyed.[38] The intervention of a medium shapes and re-shapes the message, thereby influencing the way it is received and construed by its audiences. In terms of television, Chouliaraki writes, "mediation is about putting *technical* immediacy . . . at the service of *socio-cultural* immediacy – the sense of copresence [sic] with faraway others."[39] John Tomlinson refers to this sense of connectivity or togetherness that goes with and transcends the medium as a "modality of connectivity."[40]

For Chouliaraki, the case of Amina Lawal, a Nigerian woman who was sentenced to death under the sharia law, typifies such a sense of connectivity.[41] The way it was televised as news, depicting a woman collectively mobbed by

---

35. Carroll, *Philosophy of Horror*, 158.
36. Carroll, 159.
37. Lilie Chouliaraki, *Spectatorship of Suffering* (London: Sage, 2006), 19.
38. John Tomlinson, *Globalization and Culture* (London: Sage, 1999), 154–155.
39. Chouliaraki, *Spectatorship of Suffering*, 20. Emphasis is original.
40. Tomlinson, *Globalization and Culture*, 155.
41. Chouliaraki, *Spectatorship of Suffering*, 20–21.

an enraged crowd, facilitated for its European audiences a *modal imagination*. Chouliaraki defines modal imagination as "the ability of spectators to imagine something that they have not experienced themselves as being possible for others to experience."[42] In the audience members' realm of experience, the depicted violence is an impossibility; but with the aestheticization of violence through news reporting, audience members begin to imagine that such violence is "an actual possibility for a woman out there."[43] Chourliaraki summarizes, the "mediated immediacy is about construing proximity – a sense of 'being there' that, albeit different from face-to-face contact, evokes feelings and dispositions to act 'as if' the spectator were on location."[44]

This sense of *being in solidarity with others* enables audience members to resonate with the conveyed misery, distress, and afflictions of aestheticized violence, even when the experience being depicted is existentially untrue. The mediation of immediacy could be an advantageous anthropological phenomenon for fostering a pacifist agenda and facilitating anti-violence campaigns. Aestheticizing violence can potentially discourage the perpetuation of actual brutalities and put forward amicable alternatives for human relations, thereby creating peaceful poetics.

Semiotics is an important science to consider in the attempt to aestheticize violence and create peaceful poetics.[45] Semiotics is the study of signs and symbols – what they mean and how they relate to the things or ideas to which they refer. By adjusting the semiotic conditions of an image or sign, whether moving or static, we can communicate a different story and invite the audience to view the material in a different light. For instance, by simply changing photo captions, we can render an image as humorous, emotive, tragic, and so on. Images or signs have signifiers, which are usually supplied by a context that influences their interpretation and are often based on conventions, stereotypes, and clichés. These signifiers or contextual indicators prompt and direct an audience about how to construe the material.

---

42. Chouliaraki, 20.

43. Chouliaraki, 21.

44. Chouliaraki, 21.

45. See Jorgen Dines Johansen and Svend Erik, *Signs in Use: Introduction to Semiotics*, trans. Dinda L. Gorlee and John Irons (New York: Routledge, 2002); Gunther Press, *Multimodality: A Social Semiotic Approach to Contemporary Communication* (New York: Routledge, 2010); Paul Cobley, ed., *The Routledge Companion to Semiotics and Linguistics* (New York: Routledge, 2001).

Conclusion

After the news broke about abuses committed in an American detention facility in Abu Ghraib West Baghdad, written accounts and pictures of US soldiers torturing detainees were made public. Fordham University theology professor Krista Stevens notes, "Pictures surfaced of Abu Ghraib prisoners . . . being sexually humiliated, beaten, and threatened by guard dogs."[46] This horrendous torture induced Colombian-born artist Fernando Botero to respond with a number of sketches and paintings depicting various acts of torture. Unlike Botero's previous work, his Abu Ghraib collection is poignant and disturbing. Stevens comments, the Abu Ghraib collection "is moving yet painfully disturbing, bringing to life the indignity and degradation of the prisoners in ways that the soldiers' amateur photos could not."[47] Botero's art intensifies the violence, depicting an inhumanity that is received by viewers with utter aversion.

Aestheticizing violence in art, along with strong semiotics, has the power to shape an audience's experience of violence towards a peace agenda. When the mind and the heart refuse to approve of the violence being portrayed, the violence is deemed as an unworthy option. Transforming violence into peaceable beauty can help advance anti-violence campaigns in different places and cultures, opening possibilities for peace by mediating the proximity between victims and spectators.

---

46. Krista Stevens, "The Beauty of Abu Ghraib: Art Transforming Violence," ARTS 23, no. 3 (2012): 4.

47. Stevens, "Beauty of Abu Ghraib," 4.

Section V

Partnership and Cooperation

13

Missional Engagement for Reconciliation

Local Church Builds Relationships with a Muslim Community

Glicerio M. Manzano, Jr.

This article is a case study of a collaborative effort between a mission agency working among marginalized Filipino Muslims from Rio Hondo, which was situated on the outskirts of Zamboanga City, and an urban local church from Metro Manila. Rio Hondo was a Muslim community composed of Tausug, Yakan, Samal, and Badjao people groups. It was known as a notorious area, which many visitors and even locals were afraid to visit, as if it is "synonymous to death."[1] When a team of Christians decided to begin working in this marginalized Muslim community, it marked a historical and significant reconciliation effort.

From "Mercy" Ministry to Missional Engagement

Greenhills Christian Fellowship (GCF) is a thriving local church in Metro Manila that is part of the Conservative Baptist Association of the Philippines

---

1. "Rio Hondo: The Other Face of Zamboanga City," *Love Mindanao*, March 2013, accessed February 1, 2016, http://www.lovemindanao.com/2013/03/RioHondo.html.

(CBAP) denomination. The church was founded in 1976 by Rev David and Patty Yount, an American missionary couple. Over the years, the congregation has grown and has planted a number of churches in the Philippines and overseas.

Greenhills Christian Fellowship-Operation Compassion (GCF-OC) is a ministry of this local church, which consists of medical and dental doctors, paramedics, and auxiliary volunteers. GCF organized this ministry in the 1980s to do once-a-year medical missions in needy areas within Luzon, using donated medicines and medical supplies from pharmaceutical companies.

In the mid-1990s, GCF-OC reorganized and expanded its ministry, conducting four regular medical/dental missions annually – three within the island of Luzon, where GCF is located, and one in either Visayas or Mindanao, or sometimes outside the Philippines. During this time, GCF-OC expanded its volunteer base to include non-GCF members in order to form ministry partnerships with various local churches, denominations, and mission organizations and to train them in conducting medical missions. In order to prevent over-dependence on pharmaceutical companies, which initially provided the drugs and medical supplies that were used during medical missions, GCF-OC also sought to provide quality medical service programs and projects that would be fully supported by GCF and its partners.

Emerging Missional Clarity

GCF-OC has evolved from being a "mercy" ministry to an evangelistic and missional ministry, with the specific goal of proclaiming and demonstrating the love of God to the poor, oppressed, and suffering through its medical, dental, and surgical missions, as well as its relief operations. Theologically, GCF-OC sets aside religious and denominational boundaries, believing that as God's people, we are called to manifest and demonstrate God's love and compassion to all peoples (Matt 22:37; Luke 10:27), bear witness to the glorious gospel and presence of God to all the world (Acts 1:8; Matt 5:16), and lead and usher people to Christ and into his kingdom (Matt 28:16–20).

Missiologically, GCF-OC provides mission engagement opportunities to both GCF and non-GCF members so that they can minister to their neighbors in a holistic and culturally sensitive manner. Operationally, it aims to provide quality medical services by partnering with local churches and mission agencies in order to deepen and sustain relationships with the local community and, over time, establish and strengthen a local body of believers.

Outreach to Muslim Communities

A central focus that has emerged for the ministry outreaches of GCF-OC is on the unreached people groups of Mindanao in Southern Philippines. Mindanao is a place of continuing conflict between Muslims and Christians. Religious, political, economic, and ethnic tensions intensified into a full-blown war in the 1960s that continues to this day.[2] To Muslims in Mindanao, "Christians" are the people from Luzon and Visayas who have migrated to Mindanao. Thus, from their perspective, Christians are the invaders, potential enemies, and land-grabbers. To Muslims in Mindanao, the government is basically "Christian." "Christians," on the other hand, consider the Muslims a threat, *"traitors"* (betrayers) who cannot be trusted, and religious bigots who are ready to kill their opponents.[3]

In light of this tension, GCF-OC conducted several medical mission activities in different Muslim communities in Mindanao in partnership with various local churches and mission organizations. In 2002, GCF-OC began to form a team to establish its first mission in Rio Hondo, a *barangay* (small administrative unit within a city or a municipality) situated at the edge of the highly urbanized city of Zamboanga in Mindanao.

The Context for Mission: Rio Hondo, Zamboanga City

Rio Hondo (Deep River) was named four and a half centuries ago by Spanish settlers because of the rivers that surround the area. In 1965, Rio Hondo was officially established as the site for the first Muslim community in the

2. Rizal G. Buendia, "The Mindanao Conflict in the Philippines: Ethno-Religious War or Economic Conflict?" accessed November 14, 2017, http://www.academia.edu/1433739/Mindanao_Conflict_in_the_Philippines_Ethno-Religious_War_or_Economic_Conflict. There are many scholarly sources on Christian-Muslim relations in the Philippines, such as Bobby M. Tuazon, ed., *The Moro Reader: History and Contemporary Struggles of the Bangsamoro People* (Diliman, Quezon City: Policy Study Publication and Advocacy, Center for People Empowerment in Governance in partnership with Light a Candle Movement for Social Change, 2008); Hilario Gomez, Jr., *The Moro Rebellion and the Search for Peace: A Study on Christian-Muslim Relations in the Philippines* (Zamboanga City, Phils.: Silsilah Publications, 2000); Marites D. Vitug and Glenda M. Gloria, *Under the Crescent Moon: Rebellion in Mindanao* (Quezon City: Ateneo Center for Social Policy and Public Affairs, 2000).

3. Mr Victor, "Causes of Conflict Between Christians and Muslims in the Philippines, Part 1," July 4, 2005, accessed November 12, 2017, http://www.iiipeace.org/Philippines%20Causes%20of%20Conflict%20between%20Christians%20and%20Muslims.htm.

Philippines by the Philippine President at the time, Diosdado Macapagal.[4] In the early 1980s, the population in this small settlement boomed as people from Sulu migrated due to the constant war between the government and Muslim rebels.[5] At its peak, the population reached approximately twelve thousand.

The population is mostly comprised of Muslim migrants from different tribes and localities in Mindanao – the Tausug, Yakan, Samal, and Badjao tribes, who came from the provinces of Jolo, Sulu, Basilan, and Tawi-Tawi.[6] Zamboanga City dwellers generally despised Rio Hondo for being a Muslim community. In addition to the conflict that Rio Hondo residents experience with Christians living outside the area, there are also inter- and intra-tribal conflicts within the community itself, since Rio Hondo has seven *sitios* (hamlets) – Laud-Laud, Lupa-Lupa, Kabingaan, Hongkong, Fishpond, Campo Muslim, and Aplaya – and each *sitio* is occupied by a homogenous tribal group.[7]

Economically, Rio Hondo is an urban poor community, whose dwellers are mostly small fisherfolk and traders. Some work as private or government employees, while others are Overseas Filipino Workers (OFWs) in the Middle East. Some are unemployed due to various reasons, including discrimination against Muslims by "Christian" employers in the city.

Most people, including tricycle and jeepney drivers, dread driving into Rio Hondo, so they generally refuse to take passengers there. Those who agree to do so will often drive to a certain point outside the *barangay,* and then make people walk the rest of the way. The following anecdote, commonly told by residents, illustrates Rio Hondo's notorious reputation. A tricycle driver drove a passenger to Rio Hondo, where the passenger lived. Upon reaching Rio Hondo, the passenger asked how much the fare was. When the driver said "forty-five," meaning forty-five pesos, the passenger pulled out a .45 caliber handgun and shot the poor driver dead.

---

4. "Rio Hondo, Zamboanga City, Philippines," www.zamboanga.com, accessed February 1, 2016, http://www.zamboanga.com/z/index.php?title=Rio_Hondo_Zamboanga_City_Philippines.

5. "Rio Hondo: The Other Face of Zamboanga City."

6. "Rio Hondo: The Other Face of Zamboanga City."

7. "Rio Hondo," City Government of Zamboanga, accessed February 1, 2016, http://www.zamboanga.gov.ph/index.php?option=com_content&view=article&id=396:rio-hondo&catid=1313:political-boundaries&Itemid=326.

Missional Focus: Reconciliation

In October 2002, a militant Muslim group allegedly bombed the center of Zamboanga City. Earlier that year, in June 2002, Martin Burnham, a US missionary, was taken hostage and then killed in Zamboanga del Norte during an encounter between the Muslim militants and the rescuing government forces.[8]

Because of these incidents, the GCF-OC team knew that pushing through the planned medical mission to Rio Hondo would entail grave risks. Yet the team bonded together as they depended on God, prayed, and prepared spiritually and culturally for the mission. The team also enjoined the entire church to intercede for them in their ministry engagement.

On the first day of the medical mission at Rio Hondo, the community was skeptical of the mission team and their activities, so only a few people came in the morning. The people were already tired of and frustrated with medical groups who had provided mediocre services. However, as word spread about the team's professional demeanor and the quality of their medical care, people started streaming into the mission that afternoon and in the following days.

During that first visit to Rio Hondo, those who came for medical services lived in the area dominated by the influential Tausug and Yakan tribes. Other tribes from the rest of the *sitios* did not come, mainly due to tribal animosities. Thus on succeeding visits, the team, along with the local community leaders, began to conduct medical operations in different *sitios* of the *barangay*, so that other tribal groups could access medical services. This strategy promoted goodwill among the factious Muslim tribes.

The team did not conceal their Christian identity, nor that they came from a Christian church in Manila. Each day, before starting any activity, they prayed with the local community in the name of *Isa Al Masih* (Jesus the Messiah). The doctors also prayed with the patients whenever the opportunity arose. Because of this, trust was built, relationships were established, and the team was welcomed back repeatedly. In one of the team's trips, they presented the Christmas story to the children and their accompanying parents. They were also able to leave a copy of the Bible in the school library.

As the people saw God's mercy and compassion through these Christians from Manila, a community leader commented:

---

8. "US Missionary Killed in the Philippines," *Bible Doctrine News,* accessed February 1, 2016, http://www.biblenews1.com/history2/20020607.htm. See also Gracia Burnham, *In the Presence of My Enemies* (Wheaton, IL: Tyndale House, 2004).

"Ang akala ko, ang mga Kristiano pare-pareho lang. Ngayon, alam na namin na may mga Kristiano na tunay na nagmamahal sa aming mga Muslim. Salamat sa inyo na bagama't alam ninyo ang lahat na masasamang sinasabi ng mga tao tungkol sa amin at sa aming komunidad, pumunta at tumulong kayo sa amin ng walang hinihintay na kapalit."

(I thought that all Christians were the same. Now we know that there are true Christians who really love us Muslims. Thank you because in spite of all the bad things people say about us and our community, you still came and helped us without expecting anything in return.)

Yet when GCF-OC attempted to ask some local churches in Zamboanga City to help in the ministry at Rio Hondo, they all refused. Even the officers of the Philippine Air Force Base in Zamboanga were surprised to learn that the GCF-OC team went into Rio Hondo and departed alive!

Several years later, in 2009, GCF-OC adopted Rio Hondo, Zamboanga City into its "short-term-long-term" program in partnership with the *Taytayan* ("Bridge") Foundation Project of Overseas Missionary Fellowship (OMF)-Philippines. The program is "short-term" because each visit runs for two or three days in order to accommodate the schedules of the volunteer medical doctors and other personnel. The program is also "long-term" because GCF-OC visits the same community three to four times a year in order to build trust and establish relationships.

Missional Response: Relief Operations After the 2013 Zamboanga Siege

In September 2013, the Moro National Liberation Front (MNLF) army put Zamboanga City under siege for twenty days and obliterated Rio Hondo, burning and razing houses to the ground, and using the residents of Rio Hondo as human shields against the government soldiers. The clash caused numerous deaths and enormous damages, destroying thousands of structures in Rio Hondo and other surrounding Muslim settlements and displacing around 120,000 people, who were forced to evacuate to other places.[9] The displaced

---

9. International Committee of the Red Cross, "Philippines: Moving on in Zamboanga," November 30, 2015, accessed February 1, 2016, https://www.icrc.org/en/document/philippines-moving-zamboanga; "Timeline: Crisis in Zamboanga City," Andrei Medina, September 10,

camped out in various government evacuation centers, which lacked adequate basic facilities.

About thirty people from Rio Hondo took refuge in the tiny home of a resident OMF missionary. In addition, about a hundred more Rio Hondo contacts came for lunch. In partnership with OMF-Philippines, GCF helped in the relief operations, gathering financial and material resources to help the victims of the armed conflict. Another local church in Zamboanga City – one that had previously refused to help the team in earlier missions – also mobilized their congregation to provide lunch packs, sanitation kits, and medicines to the people camped at the OMF center and in government evacuation centers.

Theological and Missiological Reflections

Through these intentional mission engagements, GCF built bridges within the local community and began to tear down some of the dividing walls between Christians and Muslims. Although there were no overt evangelistic activities, the people saw and felt Christ's love and compassion through the team's sincerity, sensitivity, and professionalism; hence, they responded warmly.

As a result of these efforts by OMF-Philippines and GCF-OC, a community of believers was established. However, due to the 2013 Zamboanga siege, Rio Hondo no longer exists as a community, and so the new believers have scattered into different places and settlement sites. Nevertheless, the *Taytayan* Project of OMF-Philippines continues to work among the believers. Up to the present, they continue to reach out to the dispersed people of Rio Hondo and to new Muslim communities in Zamboanga. GCF also continues to partner with OMF-Philippines as opportunities arise.

We often ask God to restore peace and harmony in the country, and we pray for divine intervention. But in the parable of the Good Samaritan (Luke 10:30–37), Jesus points out that fostering peace and harmony lies in the hands of the "good neighbor." Thus God reaches out to others through God's people. Instead of being indifferent like the priest (v. 31) and the Levite (v. 32) in the parable, local churches have a God-given responsibility to love and bless others, trusting God to provide the resources needed to bring unity, peace, and harmony into places of violence and tension. For the faith community to act as the "good neighbor," the local church must intentionally reach out to its hurting, hostile, or estranged neighbors in order to initiate the process

---

2013, accessed November 14, 2017, http://www.gmanetwork.com/news/news/regions/325855/timeline-crisis-in-zamboanga-city/story/.

of healing and reconciliation. The church as God's agent must, like the GCF, seek to tear down barriers and reconcile with enemies, even if it means going the extra mile.

14

The Philippine Bible Society and Interconfessional Bible Translation

An Avenue for Dialogue and Cooperation in the Filipino Christian Church

Christine Joy N. Martinez and Leizl S. Ocampo

Waves of colonial rule brought various faces of the Christian faith to the Philippines: Roman Catholicism during the Spanish rule (1521–1898), and then several mainstream Protestant denominations under the US occupation (1898–1946). The following decades (1950s–1960s) saw an increase in evangelical and Pentecostal movements. The doctrinal and theological divide between the major Christian traditions, and even among different denominations within the same tradition, remains to this day. In the ministry of the Philippine Bible Society (PBS), this division is witnessed by its workers as they engage individuals, groups, and churches coming from different faith and denominational communities in Scripture-related activities. PBS is perceived as "Catholic" by some Protestant groups and as "Protestant" by some Catholic groups. Beyond traditional labels, differences cover a variety of matters – from doctrinal issues, to the style of worship and music, to rituals of baptism and communion. These differences may have contributed to the tendency of many Christians to remain entrenched in their own groups.

Uniquely, PBS, under the mandate of the United Bible Societies (UBS), has been deliberately working towards interconfessional cooperation in its ministry, which means that PBS fosters an environment and an avenue for Christian churches of different faith traditions to work together in expanding the reach of God's Word in the country. PBS believes that its vision of "A Transformed Filipino People Through God's Word" can be more efficiently realized through one of its main core values – interconfessional cooperation – thereby encouraging strong partnerships and the involvement of most, if not all, Christian communities in the Philippines. As part of this commitment, PBS leadership includes a highly competent and interconfessional Board of Trustees, who are nominated by their own communities. Five are from the Philippine Council of Evangelical Churches (PCEC), five from the National Council of Churches in the Philippines (NCCP), five from the Roman Catholic Church through the Catholic Bishops' Conference of the Philippines' Episcopal Commission on Biblical Apostolate (CBCP-ECBA), and three from independent denominations (groups not aligned to any of the previous three).

Through its interconfessional ministry, PBS aims to foster a spirit of community and camaraderie. PBS recognizes that in spite of doctrinal differences, it is in the best interest of the Filipino people and the Christian Church as a whole to recognize that, through community and unity, we attain the mind of Christ. In the light of God's Word and how God is working in each of us, we are all equal and we all stand on level ground.

Bible Society Work in the Philippines

November 2016 marked the 117th year that the ministry of the Bible Society officially commenced in the Philippines. Throughout the years, PBS has been committed to responding to the Scripture needs of the Filipino Christian churches by providing Bible translations that are faithful to the original biblical languages, easy to understand, and in formats that people appreciate. Before the establishment of Bible Societies, Bible ministry – specifically Bible translation in the Philippines – started as a scattered enterprise by different individuals and communities. Though the official involvement of the British and Foreign Bible Society in the Philippines started in 1899, Bible translation efforts began long before. As early as the 1500s to the 1700s, portions of Scripture were translated in Tagalog, Cebuano, and Ilokano in the Baybayin script.[1]

---

1. Edgar Ebojo, *Light to the Nations* (Manila: Philippine Bible Society, 2015), 3.

The first translation of a whole book of the Bible into a Philippine language was by a former Dominican priest, Don Manrique Alonzo Lallave, who translated the Gospel of Luke into the Pangasinan language in 1873.[2] Later translations of portions of the Bible were completed in different languages, such as Bikol (F. D. Cayetano) and Hiligaynon (Rev Erick Lund).[3] During this time, Bible translation and distribution was difficult, since ports and market lines were controlled by the Spanish colonizers. Concerned that lay people might incorrectly translate and interpret the Scriptures without consulting the clergy, the Catholic Church at that time restricted its members' access to the Bible in order to protect the unity of the Church and the purity of its doctrine.[4] As a ripple effect of this prohibition, most efforts to propagate, distribute, and translate the Bible in the Philippines were done in secret.

At last, on September 6, 1898, weeks after Spain surrendered the Philippines to America, Charles Randall, under the auspices of the British and Foreign Bible Society (BFBS), came to the Philippines with hundreds of copies of portions of the New Testament in Tagalog, Ilokano, and Bikolano. Likewise, the American Bible Society (ABS) sent Rev Jay C. Goodrich as their agent in the Philippines in November 1899.[5] Together, the BFBS and ABS began to translate the Bible into the major languages of the Philippines: the Tagalog Bible in 1905; the Ilokano Bible, which became known as the Union Version, in 1909; the Hiligaynon Bible in 1912; the Bikol Bible in 1914; the Pangasinan Bible in 1915; the Pampango Bible in 1917; the Cebuano Bible in 1919; and the Samarenyo Bible in 1937.[6]

In 1919, ABS became responsible for the Bible ministry in the Philippines in order to let BFBS focus its attention on the work in Korea. The local Bible Agency later came to be known as the Philippine Bible House.[7]

Meanwhile, the BFBS and other Bible Societies have served Protestant communities for years. They dreamed of reaching out to the Catholic Church, but approaches for partnership were denied repeatedly in light of the Scripture restrictions within the Catholic community.[8]

---

2. Ebojo, *Light to the Nations*, 4.

3. Philippine Bible Society, *A Brief History of the Bible Movement in the Philippines* (Manila: Philippine Bible Society, 1984), 3.

4. Edwin Robertson, *Taking the Word to the World: 50 Years of the United Bible Societies* (Nashville: Thomas Nelson Publishers, 1986), 104.

5. Ebojo, *Light to the Nations*, 6.

6. Philippine Bible Society, *A Brief History*, 4–5.

7. Philippine Bible Society, 5.

8. Robertson, *Taking the Word to the World*, 103.

The Philippine Bible House became an autonomous institution in 1966 and was renamed the Philippine Bible Society. Since 1919, its headquarters have remained at No. 636 Isaac Peral Street, which is now known as 890 United Nations Avenue in Ermita, Manila.

Vatican II: *Nostra Aetate* and *Dei Verbum*

The breakthrough of God's grace came with a fresh wind from the second Vatican Council, which was initiated by the late Pope John XXIII in 1962, and later followed by Pope Paul VI. Among the official documents to emerge in the 1963–1965 Council, which became pivotal in the Catholic Church's involvement in the Bible movement, were the *Nostra Aetate* and the *Dei Verbum*.[9]

The *Nostra Aetate: Declaration on the Relation of the Church to Non-Christian Religions*, states:

> In her task of promoting unity and love among men, indeed among nations, she considers above all in this declaration what men have in common and what draws them to fellowship . . . The Church reproves, as foreign to the mind of Christ, any discrimination against men or harassment of them because of their race, color, condition of life, or religion. On the contrary, following in the footsteps of the holy Apostles Peter and Paul, this sacred synod ardently implores the Christian faithful to "maintain good fellowship among the nations" and if possible to live for their part in peace with all men, so that they may truly be sons of the Father who is in heaven (1 Pet 2:12).[10]

The *Dei Verbum Dogmatic Constitution on Divine Revelation* takes the Council even further, saying,

> Easy access to Sacred Scripture should be provided for all Christian faithful. But since the Word of God should be available at all times, the Church with maternal concern sees to it that suitable and correct translations are made into different languages, especially from the original texts of the sacred books . . . if given

---

9. Robertson, 109–110.

10. Vatican Council, *Nostra Aetate: Declaration on the Relation of the Church to Non-Christian Religions,* proclaimed by Pope Paul VI on October 28, 1965, nos. 1 and 3. Accessed January 10, 2016, http://www.vatican.va/archive/hist_councils/ii_vatican_council/documents/vat-ii_decl_19651028_nostra-aetate_en.html.

the opportunity and the approval of the Church authorities, these translations are produced in cooperation with the separated brethren as well; all Christians will be able to use them.[11]

The pioneer and founder of the Catholic Secretariat for Christian Unity, Cardinal Augustin Bea, S.J., later on says that this possibility of interconfessional cooperation is one of the most important highlights of Christian history, for this pivotal event breaks generations of "suspicion and hostility." He then challenges the Catholic Church to look and search within itself as she embarks on a new and valuable quest to bring God's Word to God's people.[12]

Philippine Bible Society and Interconfessional Translations

As a response to Vatican II, a parallel relationship between the Bible Societies and the Catholic Church began to be forged internationally and locally. In the United Bible Societies (UBS), various consultations and meetings were held to set the pace of the Bible Movement to respond to the needs of the Protestant and Catholic communities.[13] One of the many results of these convocations was the document, "Guidelines for Interconfessional Cooperation in Translating the Bible." In summary, it states that translations will continue to be

> based on the Hebrew Text of the OT and the Greek Text of the NT which have been agreed by scholars from various church traditions. Drafting and reviewing the translations is to be carried out in close cooperation with the aim that the new text will be acceptable to, and be used by, all Christians and Christian communities who speak the language into which the translation is being made.[14]

Rev Fr Walter Abbott, S.J., was appointed as Cardinal Bea's assistant in implementing Vatican II and its implication for interconfessional partnerships.[15]

---

11. Vatican Council, *Dei Verbum: Dogmatic Constitution on Divine Revelation,* proclaimed by Pope Paul VI on November 18, 1965, no. 22. Accessed January 10, 2016, http://www.vatican. va/archive/hist_councils/ii_vatican_council/documents/vat-ii_const_19651118_dei-verbum_en.html.

12. Robertson, *Taking the Word to the World,* 112.

13. Robertson, 112–114.

14. The Secretariat for Christian Unity and the United Bible Societies, "Guidelines for Interconfessional Cooperation in Translating the Bible," Vatican City, 1987, http://www.vatican. va/roman_curia/pontifical_councils/chrstuni/general-docs/rc_pc_chrstuni_doc_19871116_guidelines-bible_en.html.

15. Robertson, *Taking the Word to the World,* 113.

In 1967, Fr Abbott arrived in the Philippines with a copy of the Good News Translation (New Testament). This version was a new widely popular translation published by the American Bible Society, which was based on the principles of dynamic translation promulgated by Dr Eugene Nida.[16] Previously, members of the Catholic Bishops' Conference of the Philippines (CBCP) met with PBS Board members, to request permission to use PBS translations for the Catholic Bible mandate in the Philippines. PBS was a willing partner in this new relationship, but expressed that the PBS translations were outdated and needed to be revised.[17] Coincidentally, Dr Nida was in the Philippines in 1963 to train the Philippine translation team on the new principles of dynamic translation.[18] PBS proposed a new translation, based on the new principles of Nida's dynamic translation.[19] On February 14, 1967, the historic partnership between CBCP and PBS commenced, as witnessed by Rev Fr Abbott and the PBS leadership. Through this partnership, PBS became one of the first Bible Societies to embark on a truly interconfessional cooperation worldwide.[20]

To respond to the need of new translations, a month-long intensive workshop was conducted in Baguio City, with Dr Nida as chief trainer and some UBS translation consultants. There were a hundred and twenty-five Asian partners in attendance, of which thirty-five were Filipinos, representing both the Catholic and Protestant communities.[21] Bible translation workshops were also held regionally to train local native speakers in the discipline of dynamic Bible translations. Participants were invited from the Philippine Council of Evangelical Churches (PCEC), National Council of Churches in the Philippines (NCCP), the Roman Catholic Church (RCC), and other denominations, provided that they were vouched for and recommended by their church leaders. (Such affirmation by church leaders is still required for those who are participating in current Bible translations.) Out of these intensive training workshops, individuals handpicked from the group of participants formed the translation teams for various language projects. Participants who

---

16. Eugene Nida and Charles Taber, *The Theory and Practice of Translation* (Leiden: E.J. Brill, 1982), 42.

17. Anne Kwantes, *Chapters in Philippine Church History* (Manila: OMF Literature, 2001), 475.

18. Bishop Daniel C. Arichea Jr. (PBS translation consultant), in discussion with the authors, February 3, 2016.

19. Kwantes, *Chapters in Philippine Church History*, 475.

20. Bishop Arichea, February 3, 2016.

21. Kwantes, *Chapters in Philippine Church History*, 476.

were not part of the main team comprised the external review committee that later read and evaluated the drafts of the team.

In 1968, through the leadership of Dr Daniel C. Arichea Jr., five translation teams were formed – the Tagalog, Cebuano, Hiligaynon, Ilokano, and Bikol. In 1971, teams for the Pangasinan, Pampango, and Samarenyo were organized. As a result, the Magandang Balita Biblia, or Meaning-Based Bibles (MBB), were later published in eight major languages: Tagalog (1980), Cebuano (1981), Hiligaynon (1982), Ilokano and Pangasinan (1983), Samarenyo (1985), Bicol (1992), and Pampango (1994).[22]

The Role of Interconfessional Work in Bible Translation

Throughout the years, using interconfessional cooperation in Bible translation, PBS has produced texts that are faithful to the original languages and can be easily understood by both novice and experienced Bible readers. Moreover, PBS has fostered a spirit of family, community, and camaraderie among the Filipino Christian communities from different denominational traditions.

Dealing with Doctrinal Biases

Interconfessional work in Bible translation is vital, for it allows the people, as represented by the members of the translation teams and review committees, to go back to the meaning of the text in the original languages and allow it to speak for itself. As part of an interconfessional team, a translator must come to terms with his or her own doctrinal presuppositions and be willing to let go of them in order to produce a community-based, faithful, and – as much as possible – unbiased translation. One of the main values of a UBS Bible translation is to provide a version that has no doctrinal comment, is faithful to the meaning of the original languages, and is not biased towards any denomination or religion.

To give an example, the following passages provide difficulty in translation because of various presuppositions from different faith groups. In the NRSV, Matthew 1:25 is translated: "but had no marital relations with her until she had borne a son; and he named him Jesus." The use of the conjunction/preposition "until" implies that after Mary bore a son, she and Joseph had marital relations. Catholics do not accept this, as they believe in Mary's perpetual virginity. In order to resolve this, the interconfessional translation groups followed the

---

22. Kwantes, 476.

Good News Translation (GNT) as a model: "But he had no sexual relations with her *before* she gave birth to her son. And Joseph named him Jesus." This allowed the different church traditions to interpret what happened after Jesus was born. The preposition *heos* (until or before) can be either of the two translations. On the other hand, the PBS Ilocano[23] translation reads, "*Ngem saanna a dinennaan ni Maria sakbay a nangipasngay iti anak a lalaki a pinanaganan ni Jose iti Jesus.*"[24] (But he did not have intimate relations with Mary while she was pregnant with the son whom Joseph named Jesus). *Sakbay* here can be translated "while" which, like the GNT, does not specify that Joseph and Mary had intimate relations after Mary's pregnancy. The interpretation is left to the reader.

Another difficult translation appears in Matthew 26:26–30, Mark 14:22–26, Luke 22:14–20, 1 Corinthians 11:23–25 (The Lord's Supper), where Jesus says, "This is my body" and "This is my blood." Non-Catholics and non-Lutherans interpret the bread and the drink as symbols of Christ's body and Christ's blood, and so some evangelical translators insist that the translation should be rendered as "symbol of my body," "symbol of my blood," because their translations were meaning-based anyway.[25] However, PBS translations retain the form of the original languages. For example, the Tagalog translation of Matthew 26:30 reads, "*Kunin ninyo ito at kainin. Ito ang aking katawan . . . Ito ang aking dugong ibinubuhos para sa kapatawaran . . .*"[26] (Take this and eat. This is my body . . . This is my blood that was poured out for forgiveness . . .). Whether the interpretation is symbolic or literal is left to the faith communities.

These examples reveal how the translation committee, under the guidance of an assigned translation consultant, developed a translation principle: where there is a problem with theological implications in a translation, the text should be translated literally and retain its ambiguity, so that the interpretation may be left to the churches.

A Place for Scholarly Dialogue

Through interconfessional cooperation in Bible translation, the team members, consisting of representatives from the major Christian traditions, are given

---

23. Ilocano is one of the Philippines' major languages.

24. Philippine Bible Society, *Naimbag Adamag Biblia* (Manila: Philippine Bible Society, 1996).

25. Bishop Arichea, February 3, 2016.

26. Philippine Bible Society, *Magandang Balita Biblia-Tagalog* (Manila: Philippine Bible Society, 2012).

the opportunity to discuss translation issues through committee meetings in the translation process. Each translator is provided with translator tools and other aids, such as the UBS Translators' Handbook[27] and a software package called Paratext, a software developed by the UBS and the Summer Institute of Linguistics (SIL).[28] Paratext includes several useful functions, such as the encoding and reviewing of drafts; real-time editing views; access to biblical source texts, selected model translations, the UBS Translator's Handbook, and other resources; and eases basic checks for biblical terms, proper names, etc.

Through intensive training, a UBS scholarship, translation tools, and the help of local translation consultants, translators are equipped to answer and face difficult translation questions and inquiries. As a team, they are encouraged to discuss difficult passages with each other and are required to come to a decision that minimizes the role played by their personal faith biases. This committee discussion allows for dialogue, but the aim is to complete the translation rather than prove who is wrong and who is right. Through this exchange, translators become more objective as they allow others to voice their opinions on neutral grounds.

A Community Effort

Through interconfessional cooperation, the process of Bible translation assures that the end product is a community output and not the work of one individual. One common reflection from PBS translation consultants is, "We do not entrust the quality of the translation to human beings, but we trust the process of translation to assure the quality and faithfulness of our work."

Each new translation goes through at least eight stages. After getting a list of assigned books, the translators produce the initial or *preliminary draft.* Then they review each other's work as part of the *internal review.* Based

---

27. The UBS Translators' Handbook is a consortium of detailed commentaries prepared by the United Bible Societies especially for translators. This series of books help the translators by providing them with the necessary exegetical, contextual, historical, and linguistic data to assist them in writing translations which are free from doctrinal bias.

28. "Paratext is a tool designed to help translators, exegetical advisors, translation consultants, project support staff produce quality translations from the point of view of both format and content. The program enables the translator to input a first or revised draft of the text and check and review that draft against the biblical source texts and a selection of model translations and resource materials in electronic format. The UBS Translation Handbook Series complement and enhance the resources of the major Bible versions included with Paratext. The Handbooks are detailed commentaries providing exegetical, historical, cultural, and linguistic information on the books of the Bible. They are prepared primarily to assist Bible translators" (UBS, January 20, 2016).

on the comments from their reviewers, they come up with a *revised draft*. The translators meet together as a committee to read the revised drafts and discuss any points of concern, and then produce the *committee draft*. The committee draft is checked by the translation consultant (TC), though a TC check can be done at any stage of translation. Based on the TC's comments, the committee creates a *revised committee draft*. This draft is sent to selected individuals outside the core translation team for *external review*. After taking all external comments into account, the team then produces the *final draft*, which undergoes *copyediting* to ensure the consistency, clarity, and completeness of the text.

Ownership of the Text Belongs to the Community

Interconfessional cooperation also makes sure that nobody has a monopoly on the translated text. God's Word is for all, and the PBS ministry assures that each Christian tradition is given equal opportunity to become part of the translation process and, at the same time, make God's Word accessible to their communities. PBS respects the canonical traditions of Christian communities, which means that PBS is committed to respond to the needs of the church, whether Catholic or Protestant.

Moreover, the Bible Society's policy is to leave out the names of the translators in the published edition. This protects individual translators from being bombarded with translation queries. While acknowledging the partnership, efforts, and time investment of translators, PBS takes full accountability for the translations it publishes and produces. As such, the ownership of the text belongs to the community of Christian believers rather than the translators or a particular church tradition.

Community Activities

Outside of the translation office, interconfessional cooperation is the work of the Bible Society as it engages the rest of the community.

May They Be One Bible Campaign

First launched on September 30, 2008, the *May They Be One (MTBO) Bible Campaign* is a nationwide endeavor that aims to put a Bible in every home and encourages Filipinos to read and live out the Word to transform the nation. The program is a response to the prayer of Christ for all God's children to "be one" (John 17:21), recognizing that the unity of Christ's Body is essential in making God's Word accessible and relevant to all. This same unity is needed in families, communities, and different sectors of society in working for national transformation. The goal is to raise sufficient funds for the printing and distribution of Bibles so that five million homes can be provided with a copy of the Word of God. About a fifth of the total number of Bibles to be printed are given away free at the discretion of affiliated local parish priests and pastors.

National Bible Week

The Philippines has been celebrating *National Bible Week (NBW)* every year, starting in 1982, with the signing of Proclamation No. 2242 by former president Ferdinand E. Marcos:

> Whereas, the Bible has been recognized by both Christians and Non-Christians alike as an excellent source of principles for the development of moral character and personal discipline; whereas, Christian churches throughout the country celebrate Bible Sunday every year to encourage the reading of the Holy Bible as an instrument to develop moral character, personal discipline, understanding and unity among our people.[29]

This proclamation was amended by former president Corazon C. Aquino in 1986 through Proclamation No. 44, which moved the date of the celebration from the first Sunday of Advent to the last week of January.[30] Later, former president Fidel V. Ramos reinforced the earlier proclamations through Proclamation No. 1067, which states that "it is fitting and proper that national attention be focused on the importance of reading and studying the Bible in molding the spiritual, moral, and social fiber of our citizenry."[31]

During this week-long celebration, churches come together and proclaim the year's Bible week theme in different ways: fun runs, parades, motorcades, *i-Proclaim* (continuous oral reading of chosen Scripture passages in public places, such as town plazas), and others. On National Bible Sunday, sermons

---

29. Philippine President, Proclamation No. 2242, s. 1982, "Declaring the Last Sunday of November as Bible Sunday and the Week Following as National Bible Week and Every Year Thereafter, *Official Gazette of the Republic of the Philippines* (Nov 19, 1982), http://www.officialgazette.gov.ph/1982/11/19/proclamation-no-2242-s-1982-2/.

30. Philippine President, Proclamation No. 44, s. 1986, "Amending Proclamation No. 2242," *Official Gazette of the Republic of the Philippines* (Nov 21, 1986), http://www.officialgazette.gov.ph/1986/11/21/proclamation-no-44-s-1986/.

31. Philippine President, Proclamation No. 1067, s. 1997, "Declaring the Last Week of January of Every Year as National Bible Week," *Official Gazette of the Republic of the Philippines* (Aug 26, 1997), http://www.officialgazette.gov.ph/1997/08/26/proclamation-no-1067-s-1997/.

and homilies across the nation focus on the role of the Bible in transforming people's lives.

Bible Relevance in Modern Times

The Bible Relevance in Modern Times Seminar (BRIMS) is an endeavor designed to equip local church leaders and workers across the nation, both Catholic and Protestant, to be more effective in their ministry by training them in various areas related to the Word of God. The seminar covers a range of topics, including hermeneutics, homiletics, ministering to children, *Dei Verbum*, among others, and is taught by respected Bible scholars.

Conclusion

As the need for new Bible translations and revisions in Philippine languages increases, interconfessional Bible translation work continues to serve as a nexus that brings together not only biblical scholars and linguistic experts from different branches of the Christian faith, but also the rest of their communities as one big family, which is the Filipino Christian church. May every effort be a step in response to the prayer of our Lord Jesus Christ in John 17:21, "I pray that they may all be one. Father! May they be in us, just as you are in me and I am in you. May they be one, so that the world will believe that you sent me" (GNT).[32]

---

32. The *Good News Translation* was first published as a full Bible in 1976 by the American Bible Society. The version was earlier called *Good News for Modern Man* (New Testament) and *Today's English Bible* (the complete Bible) later on. This version aims to present a biblical text that is clear in modern English and second-language English speakers, yet faithful to the original languages. It applies the principles of dynamic translation introduced by Eugene Nida.

Bibliography

Acolola, Gari. "Forced to Flee: How Many Have Been Displaced Due to Conflict?" *Rappler.com*, July 11, 2017. https://www.rappler.com/newsbreak/iq/175236-fast-facts-world-population-internally-displaced-persons-conflict.

Agyenta, Alfred. "When Reconciliation Means More than 'Re-Membering' of Former Enemies." *Ephemerides Theologicae Lovanienses* 83, no. 1 (2007): 123–134.

Aligan, Rodel E. *The Biblical and Folkloric Elements of the First Tagalog Pasyon*. Manila: UST Publishing House, 2001.

Allan, Kenneth. *Contemporary Social and Sociological Theory: Visualizing Social Worlds*. 2nd edition. Los Angeles: Sage, 2011.

Alter, Robert. *The Art of Biblical Narrative*. Revised edition. New York: Basic Books, 2010.

American Psychiatric Association. *Diagnostic and Statistical Manual of Mental Disorders*. 5th edition. Arlington, VA: American Psychiatric Publishing, 2013.

Amit, Yairah. *Reading Biblical Narratives*. Minneapolis, MN: Fortress Press, 2001.

Amos, Clare. "The Genesis of Reconciliation: The Reconciliation of Genesis." *Mission Studies* 23, no. 1 (2006): 9–26.

Anasarias, Ernesto A. "Children as Zones of Peace: Child Centered Organizing and Development in Conflict-Affected Communities in Pikit, North Cotabato." Master's thesis, University of the Philippines, 2008.

———. *Rebuilding Communities*. Quezon City, Phils: Balay Rehabilitation Center, 2005.

Andrews, Dave. *The Jihad of Jesus*. Eugene, OR: Wipf & Stock, 2015.

"Archbishop Urges Peace Building at Grassroots Level." *CBCP News*, Oct 10, 2012. http://www.cbcpnews.com/cbcpnews/?p=5342.

Aristotle. *Politics*. Translated by Benjamin Jowett. Kitchener: Batoche, 1999.

Ashmore, Richard D., Lee Jussim, and David Wilder, eds. *Social Identity, Intergroup Conflict, and Conflict Reduction*. Oxford: Oxford University Press, 2001.

Atkins, Thomas R., ed. *Graphic Violence on Screen*. New York: Simon & Schuster, 1976.

Augsburger, David. *Conflict Mediation across Cultures: Pathways and Patterns*. Louisville, KY: Westminster John Knox Press, 1992.

———. *Dissident Discipleship: A Spirituality of Self-Surrender, Love of God, and Love of Neighbor*. Grand Rapids: Brazos Press, 2006.

———. *Helping People Forgive*. Louisville, KY: Westminster John Knox Press, 1996.

Austin, Alexander, and N. Ropers, eds. *Berghof Handbook for Conflict Transformation*. Berlin: Berghof Research Center for Constructive Conflict Management, 2001.

The Australian Hymn Book: With Catholic Supplement. Sydney: Collins, 1977.

Balay Rehabilitation Center. "People's Declaration: GiNaPaLaDTaKa Space for Peace and Children as Zones of Peace [video]." https://balayph.net/multimedia/videos?start=8.

Barash, David P., and Charles Webel. *Peace and Conflict Studies*. Thousand Oaks, CA: Sage Publications, 2002.

Bar-Efrat, Shimon. *Narrative Art in the Bible*. Sheffield: Sheffield Academic Press, 1989, 1997.

Barnes, Catherine. "Democratizing Peacemaking Processes: Strategies and Dilemmas for Public Participation." *Accord* 13 (2002): 6–13.

Bartholow, Bruce D., and Craig A. Anderson. "Effects of Violent Video Games on Aggressive Behavior: Potential Sex Differences." *Journal of Experimental Social Psychology* 38, no. 3 (May 2002): 283–290.

Bartlett, John. *Bartlett's Familiar Quotations*. 14th edition. London: Macmillan, 1977.

Baudrillard, Jean. *The Transparency of Evil: Essay on Extreme Phenomena*. London: New Left, 1993.

Beardsley, Monroe. *Aesthetics*. New York: Harcourt Brace, 1958.

Berliner, Peter, Ernesto Anasarias, and Elena de Casas Soberón. "Religious Diversity as Peacebuilding: The Space for Peace." *Journal of Religion, Conflict, and Peace* 4, no. 1 (2010): 2–10.

Boff, Leonardo. *Saint Francis: A Model of Human Liberation*. Quezon City: Claretian, 1984.

Bok, Sissela. *Mayhem: Violence as Public Entertainment*. Boston: Addison-Wesley, 1998.

Boltanski, Luc. *Distant Suffering: Morality, Media and Politics*. Cambridge: Cambridge University Press, 1999.

Bonaventure. *The Life of St. Francis*. New York: HarperOne, 2005.

The Book of Alternative Services of the Anglican Church of Canada. Toronto: Anglican Book Centre, 1985.

The Book of Common Prayer. New York: Oxford University Press, 1990.

Book of Worship. Geelong: Reformed Churches Publishing House, 1990.

Bosch, David J. *Transforming Mission: Paradigm Shifts in Theology of Mission*. Maryknoll, NY: Orbis, 1991.

Boutros-Ghali, Boutros. "An Agenda for Peace: Preventive Diplomacy, Peacemaking and Peace-keeping: Report of the Secretary-General, 17 June 1992, United Nations." http://www.un-documents.net/a47-277.htm.

Braswell, Michael, John Fuller, and Bo Lozoff. *Corrections, Peacemaking, and Restorative Justice: Transforming Individuals and Institutions*. New York: Routledge, 2015.

Bruder, Margaret Ervin. "Aestheticizing Violence, or How to Do Things with Style." *Postmodern Discourses* (1998). http://www.gradnet.de/papers/pomo98.papers/mtbruder98.hhtm.

Brueggemann, Walter. *The Covenanted Self: Explorations in Law and Covenant*. Minneapolis: Fortress Press, 1999.

———. *Genesis*. Atlanta, GA: John Knox Press, 1982.

Buendia, Rizal G. "The Mindanao Conflict in the Philippines: Ethno-Religious War or Economic Conflict?" http://www.academia.edu/1433739/Mindanao_Conflict_in_the_Philippines_Ethno-Religious_War_or_Economic_Conflict.

Burgess, Guy, and Heidi Burgess, eds. *Beyond Intractability*. Boulder, CO: Conflict Information Consortium, University of Colorado, 2003. https://www.beyond intractability.org/essay/hierarchical_intervention_levels.

Burnham, Gracia. *In the Presence of My Enemies*. Wheaton, IL: Tyndale House, 2004.

Butigan, Ken, Mary Litell, and Louis Vitale. *Franciscan Nonviolence: Stories, Reflections, Principles, Practices, and Resources*. Las Vegas, NV: Pace e Bene, 2003.

Carroll, Noël. *Philosophy of Horror or Paradoxes of the Heart*. New York: Routledge, 1990.

Catechism of the Catholic Church. Manila: ECCCE, Word of Life Publications, 1994.

Celtic Daily Prayer: From the Northumbria Community. New York: HarperOne, 2002.

Celtic Daily Prayer, Book Two: Farther Up and Farther In. London: William Collins, 2015.

Chouliaraki, Lilie. *Spectatorship of Suffering*. London: Sage, 2006.

Claydon, David, ed. *A New Vision, A Renewed Heart, A Renewed Call (Vol. 2): Lausanne Occasional Papers*. Pasadena, CA: William Carey Library Books, 2005.

CNN Philippines. "Timeline: The Marawi Crisis." Last updated Oct 28, 2017. http://cnnphilippines.com/news/2017/05/24/marawi-crisis-timeline.html.

Coats, George W. *Genesis: with an Introduction to Narrative Literature*. Grand Rapids: Eerdmans, 1983.

Cobley, Paul, ed. *The Routledge Companion to Semiotics and Linguistics*. New York: Routledge, 2001.

Cohn, Robert L. "Narrative Structure and Canonical Perspective in Genesis." *JSOT* 25 (1983): 3–16.

Conciliation Resources. "History: Mindanao Conflict and the Moro Islamic Liberation Front." http://www.c-r.org/where-we-work/southeast-asia/history-mindanao-conflict-and-moro-islamic-liberation-front.

Conteh-Morgan, Earl. "Peacebuilding and Human Security: A Constructivist Perspective." *International Journal of Peace Studies* 10, no. 1 (2005): 69–86. http://www.gmu.edu/programs/icar/ijps/vol10_1/Conteh-Morgan_101IJPS.pdf.

Coronel-Ferrer, Miriam. "Civil Society Institutional Response: Peaceful Intervention to Resolve Armed Conflicts." *Policy Notes* 3 (2006): 1–10.

———. *Framework and Synthesis of Lessons Learned in Civil-Society Peacebuilding*. Quezon City: UP Center for Integrative and Development Studies in partnership with the United Nations Development Programme, 2005.

Crosby, Michael H. *Finding Francis, Following Christ*. Maryknoll, NY: Orbis, 2007.

Dallaire, Romeo. *Shake Hands with the Devil: The Failure of Humanity in Rwanda*. Toronto: Random House Canada, 2003.

De Guzman, Judith M., and Charlie Inzon. "Shared and Contested Meaning in the Mindanao Conflict: Exploring People's Understanding of Bangsamoro." *Philippine Journal of Psychology* 44, no. 1 (2011).

Delio, Ilia. *Franciscan Prayer*. Cincinnati, OH: St. Anthony Messenger Press, 2004.

Dickie, George. *Art and the Aesthetic: An Institutional Analysis*. Ithaca, NY: Cornell University, 1974.

———. *The Art Circle*. New York: Haven, 1984.

Drisko, James W., and Tina Maschi. *Content Analysis: Pocket Guide to Social Work Research* Methods. New York: Oxford University Press, 2016.

Dymock, Darryl. *A Sweet Use of Adversity*. Armidale: University of New England Press, 1995.

Ebojo, Edgar. *Light to the Nations*. Manila: Philippine Bible Society, 2015.

Engelhardt, Christopher R., Micah O. Mazurek, Jospeh Hilgard, Jeffery N. Rouder, and Bruce D. Bartholow. "Effects of Violent Video Game Exposure on Aggressive Behavior, Aggressive-Thought Accessibility, and Aggressive Affect among Adults with and without Autism Spectrum Disorder." *Psychological Science* 26, no. 8 (August 2015): 1187–1200.

Evans, Keith, Sam Stockley, Calvin Taylor, Julie Brown, Maryam Rab, Sumbul Khan. *Cultural and Creative Industries in Pakistan*. London: British Council, 2004.

Fass, David. "Jacob's Limp." *Judaism* 38 (1989): 143–150.

Ferrer, Oscar P. "Community Governance: Understanding Community Processes and Initiatives: Four Case Studies on Local Initiatives in Public Administration and Governance." PhD dissertation, University of the Philippines, 2006.

Francis of Assisi. *Francis and Clare: The Complete Works*. New York: Paulist Press, 1982.

Franks, Anne, and John Meteyard. "Liminality: The Transforming Grace of In-Between Places." *The Journal of Pastoral Care and Counseling* 6, no. 3 (Fall 2007): 215–222.

Freedman, D. N., J. R. Lundbom, and H. J. Fabry. "*ḥānan*." In *TDOT* 5:24.

Gadamer, Hans-Georg. *Truth and Method*. 2nd edition. London: Sheed & Ward, 1993.

Galli, Mario von. *Living Our Future: Francis Assisi and the Church Tomorrow*. Chicago: Franciscan Herald Press, 1972.

Galtung, Johan, ed. *Peace, War and Defense: Essays in Peace Research, vol. 2*. Copenhagen: Christian Ejlers, 1976.

Gaspar, Karl, Elpidio A. Lapad, and Ailynne J. Maravillas. *Mapagkamalinawon: A Reader for the Mindanawon Peace Advocate*. Davao City: Alternate Forum for Research in Mindanao and Catholic Relief Services, 2002.

GMA News. "FAQs about the Bangsamoro Basic Law." Sept 10, 2014. http://www.gmanetwork.com/news/news/nation/378530/faqs-about-the-bangsamoro-basic-law/story/.

Gomez, Hilario, Jr. *The Moro Rebellion and the Search for Peace: A Study on Christian-Muslim Relations in the Philippines*. Zamboanga City, Phils: Silsilah Publications, 2000.

Gorospe, Athena. *Narrative and Identity: An Ethical Reading of Exodus* 4. Leiden: Brill, 2007.

————. "Old Testament Narratives in Context: Moses' Reverse Migration and a Hermeneutics of Possibility." In *The Gospel in Culture: Contextualization Issues through Asian Eyes*, edited by Melba Padilla Maggay. Mandaluyong: OMF Literature, 2013.

Granot, Hayim. "Jacob and the Angel: Terror and Divine Providence." *JBQ* 40 (2012): 125–127.

Grootaert, Christiaan, and Thierry van Bastelaer, eds. *Understanding and Measuring Social Capital: Multidisciplinary Tools for Practitioners*. Washington, DC: The World Bank, 2002.

Guetzkow, Joshua. *How the Arts Impact Communities: An Introduction to the Literature on Arts Impact Studies*. Princeton: Princeton University, 2002.

Hahn, Thich Nhat. *True Love: A Practice for Awakening the Heart*. Boston: Shambhala Publications, 1997.

Hall, Douglas John. *The Stewardship of Life in the Kingdom of Death*. Grand Rapids: Eerdmans, 1992.

Hamilton, Victor P. *The Book of Genesis*. Grand Rapids: Eerdmans, 1995.

Hancock, Landon E., and Christopher Mitchell, eds. *Zones of Peace*. Bloomfield, CT: Kumarian Press, 2007.

Helmick, Raymond G., and Rodney L. Petersen, eds. *Forgiveness and Reconciliation: Religion, Public Policy, and Conflict Transformation*. West Conshohocken, PA: Templeton Foundation Press, 2002.

Herman, Judith L. *Trauma and Recovery: The Aftermath of Violence – From Domestic Abuse to Political Terror*. Philadelphia: Basic Books, 2015.

Horan, Daniel P. *The Franciscan Heart of Thomas Merton*. Notre Dame: Ava Maria Press, 2014.

Ignatieff, Michael. *The Needs of Strangers*. New York: Picador, 2001.

International Committee of the Red Cross. "Philippines: Moving on in Zamboanga." November 30, 2015. https://www.icrc.org/en/document/philippines-moving-zamboanga.

Iyer, Pushpa. "Peace Zones of Mindanao, Philippines: Civil Society Efforts to End Violence." Case study, CDA Collaborative Learning Projects, 2004. http://cdacollaborative.org/wordpress/wp-content/uploads/2016/01/Peace-Zones-of-Mindanao-Philippines-Civil-Society-Efforts-to-End-Violence.pdf.

Jaafar, Ghazali B. "Peacetalk: This Bangsamoro Basic Law Is Our New Formula for the Very Elusive Peace in Mindanao." *MindaNews*, July 22, 2017. http://www.mindanews.com/mindaviews/2017/07/peacetalk-this-bangsamoro-basic-law-is-our-new-formula-for-the-very-elusive-peace-in-mindanao/.

Javellana, Rene B. "The Sources of Gaspar Aquino de Belen's Pasyon." *Philippine Studies* 32 (1984): 305–321.

Jegen, Mary Evelyn. *Just Peacemakers: An Introduction to Peace and Justice*. New York: Paulist Press, 2006.

Johansen, Jorgen Dines, and Svend Erik. *Signs in Use: Introduction to Semiotics*. New York: Routledge, 2002.

Johnston, Patricia, ed. *Seeing High and Low: Presenting Social Conflict in American Visual Culture*. Berkeley: University of California, 2006.

Jorgenson, Jorgen. *Saint Francis of Assisi: A Biography*. New York: Longmans, Green & Co., 1913.

Kagsabuwa Inc. and German Development Service (DED). *Batasan Adansil: Customary Laws of the Higaonon Tribe in Iligan City*. Intellectual Property of the Higa-onon Tribe of Iligan City, n.d.

Kalantzis, George. *Caesar and the Lamb: Early Christian Attitudes on War and Military Service*. Eugene, OR: Cascade Books, 2012.

Kaufman, Stuart. "Symbolic Politics and Ethnic War in the Philippines." Lecture presented at the International Studies Association 48th Annual Convention, Chicago, IL, March 2007.

Kidner, Derek. *Genesis*. Downers Grove, IL: InterVarsity Press, 1967.

Kirk, Alan. "Love Your Enemies, The Golden Rule and Ancient Reciprocity (Luke 6:27–35)." *JBL* 122 no. 4 (2003): 667–686.

Knight, Henry F. "Meeting Jacob at Jabbok: Wrestling with a Text – A Midrash on Genesis 32:22–32." *JES* 29 (1992): 451–460.

Kwantes, Anne. *Chapters in Philippine Church History*. Manila: OMF Literature, 2001.

The Lausanne Movement. "The Cape Town Commitment: A Confession of Faith and a Call to Action." 2011. https://www.lausanne.org/content/ctc/ctcommitment.

Layson, Roberto C. "Peacetalk: It's Because We Are Different That We Have So Much to Share." *MindaNews*, 9 June 2014. http://www.mindanews.com/mindaviews/2014/06/peacetalk-its-because-we-are-different-that-we-have-so-much-to-share/.

Lederach, John Paul. *Building Peace: Sustainable Reconciliation in Divided Societies*. Washington, DC: United States Institute of Peace Press, 1997.

Ledesma, Antonio J. *Panagtagbo sa Kalinaw: A Basic Orientation Manual Towards a Culture of Peace for Mindanao Communities*. Manila: UNICEF, 1998.

Levin, Schneir. "Jacob's Limp." *Judaism* 44 (1995): 325–327.

Levinas, Emmanuel. "Ethics and Infinity." *Cross Currents* 34, no. 2 (1984): 191–203.

———. *Humanism of the Other*. Chicago: University of Illinois Press, 2006.

———. *Otherwise Than Being*. Translated by Alfonso Lingis. Dordrecht: Kluwer Academic Publishers, 1991.

———. *Totality and Infinity: An Essay on Exteriority*. Translated by Alphonso Lingis. Boston: Martinus Nijhoff Publishers, 1979.

Liechty, Daniel, ed. *Early Anabaptist Spirituality: Selected Writings*. New York: Paulist Press, 1994.

Linn, Dennis, Sheila Fabricant Linn, and Matthew Linn. *Don't Forgive Too Soon: Extending the Two Hands That Heal*. New York: Paulist Press, 1997.

Lisbon, Monique. *Fragments of Home*. Melbourne: Braidwood Press, 2008.

Lund, Jerome A. "On the Interpretation of the Palestinian Targumic Reading of WQHT in Gen 32:25." *JBL* 105 (1986): 99–103.

Maggay, Melba Padilla, ed. *The Gospel in Culture: Contextualization Issues through Asian Eyes*. Mandaluyong: OMF Literature, 2013.

Manalo, Fermin, Jr. "Community Development Animating Peacebuilding from Below: The Case of GiNaPaLadTaKa Space for Peace in Pikit, North Cotobato." *Philippine Journal of Social Development* 15 (2013): 112–142.

Mann, Thomas. *The Book of the Torah: The Narrative Integrity of the Pentateuch*. Atlanta, GA: John Knox Press, 1988.

Martens, Paul, Matthew Porter, and Myles Werntz, eds. *Nonviolence: A Brief History*. Waco: Baylor University Press, 2010.

Martin, Ralph P. *Reconciliation: A Study of Paul's Theology*. London: Marshall, Morgan & Scott, 1981.

May, Rollo. *Power and Innocence: A Search for the Sources of Violence*. New York: Norton & Company, 1972.

McKay, Heather. "Jacob Makes It across the Jabbok: An Attempt to Solve the Success/Failure Ambivalence in Israel's Self-Consciousness." *JSOT* 38 (1997): 3–13.

McKenzie, Steve. "You Have Prevailed: The Function of Jacob's Encounter at Peniel in the Jacob Cycle." *RQ* 23, no. 4 (1980): 225–231.

McKeon, Celia. *From the Ground Up: Exploring Dichotomies in Grassroots Peacebuilding*. UK Conciliation Resources, 2003. http://www.c-r.org/downloads/FromTheGroundUp_200310_ENG.pdf.

Medina, Andrei. "Timeline: Crisis in Zamboanga City." September 10, 2013. http://www.gmanetwork.com/news/news/regions/325855/timeline-crisis-in-zamboanga-city/story/.

Molito, Alvin. "From Jacob to 'Israel,' Transformation Through Divine Confrontation: Narrative, Ritual, and Etiological Analysis of Genesis 32:23–33." Master's thesis, Asian Theological Seminary, 2015.

———. "Transformation in the Context of Divine-Human Confrontation: A Narrative Reading of Genesis 32–33." *Phronesis* 17–20 (2010–2013): 111–130.

Munayer, Salim. *Musalaha: A Curriculum of Reconciliation*. Jerusalem: Musalaha Ministry of Reconciliation, 2011, 2014.

Munayer, Salim, and Lisa Loden. *Through My Enemy's Eyes*. Milton Keynes, UK: Paternoster, 2014.

Murray, John B. "Psychological Profile of Pedophiles and Child Molesters." *The Journal of Psychology* 132, no. 2 (2000): 211–224.

Murray, Stuart. *The Naked Anabaptist: The Bare Essentials of a Radical Faith*. Scottdale, PA: Herald Press, 2010.

National Disaster Risk Reduction and Management Council (NDRRMC). "Situational Report re Emergency Management for the Displaced Persons Resulting from Armed Conflict in Zamboanga City and Basilan Province." Sept 25, 2013, 2–3. http://www.ndrrmc.gov.ph/attachments/article/2655/Emergency_Management_for_the_Displaced_Person_Resulting_from_Armed_Conflict_in_Zamboanga_City_and_Basilan_Province_as_of_25SEP2013_0800H.pdf.

Newbigin, Lesslie. *The Gospel in a Pluralist Society.* Grand Rapids: Eerdmans, 1989.

Nida, Eugene, and Charles Taber. *The Theory and Practice of Translation.* Leiden: Brill, 1982.

O'Brien, David J., and Thomas A. Shannon, eds. *Catholic Social Thought: The Documentary Heritage.* Maryknoll, NY: Orbis, 1992.

O'Brien, P. T. *The Letter to the Ephesians.* Grand Rapids: Eerdmans; Leicester: Apollos, 1999.

Oda, Hiroshi. "Peacebuilding from Below: Theoretical and Methodological Considerations Toward an Anthropological Study on Peace." *Journal of the Graduate School of Letters* 2, no. 1 (2007): 1–16. http://eprints.lib.hokudai.ac.jp/dspace/bitstream/2115/20475/1/ODA.pdf.

Omar, Irfan A., and Michael K. Duffy. *Peacemaking and the Challenge of Violence in World Religions.* Oxford: Wiley Blackwell, 2015.

Oropeza, B. J. "Apostasy in the Wilderness: Paul's Message in the Corinthians in Eschatological Liminality." *JSNT* 75 (1999): 74–75.

Paredes, Oona. *A Mountain of Difference: The Lumad in Early Colonial Mindanao.* New York: Cornell University, 2013.

Philippine Bible Society. *A Brief History of the Bible Movement in the Philippines.* Manila: Philippine Bible Society, 1984.

———. *Magandang Balita Biblia-Tagalog.* Manila: Philippine Bible Society, 2012.

———. *Naimbag Adamag Biblia.* Manila: Philippine Bible Society, 1996.

Philippine President, Proclamation No. 44, s. 1986. "Amending Proclamation No. 2242." *Official Gazette of the Republic of the Philippines* (Nov 21, 1986). http://www.officialgazette.gov.ph/1986/11/21/proclamation-no-44-s-1986/.

———. Proclamation No. 2242, s. 1982. "Declaring the Last Sunday of November as Bible Sunday and the Week Following as National Bible Week and Every Year Thereafter." *Official Gazette of the Republic of the Philippines* (Nov 19, 1982). http://www.officialgazette.gov.ph/1982/11/19/proclamation-no-2242-s-1982-2/.

———. Proclamation No. 1067, s. 1997. "Declaring the Last Week of January of Every Year as National Bible Week." *Official Gazette of the Republic of the Philippines* (Aug 26, 1997). http://www.officialgazette.gov.ph/1997/08/26/proclamation-no-1067-s-1997/.

Philippines, Republic of the. "Republic Act 8371: The Indigenous Peoples Rights Act (IPRA) of 1997." http://www.lawphil.net/statutes/repacts/ra1997/ra_8371_1997.html.

Picardal, Amado L. "Christian-Muslim Dialogue in Mindanao." *Asian Christian Review* 2 (2008): 54–72. http://www.asianchristianreview.org/acr_pdf/acr_pdf_0202-03_08picardal.pdf.

Plato. *The Portable Plato*. Edited by Scott Buchanan. New York: Penguin, 1976.

Pobre, Cesar, and Raymund Quilop, eds. *In Assertion of Sovereignty, vol. 1: The 2000 Campaign Against the MILF*. Quezon City: Office of Strategic and Special Studies, Armed Forces of the Philippines, 2008. https://www.academia.edu/184241/In_Assertion_of_Sovereignty_The_2000_Campaign_Against_the_MILF.

Postman, Neil. *Amusing Ourselves to Death: Public Discourse in the Age of Show Business*. London: Penguin, 1986.

Press, Gunther. *Multimodality: A Social Semiotic Approach to Contemporary Communication*. New York: Routledge, 2010.

Ramsbotham, Oliver, Tom Woodhouse, and Hugh Miall. *Contemporary Conflict Resolution: The Prevention, Management and Transformation of Deadly Conflicts*. Cambridge, UK: Polity Press, 2011.

Ringma, Charles. "Contemplation in a World of Action." https://www.northumbria community.org/wp-content/uploads/2015/06/Contemplation-in-a-World-of-Action.pdf.

———. *Gadamer's Dialogical Hermeneutics*. Heidelberg: Universitätsverlag C. Winter, 1999.

———. *Resist the Powers with Jacques Ellul*. Vancouver: Regent College Publishing, 2009.

"Rio Hondo." City Government of Zamboanga. http://www.zamboanga.gov.ph/index.php?option=com_content&view=article&id=396:rio-hondo&catid=1313:political-boundaries&Itemid=326.

"Rio Hondo: The Other Face of Zamboanga City." *Love Mindanao*. March 2013. http://www.lovemindanao.com/2013/03/RioHondo.html.

"Rio Hondo, Zamboanga City, Philippines." www.zamboanga.com. http://www.zamboanga.com/z/index.php?title=Rio_Hondo_Zamboanga_City_Philippines.

Rivera, Elena Zarco. "Christ in the Tagalog Pasyon." Master's thesis, University of the Philippines, 1976.

Roberts, Gregory. "It's Our Humanity That Dies in an Execution." *Sydney Morning Herald*, August 14, 2003.

Robertson, Edwin. *Taking the Word to the World: 50 Years of the United Bible Societies*. Nashville: Thomas Nelson Publishers, 1986.

Rohr, Richard. "Transforming Our Pain." Center for Action and Contemplation, Feb 26, 2016. https://cac.org/transforming-our-pain-2016-02-26/.

Rudolfsson, Lisa, and Inga Tidefors. "I Have Cried to Him a Thousand Times, But It Makes No Difference: Sexual Abuse, Faith, and Images of God." *Mental Health, Religion & Culture* 17, no. 9 (2014): 910–922. http://dx.doi.org/10.1080/136746 76.2014.950953.

Santos, Soliman M. *Peace Zones in the Philippines: Concept, Policy, and Instruments.* Quezon City: Gaston Z. Ortigas Peace Institute, 2005.

Schlegal, Stewart. *Tiruray Justice: Traditional Tiruray Law and Morality.* London: University of California Press, 1970.

———. *Wisdom from a Rainforest: The Spiritual Journey of an Anthropologist.* Manila: Ateneo de Manila University Press, 1999.

Schmidt, Nathaniel. "The Numen of Penuel." *JBL* 45 (1926): 260–279.

The Secretariat for Christian Unity and the United Bible Societies. "Guidelines for Interconfessional Cooperation in Translating the Bible." Vatican City, 1987. http://www.vatican.va/roman_curia/pontifical_councils/chrstuni/general-docs/rc_pc_chrstuni_doc_19871116_guidelines-bible_en.html.

Short, Rendle. *The Bible and Modern Medicine.* London: Paternoster Press, 1953.

Short, William J. *Poverty and Joy: The Franciscan Tradition.* Maryknoll, NY: Orbis, 1999.

Simons, Jeremy. "Guardians of the Sacred Oil and Comb: Towards an Understanding of Talaandig Spirituality, Cosmology, and Peace Practices." Unpublished manuscript, 2010.

Skrabalo, Marina. "Documenting the Impact of Community Peacebuilding Practices in the Post Yugoslav Region as a Basis for Policy Framework Development." Project paper, Centre for Peace Studies, Zagreb, Croatia, 2003. http://www.policy.hu/skrabalo/rp.html.

Smedes, Lewis B. *The Art of Forgiving: When You Need to Forgive and Don't Know How.* Milton Keynes, UK: Summit Publishing, 1996.

A Sourcebook on Alternatives to Formal Dispute Resolution Mechanisms. Manila: National Judicial Institute, 2008.

Stassen, Glen H., Mark Thiessen Nation, and Matt Hamsher, eds. *The War of the Lamb: The Ethics of Nonviolence and Peacemaking.* Grand Rapids: Brazos Press, 2009.

Stevens, Krista. "The Beauty of Abu Ghraib: Art Transforming Violence." *ARTS* 23, no. 3 (2012): 4–10, 37.

Steward, Desmond. *The Monks of War: The Military Orders.* London: The Folio Society, 2000.

Steward, John. *From Genocide to Generosity: Hatreds Heal on Rwanda's Hills.* Carlisle: Langham Global Library, 2015.

Stott, John R. W., ed. *Making Christ Known: Historic Mission Documents from the Lausanne Movement, 1974–1989.* Grand Rapids: Eerdmans, 1996.

"Striving for a Just Peace, the Moral Road." *CBCP News,* July 11, 2015. http://www.cbcpnews.com/cbcpnews/?p=59874.

Together in Song: Australian Hymn Book II. East Melbourne: Harper Collins Religious, 1999.

Tomlinson, John. *Globalization and Culture.* London: Sage, 1999.

Tuazon, Bobby M., ed. *The Moro Reader: History and Contemporary Struggles of the Bangsamoro People.* Diliman, Quezon City: Policy Study Publication and

Advocacy, Center for People Empowerment in Governance in partnership with Light a Candle Movement for Social Change, 2008.

Turner, Victor. *Forest of Symbols: Aspects of Ndembu Ritual*. Ithaca, NY: Cornell University Press, 1967.

———. *Ritual Process: Structure and Anti-Structure*. New York: Cornell University Press, 1991.

United Nations Trust Fund for Human Security (UNTFHS). *Human Security in Theory and Practice*. New York: UNTFHS, 2009.

United Nations High Commissioner for Refugees (UNHCR). "UNHCR Guiding Principles on Internal Displacement." http://www.unhcr.org/protection/idps/43ce1cff2/guiding-principles-internal-displacement.html.

"US Missionary Killed in the Philippines." *Bible Doctrine News*. http://www.biblenews1.com/history2/20020607.htm.

Van Gennep, Arnold. *The Rites of Passage*. Translated by Monika B. Vizedom and Gabrielle L. Caffee. Chicago: University of Chicago Press, 1960.

Vatican Council. *Dei Verbum: Dogmatic Constitution on Divine Revelation*. Proclaimed by Pope Paul VI on November 18, 1965, no. 22. http://www.vatican.va/archive/hist_councils/ii_vatican_council/documents/vat-ii_const_19651118_dei-verbum_en.html.

Vatican Council. *Nostra Aetate: Declaration on the Relation of the Church to Non-Christian Religions*. Proclaimed by Pope Paul VI on October 28, 1965, nos. 1 and 3. http://www.vatican.va/archive/hist_councils/ii_vatican_council/documents/vat-ii_decl_19651028_nostra-aetate_en.html.

Victor, Mr. "Causes of Conflict between Christians and Muslims in the Philippines, Part 1." July 4, 2005. http://www.iiipeace.org/Philippines%20Causes%20of%20Conflict%20between%20Christians%20and%20Muslims.htm.

Vitug, Marites D., and Glenda M. Gloria. *Under the Crescent Moon: Rebellion in Mindanao*. Quezon City: Ateneo Center for Social Policy and Public Affairs, 2000.

Voiss, James. *Rethinking Christian Forgiveness: Theological, Philosophical, and Psychological Explorations*. Collegeville, MN: Liturgical Press, 2015.

Volf, Miroslav. *Exclusion and Embrace: A Theological Exploration of Identity, Otherness, and Reconciliation*. Nashville: Abingdon, 1996.

Voltaire. *Candide and Other Stories*. Translated by Roger Pearson. Oxford: Oxford University, 2006.

Von Rad, Gerhard. *Genesis: A Commentary*. Philadelphia, PA: Westminster Press, 1972.

"Von Weizsäckers berühmte Rede vom 8. Mai 1985." *Welt*, January 1, 2015, https://www.welt.de/politik/deutschland/article136982300/Von-Weizsaeckers-beruehmte-Rede-vom-8-Mai-1985.html.

Walsh, Jerome T. *Style and Structure in Biblical Hebrew Narrative*. Collegeville, MN: Liturgical Press, 2001.

Webel, C. P., and J. Johansen, eds. *Peace and Conflict Studies: A Reader*. London: Routledge, 2012.

Wenham, Gordon. *Genesis 16–50*. Dallas, TX: Word Books, 1994.

"What Went Before: The MNLF Siege of Zamboanga City," *Philippine Daily Inquirer*, Sept 8, 2014, http://newsinfo.inquirer.net/635995/what-went-before-the-mnlf-siege-of-zamboanga-city.

Wolterstorff, Nicholas. *Justice: Rights and Wrongs*. Princeton, NJ: Princeton University Press, 2008.

Yoder, Carolyn. *The Little Book of Trauma Healing*. Intercourse, PA: Good Books, 2005.

About the Editors and Contributors

Athena E. Gorospe teaches in the areas of Old Testament, Hebrew Language, and Theology at Asian Theological Seminary in Manila, Philippines, where she is also Program Director for the newly launched PhD in Contextual Theology. She has published articles from the biblical perspective on various social issues. Athena graduated from Fuller Theological Seminary in Pasadena, California, USA, with a PhD in Theology (Old Testament concentration). She is the author of *Narrative and Identity: An Ethical Reading of Exodus 4* (Leiden: Brill, 2007) and *Judges* for the Asia Bible Commentary Series (Carlisle: Langham Global Library, 2016).

Ronaldo Magpayo is the pastor of Sumapa Christian Church in Malolos, Bulacan. He completed his MDiv in Biblical Studies at Asian Theological Seminary (ATS) and received his ThM in Theological Studies at Asia Graduate School of Theology, Philippines. He is a faculty member of Penuel School of Theology and a visiting professor of the Theology Department at ATS.

Annabel M. Manalo is Associate Professor, Chair of the Counseling Department, and Director of the Counseling Center at Asian Theological Seminary. She heads its Psychosocial Support Training Program. She completed her AB at the University of the Philippines Diliman, MA in Christian Leadership at ATS, and MA in Counseling Psychology and PhD in Clinical Psychology at the Ateneo de Manila University. She is a licensed psychologist and a certified clinical, counseling, and assessment psychologist.

Fermin P. Manalod Jr. is an Assistant Professor at the University of the Philippines College of Social Work and Community Development and Center for International Studies. He is a visiting faculty of the Transformational Urban Leadership program at Asian Theological Seminary.

Glicerio (Jojo) Manzano Jr., DMiss, served as a missionary in Nepal with International Nepal Fellowship before serving with OMF International as General Secretary of the Philippine Home Council of OMFI. He is a graduate of Laidlaw College, New Zealand; Australian College of Theology, Sydney; and Asia Graduate School of Theology (AGST), Philippines. He is currently an Adjunct Professor at Asian Theological Seminary Intercultural and Urban Studies Department, which he formerly chaired before he retired. He is also the Director of the Doctor of Intercultural Studies Program of AGST-Philippines.

Christine Joy N. Martinez is the Translation Supervisor of the Philippine Bible Society, currently on study leave to finish her PhD in Biblical Theology at the Ateneo de Manila University's Loyola School of Theology. She finished her MDiv in Biblical Studies with honors at Asian Theological Seminary and completed her undergraduate degree in Linguistics at the University of the Philippines, Diliman.

Tricia Mazo is a licensed social worker with over twenty years of experience. She is a graduate of ATS with a degree in Master of Arts in Pastoral Counseling. She worked as a social welfare specialist and program developer with the Department of Social Welfare and Development and was the program manager of the Institute in Basic Life Principles, a Christian ministry in Manila, where she journeyed with girls and boys who were abused, abandoned, and exploited. She is currently the Protection Specialist for Middle East Response of Tearfund UK.

Alvin M. Molito completed his BA in Theology at the Philippine Missionary Institute and his MDiv in Biblical Studies at ATS. He works as a translator of the Philippine Bible Society, as visiting faculty of ATS and Penuel School of Theology, and as pastor of the Community Baptist Church in Las Piñas City.

Salim J. Munayer is executive director and founder of Musalaha Ministry of Reconciliation, which has been bringing Israelis and Palestinians together since 1990 and creating a forum for reconciliation. Salim is a Palestinian-Israeli born in Lod, and received his BA from Tel Aviv University in History and Geography, his MA from Fuller Theological Seminary, and his PhD from the Oxford Center of Mission Studies, UK. He also did graduate studies in New Testament at Pepperdine University. He has published books on reconciliation, the Israeli-Palestinian conflict, and Christians in Israel and the Palestinian Authority. His most recent work is *Through My Enemy's Eyes: Envisioning Reconciliation in Israel-Palestine* (Milton Keynes: Paternoster, 2014) co-authored with Lisa Loden. Salim served as academic dean and professor at Bethlehem Bible College from 1989 to 2008. He is adjunct professor at Fuller Theological Seminary and The Hebrew University of Jerusalem.

Takamitsu Muraoka was born in Hiroshima in 1938. He has a BA in English, an MA in linguistics from Tokyo Kyoiku University, and a PhD in Hebrew from The Hebrew University in Jerusalem. He was Professor of Hebrew at the Leiden University, The Netherlands, for more than ten years before retirement. Previously, he was Lecturer in Semitic Languages at Manchester University, UK, and Professor in Middle Eastern Studies, Melbourne University, Australia. In 2017, he was awarded the British Academy's Burkitt Medal for Hebrew Bible studies, in recognition of his outstanding contribution to the study of Hebrew grammar and syntax and the Septuagint.

Leizl S. Ocampo is a copyeditor for the Philippine Bible Society. She completed her degree in Linguistics as Summa Cum Laude from the University of the Philippines, Diliman.

John Robert Rances received his BA from Presbyterian Theological Seminary. He is currently an MA Theology student at ATS and adjunct faculty at Penuel School of Theology. He is the Resident Pastor of Jesus Cares Church, a member of the Presbyterian Churches of the Philippines.

Charles Ringma completed his theological training at the Reformed Theological College in Geelong, Australia. For the next twenty years, he worked in urban missions. After further training, he worked as a senior researcher in the social sciences and went on to complete his PhD in Philosophical Hermeneutics at The University of Queensland. Dr Ringma later taught at ATS and at Regent College in Vancouver, Canada. He is presently Emeritus Professor, Regent College, and Honorary Research Associate Professor, School of Historical and Philosophical Inquiry, The University of Queensland, Brisbane.

Jeremy Simons previously worked in public schools and community-based restorative justice advocacy in Denver, Colorado. After this, he lived in Mindanao for nearly ten years, where he engaged government, civil society, church, and academe as a peacebuilding consultant. He has taught conflict transformation, restorative justice, and appreciative inquiry in universities and non-governmental organizations in the Philippines and across Asia. He also co-edited a publication on transitional justice for the Bangsamoro peace process and has essays published in a variety of news publications. He is currently in New Zealand conducting doctoral research on indigenous peace and restorative justice traditions.

John Steward gained his PhD from Adelaide University after completing his honors degree in Agriculture. He received his BD (Hons) from the Melbourne College of Divinity. He then taught theology and agriculture before joining World Vision in Jakarta to create a training center for village development motivators and to facilitate adult learning for indigenous World Vision community workers from fifty countries. In 1997, John became involved in post-genocide reconstruction in Rwanda. For nine years, he revisited Rwanda every six months to mentor Rwandan peacemakers. His book, *From Genocide to Generosity* (Carlisle: Langham Global Library, 2015), which contains stories of healing and hope after trauma, is now accompanied by an online study guide, *To Live Well*. In Melbourne, John is a Spiritual Director with the Living Well Centre and is a member of Wellspring.

Christopher Wright is the International Ministries Director of Langham Partnership, which provides literature, scholarships, and preaching training for Majority World pastors and seminaries. He taught in India for five years. His books include *Old Testament Ethics for the People of God*; *The Mission of God*; *The God I Don't Understand*; and *The Mission of God's People*. Chris and family live in London and are members of All Souls Church, Langham Place.

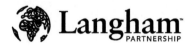

Langham Literature, with its publishing work, is a ministry of Langham Partnership.

Langham Partnership is a global fellowship working in pursuit of the vision God entrusted to its founder John Stott –

to facilitate the growth of the church in maturity and Christ-likeness through raising the standards of biblical preaching and teaching.

Our vision is to see churches in the majority world equipped for mission and growing to maturity in Christ through the ministry of pastors and leaders who believe, teach and live by the Word of God.

Our mission is to strengthen the ministry of the Word of God through:
- nurturing national movements for biblical preaching
- fostering the creation and distribution of evangelical literature
- enhancing evangelical theological education

especially in countries where churches are under-resourced.

Our ministry

Langham Preaching partners with national leaders to nurture indigenous biblical preaching movements for pastors and lay preachers all around the world. With the support of a team of trainers from many countries, a multi-level programme of seminars provides practical training, and is followed by a programme for training local facilitators. Local preachers' groups and national and regional networks ensure continuity and ongoing development, seeking to build vigorous movements committed to Bible exposition.

Langham Literature provides majority world preachers, scholars and seminary libraries with evangelical books and electronic resources through publishing and distribution, grants and discounts. The programme also fosters the creation of indigenous evangelical books in many languages, through writer's grants, strengthening local evangelical publishing houses, and investment in major regional literature projects, such as one volume Bible commentaries like the *Africa Bible Commentary* and the *South Asia Bible Commentary*.

Langham Scholars provides financial support for evangelical doctoral students from the majority world so that, when they return home, they may train pastors and other Christian leaders with sound, biblical and theological teaching. This programme equips those who equip others. Langham Scholars also works in partnership with majority world seminaries in strengthening evangelical theological education. A growing number of Langham Scholars study in high quality doctoral programmes in the majority world itself. As well as teaching the next generation of pastors, graduated Langham Scholars exercise significant influence through their writing and leadership.

To learn more about Langham Partnership and the work we do visit **langham.org**

Lightning Source UK Ltd.
Milton Keynes UK
UKHW020646040219
336711UK00010B/280/P